COMMONERS, TRIBUTE, AND CHIEFS

THE DEVELOPMENT OF ALGONQUIAN CULTURE IN THE POTOMAC VALLEY

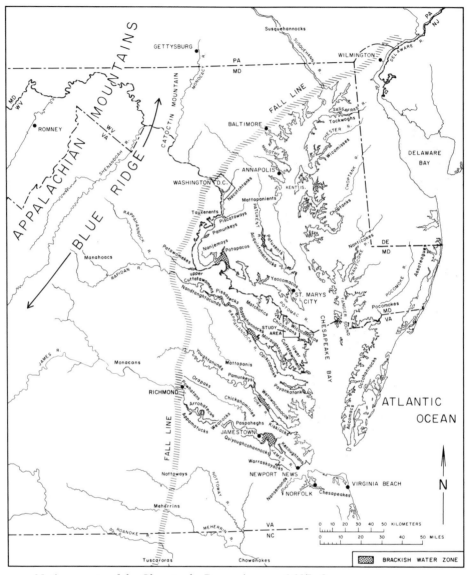

Native groups of the Chesapeake Bay region, ca. 1607–8.
(Map by G. Robert Lewis)

COMMONERS, TRIBUTE, AND CHIEFS

THE DEVELOPMENT OF ALGONQUIAN CULTURE IN THE POTOMAC VALLEY

Stephen R. Potter

UNIVERSITY PRESS OF VIRGINIA
CHARLOTTESVILLE AND LONDON

The University Press of Virginia
Copyright © 1993 by the Rector and Visitors
of the University of Virginia

First published 1993

Library of Congress Cataloging-in-Publication Data

Potter, Stephen R.
    Commoners, tribute, and chiefs: the development of Algonquian cul-
ture in the Potomac Valley / Stephen R. Potter.
        p. cm.
    Includes bibliographical references and index.
    ISBN 0-8319-1422-1
    1. Algonquian Indians—Social life and customs. 2. Indians of North
America—Potomac River Valley—Social life and customs. 3. Chiefdoms—
Potomac River Valley. 4. Algonquian Indians—Antiquities. 5. Indians of
North America—Potomac River Valley—Antiquities. 6. Potomac River
Valley—Antiquities. I. Title.
E99.A35P67   1993
975.2′01—dc20   92-28417
                                                                      CIP

Printed in the United States of America

To Diane

Contents

Figures

Tables

Acknowledgments

THIS BOOK EXISTS BECAUSE OF THE KINDNESS, generosity, and assistance of many people. Foremost is my wife, Diane E. Gelburd, whose encouragement and support kept me going. For four years she endured the disruption to our lives that the research and writing caused. Diane also provided copies of reports and articles, offered sound advice at critical times, and read the final draft manuscript. Words cannot express the depth of my gratitude to her.

Funding for the research came from a Horace M. Albright Employee Development Fund grant awarded by the National Park Foundation and administered by the National Park Service. My bosses, past and present, at the National Park Service gave me the opportunity to complete the research, while tolerating my momentary lapses of sanity. In particular, I want to thank Terry Carlstrom, Dwight Pitcaithley, Emmons ("Skip") Larson, Michael Donnelly, and the late Paul Goeldner. Also, thanks go to Robert Sonderman and Matthew Virta for managing the Regional Archaeology Program in my absence.

Much is owed to my parents, Louise and Robert Potter, who always supported, in every way they could, my interest in archaeology and anthropology. My parent-in-laws, Peggy and Irving Gelburd, along with my wife and parents, patiently understood what it meant to have a struggling author in the family.

The fieldwork in Virginia's Northern Neck was accomplished, in part, with the assistance of many members of my extended family. I am deeply indebted to Vernette Hundley and her late husband, Ralph, Geraldine and Albert Clark, Madlyn and David Hundley, Cynthia and Edward Smith, Glenn Clark, Robert Hundley, Almeda McKenney, and Sharon Clark. Without their help, and that of my parents, there would have been fewer hectares surveyed, sites discovered, soils excavated and screened, and artifacts washed and labeled.

A number of colleagues read portions of earlier drafts of this work and kindly provided me with their comments and suggestions. These include Gregory Waselkov, Helen Rountree, Jeffrey Hantman, Ives Goddard, David Pentland, Maureen Kavanagh, Dennis Curry, Richard Hughes, Paul Cissna, and Richard Dent.

In addition, I was privileged to visit excavations at nine archaeological sites relevant to my research. Colleagues who freely opened the "doors" to their excavations were Julia King, Joseph Herbert, Laurie Steponaitis, Jeffrey Hantman, Tyler Bastian, Maureen Kavanagh, Dennis Curry, Richard Dent, Michael Johnson, Charles Hodges, and Mary Ellen N. Hodges.

Numerous colleagues generously shared ideas, information, access to collections, and published and unpublished papers with me. These were Lysbeth Acuff, James Bradley, Paul Cissna, Wayne Clark, Dennis Curry, Jay Custer, Richard Dent, Andrew Edwards, Keith Egloff, J. Frederick Fausz, William Fitzgerald, William Gardner, Robert Grumet, Jeffrey Hantman, Joseph Herbert, Richard Hughes, Christine Jirikowic, Michael Johnson, Maureen Kavanagh, Martha McCartney, Howard MacCord, Sr., Douglas McLearen, Larry Moore, L. Daniel Mouer, David Pentland, David Phelps, Stuart Reeve, Leigh Rosenow, Helen Rountree, Laurie Steponaitis, R. Michael Stewart, E. Randolph Turner, III, H. Trawick Ward, J. Mark Wittkofski, and, most especially, Gregory Waselkov.

At the Smithsonian Institution, Molly Coxson of the Anthropology Department's Processing Laboratory provided access to and assistance in removing artifacts for photography, while Harold ("Doc") Dougherty and Diane Nordeck of the Smithsonian's Museum Support Center did the initial photography of artifacts curated there. Over the years T. Dale Stewart, curator emeritus of physical anthropology, regaled me with stories about the Potomac Creek site and generously allowed me access to unpublished manuscripts. Also, thanks to William Fitzhugh, curator of North American Archaeology, for his continued support of my appointment as a Research Associate with the Department of Anthropology, Smithsonian Institution.

Most of the maps were done by the skilled hand of illustrator G. Robert Lewis, while many of the black-and-white photographs were artfully produced by photographer Victor Krantz. The tables, graphs, and final printout of the manuscript were accomplished by the computer wizardry of J. D. Ross.

My thanks to the publisher and the repository for permission to reproduce plates 32, 36, and 38 from Paul Hulton, *America 1585: The*

Complete Drawings of John White, color plates copyright © The Trustees of the British Museum, copyright © 1984 by the University of North Carolina Press. Also, I would like to thank the University of Nebraska Press for permission to reproduce figure 2, p. 163 from Peter H. Wood, Gregory A. Waselkov, and M. Thomas Hatley, eds., *Powhatan's Mantle: Indians in the Colonial Southeast,* copyright © 1989 by the University of Nebraska Press.

I must especially mention John McGuigan, former Acquisitions Editor at the University Press of Virginia, whose personal enthusiasm for this work provided the initial impetus for its production. The continued support of Nancy Essig, Director of the University Press of Virginia, also deserves special thanks.

To all—family, coworkers, colleagues, and editors—I offer my heartfelt appreciation for your help.

COMMONERS, TRIBUTE, AND CHIEFS

THE DEVELOPMENT OF ALGONQUIAN CULTURE IN THE POTOMAC VALLEY

Introduction

WHEN THE ENGLISH INVADED VIRGINIA IN 1607, they unwittingly settled in the midst of one of the most politically complex Indian groups along the Atlantic coast, the Algonquian-speaking Powhatans. Named for the paramount chief who governed the majority of the Virginia Algonquians, the Powhatan chiefdom was the largest and most centralized of the southern Algonquian polities, incorporating more than thirty smaller chiefdoms or districts. One of the two goals of this book is to present the findings from the first detailed archaeological and ethnohistorical study of one of those Algonquian districts—Chicacoan.

Located along the Potomac River's southern shore, the Chicacoans were living on the natural boundary between the large and rapidly expanding Powhatan chiefdom of eastern Virginia and the smaller Algonquian-speaking Conoy chiefdom of southern Maryland (frontispiece). Previous studies have dealt with either the Powhatans or the Conoys, but rarely has the formation of one of these polities been considered in light of the other. To fully understand the development of the Chicacoans and their neighbors, one must consider both the Powhatans and the Conoys. Therefore, the second goal here is to look beyond the confines of the Chicacoan chiefdom and to construct an interpretation of the development of Algonquian Indian culture in the lower Potomac Valley. Although the Algonquian-speaking groups living below the Great Falls of the Potomac River provide the focus for this book, their development is interpreted within the larger natural and cultural world of which they were a part—the Chesapeake Bay region.

The varying degrees of political complexity shared by the early seventeenth-century Potomac River Algonquians is expressed in the title of this book by the words "commoners" and "chiefs." The Algonquian word for chief was *werowance;* but if the Algonquians had a word for the rank and file, the early English observers did not record it. Rather, Jamestown colonists like Captain John Smith (1986b:161) simply distinguished between the "better sort," referring to the chiefs, their matrilineal relatives, and other elite members of Algonquian society, and the "common sort," referring to everyone else. Consequently, the word "commoners" here denotes the men, women, and children who were the foundation upon which the Algonquian chiefdoms were built.

Another phrase from the book's title requiring explanation is "Algonquian culture." One of the first things taught to beginning anthropology students is that race, language, and culture vary independently of each other. Algonquian is one of several great Native-American language families, with many languages spoken by many different groups. Most of the coastal peoples living from southern Delaware, through Maryland and Virginia, to northeastern North Carolina spoke a variant of the Eastern Algonquian languages (Goddard 1978). They also happened to share certain cultural traits and patterns (Flannery 1939). It is for those reasons that I use the phrase "Algonquian culture" as a form of shorthand to denote the native groups of the lower Potomac Valley who probably spoke mutually understandable variants of Eastern Algonquian and shared similar cultural patterns.

Recently several archaeologists (Fiedel 1991, 1990, 1987; Luckenbach et al. 1987) have turned to historical linguistics in an effort to determine when the Algonquians arrived in the Middle Atlantic region. Unfortunately, in doing so they used glottochronology, a technique for determining the dates of the separation of related languages descended from some protolanguage which many historical linguists discounted several decades ago (Bergsland and Vogt 1962; Chretien 1962). Contrary to the archaeologists' statements, the dates derived from applying glottochronological techniques to various Algonquian languages cannot be considered reliable. Ives Goddard (personal communication 1991), a historical linguist and Algonquianist, has observed that

> all the premises of the method are suspect from the linguistic perspective, starting with the assumption that the 100-word list can be filled out and scored in an objective and replicable manner for every language. The attempts to apply the method to Algonquian data are not based on a determination of cognacy for the compared words, only similarity, . . . and omit discussions of selection problems and scoring ambiguities (though even a small

number of such problems, which always exist, would call into serious question the statistical significance of any percentages of replacement determined by the method, even when it is correctly applied).

There is general agreement, though, between most historical linguists and archaeologists on two key issues. First, Eastern Algonquian languages probably are not native to the Middle Atlantic. And second, the putative homeland for Eastern and Central Algonquian languages is somewhere in the Great Lakes region.

According to David Pentland (personal communication 1991), another historical linguist and Algonquianist, the movement of Eastern Algonquian-speakers into the Middle Atlantic region was not a single migration but consisted of several "cells" or groups of people coming into the area in succession, with the Carolina Algonquians arriving first and the Delawares last. On the other hand, Ives Goddard (personal communication 1991) sees

the differentiation of Eastern Algonquian as an in situ development, though this naturally involved a fair amount of [moving] around. For example, the extinction of intermediate dialects (by population loss, language shift, or both) may give rise to a relatively sharp linguistic boundary in the midst of a continuum of closely related languages; hence, the presence of such a break does not necessarily demonstrate a major, long-distance migration and population replacement. There was, of course, also some differentiation during the period of initial spread down the coast, and one would expect there to be fits and starts in the process. But most migrations were probably local, within the continuum that already existed.

Based upon current knowledge of the sequence of archaeological cultures from southern Delaware to northeastern North Carolina, there are two likely times when long-distance migrations of Eastern Algonquian-speakers might have occurred—at the beginning of the late Middle Woodland period, ca. A.D. 1–200, and/or at the end of the Middle Woodland and the beginning of the Late Woodland periods, ca. A.D. 700–900. To determine if long-distance migrations did occur and, if so, when will require years of careful research, the development of methodologies to distinguish migrations from other prehistoric patterns of movement (Anthony 1990), and the examination of archeological data from coastal North Carolina to the upper Delaware Valley. Given that, this volume errs on the liberal side, starting the discussion of the prehistory around A.D. 200.

Underlying this study is the concept that culture is an integrated whole; an idealized body of customs, beliefs, and values acquired and differentially shared by humans as members of society, which can be inferred from their noninstinctive, patterned behavior "and from the symbolic products of their actions, including material artifacts, language, and social institutions" (Axtell 1981:6). As such, "culture can be viewed as a system comprising a theoretically infinite number of subsystems interrelated in such a way that change" in one realm produces adjustments in other aspects of the cultural system so that equilibrium is maintained (Wells 1980:4). More broadly, cultural systems must adapt to a total environment composed of both natural elements and other cultures (Trigger 1978:147).

The book begins with an ethnohistorical examination of the Algonquians of Virginia and Maryland around the year 1608. Ethnohistory represents a union of history and anthropology, combining historical and ethnological methods to sift through historical documents for the purpose of constructing the human past based upon credible evidence (Wood 1990:84; Axtell 1981:15). Although a relative wealth of written and cartographic source material exists for the Virginia Algonquians in general, there is somewhat less for the Maryland Algonquians, and less still for the Chicacoans. To overcome the lack of a wide range of specific ethnohistorical data on the early seventeenth-century Chicacoans, it was necessary to extrapolate from the historical documentation pertaining to adjacent Algonquian groups, as well as from the Virginia Algonquians as a whole. The ethnohistory provides a standard to measure change in the archaeological record and the means to track the historic Algonquian chiefdoms back in time before they appear in written records, while the archaeology provides new interpretations of its own and a means of independently evaluating the veracity of the ethnohistorical sources.

In chapter 2, the journey back in prehistory begins with a detailed archaeological study of what was once the core of the Chicacoans' territory. Landscapes contain impressions of time, and archaeology consists, in part, of the method and set of techniques necessary to read the impressions left by past human activities. Those impressions are often quite faint, and even under the best conditions of site preservation the archaeologist is usually "attempting to pronounce on less than 15 per cent of the basic [material] culture" (Clarke 1968:370). Thus, archaeological interpretations are based on the similarities and differences within a very small sample of the artifacts that comprise the exoskeletons of extinct cultural systems.

Archaeological sites are places where past human activities left empirically observable evidence that was preserved. A single cultural manifestation at a site, such as an assemblage from a cultural zone within a stratified site or from a surface site, is called a component. An assemblage is "an associated set of contemporary artefact-types" (Clarke 1968:230). Components having similar assemblages, containing a comprehensive selection of artifact types, found within a limited geographic area, and dating to the same period of time constitute an archaeological cultural assemblage, or simply an "archaeological culture" (Clarke 1968:234).

The archaeological study of the Chicacoan locality focused on documenting changes in the distribution of the various types of archaeological components over time, from around A.D. 200 to the decade of the 1650s. Because the patterned behavior of the members of extinct human cultures is reflected (to varying degrees) in the quantity, type, and distribution of archaeological remains, it is possible to identify areal settlement patterns based on the distribution of affiliated components. The diachronic study of areal settlement patterns enables an archaeologist to observe internal changes in cultural systems, as well as the development and interaction of adaptive strategies. Thus, the Chicacoan locality serves as a detailed case study, providing data useful for comparison throughout the Potomac-Chesapeake tidewater.

The remaining chapters of the book concern the development of the Algonquian-speaking groups of the lower Potomac Valley as a whole, using data from archaeology, ethnohistory, and history. When appropriate, hypotheses are proposed concerning probable relationships between certain archaeological cultures and linguistic or ethnic groups. This it not to contradict the concept that race, language, and culture vary independently of one another. A simple one-to-one identification of all components of a particular archaeological culture with a specific linguistic or ethnic group was impossible in the past and is impossible now. Clustering components with similar assemblages, while certainly isolating linguistically and ethnically affiliated units, nevertheless will include some cultural components of other language or ethnic groups. However, as David L. Clarke (1968:373) pointed out, that "need not prevent the careful and skilful isolation of an underlying relationship between linguistic, historical, and archaeological entities within the defined limits of a probability proposition." To deny that such relationships existed is as foolish as drawing naive correlations (Clarke 1968:398). Finally, as W. Raymond Wood (1990:83–84) recently noted, "both history and prehistory are in fact constructions, not 'reconstructions,' for too much information has been lost at every point in time to make reconstructions possible in either discipline. . . . These notions are clearly consonant with modern anthropology in that we seek knowledge and generalizations based on the careful examination of all relevant evidence, realizing that 'truth' is simply the best current hypothesis—a point that indeed characterizes all fields of science."

CHAPTER 1

The
Algonquian
Country
on the
Great River, 1608

Introduction

CHESAPEAKE BAY, THE ALGONQUIAN "country on the great river" (Barbour 1971:287), is the drowned valley of the Susquehanna, formed by the rise in sea level that followed global warming and melting of the continental ice sheets, beginning 15,000 years ago (see frontispiece). Almost 290 kilometers (180 mi) long, 8–48 kilometers (5–30 mi) wide, and up to 53 meters (175 ft) deep, with over 12,900 kilometers (8,000 mi) of shoreline broken by hundreds of creeks, rivers, and bays, it is the largest estuary in the United States. A diverse and vast watershed of 191,660 square kilometers (74,000 mi²) surrounds the bay (Lippson 1973:2).

Starting on the Chesapeake's western edge, the coastal plain of Virginia is drained by four major rivers flowing generally from northwest to southeast into the bay. From south to north these rivers are the James, York, Rappahannock, and Potomac. Those rivers divide Virginia's coastal plain into four subregions: from south to north they are Southside Virginia, Virginia Peninsula (commonly referred to as "The Peninsula"), Middle Peninsula, and Northern Neck. Maryland's coastal plain, often called the western shore, is drained by the Potomac River—which separates Virginia and Maryland—and several other rivers, the largest being the Patuxent (Potter 1982:8).

All the major rivers have their origins west of the coastal plain, in the Appalachian Mountains, the Great Valley, or the hills of the piedmont. As the rivers pass over the more resistant igneous and metamorphic rocks of the piedmont onto the unconsolidated sands, gravels, and clays of the coastal plain terraces, they form a series of cataracts, known as the fall line. Below the cataracts, the rivers lie entirely in drowned channels in which the tide ebbs and flows, hence the name tidewater (Potter 1982:13–15).

Depending upon the salinity of the water, the tidal segments of the rivers can be divided into three zones: saltwater, brackish water or salt-freshwater transition, and freshwater. The salt and brackish water zones are the estuarine portion of the drainage systems, also known as the outer coastal plain. The freshwater zone is the riverine portion of the drainage systems, referred to as the inner coastal plain (Potter 1982:15).

At the head of the bay is the Susquehanna, the greatest river on the Atlantic coast (Lippson 1973:2). The east side of the bay is bordered by the Delmarva Peninsula, or Eastern Shore, a flat, expansive tongue of coastal plain sediments separating Chesapeake Bay from the Atlantic Ocean. Three states—Delaware, Maryland, and Virginia—claim portions of the peninsula, each one contributing several letters to form its name. The three largest river systems of the Eastern Shore that drain into Chesapeake Bay are, from south to north, the Pocomoke, Nanticoke, and Choptank.

The recorded view of native life in the Chesapeake region shortly after Jamestown was settled is merely a reflection of Indian images in English eyes. To remove the European filter from the historical lens, it is necessary to evaluate and interpret what the English thought they saw, rather than accepting their written accounts about the natives' way of life at face value. This chapter presents four aspects of the Algonquians' cultural system—social and political organization, demography, settlement, and subsistence—as seen by the English about the year 1608. The ethnohistory provides a reference point for studying change in the archaeological record and a way of tracing the historically documented Algonquian chiefdoms of the lower Potomac River back into prehistory.

Captain John Smith's Explorations

The earliest detailed account of the Indians of the Potomac River records the observations of Captain John Smith and other members of the Jamestown colony who accompanied him on his explorations of Chesapeake Bay. On June 16, 1608, Smith and fourteen other men entered the Potomac River aboard a two-ton open barge in search of "a glistering mettal, the Salvages told us they had from Patawomeck" (Smith 1986b:224, 227). For 48 kilometers (30 mi), they saw no natives. Then, near Nomini Bay, not far from the principal village of the Onawmanient or Matchotic Indians (fig. 1), two natives guided Smith's party up a small creek where they were ambushed by three or four hundred Indians "so strangely painted, grimed, and disguised" (Smith 1986b:227). When Smith (1986b:227) ordered some of his men to fire low, toward the Indians, "the grazing of the bullets upon the river, with the ecco of the woods so amazed them, as down went their bowes and arrowes." They exchanged hostages as a pledge of good faith and a means of preserving the peace, with James Watkins being "sent 6. myles up the woods, to their kings habitation" (Smith 1986b:227).

The size of the force that attacked Smith (1986b:148) can be questioned, since he himself estimated the total number of Matchotic bowmen at only one hundred. In later years Smith (1986c:166) inflated the number of attackers to a phenomenal three or four thousand, perhaps to glorify his exploits. Regardless of the actual count, estimates made under the stress of conflict must be considered with caution. Even if the lower figure of three or four hundred warriors is accepted, it indicates that other nearby groups were assisting the Matchotics. According to Walter Russell and Anas Todkill (Smith 1986b:227), chroniclers of this and other "accidents that happened in the Discoverie of the bay," the Matchotics "were coummaunded to betray us, by Powhatans direction." This is probable, given the likely participation of several groups in the attack, as well as the belligerent receptions Smith received at Cekakawon (also known as Chicacoan), Patawomeke, "and divers other places" (Smith 1986b:227).

It is interesting that the Chicacoans are mentioned after the encounter with the Matchotics, since Smith's barge went by Chicacoan and Wicocomoco territory on its way upriver to Nomini Bay. If Smith stayed in the center of the Potomac River channel, then it is understandable how he could bypass the Chicacoans and Wicocomocos since the river is 14.5 kilometers (9.0 mi) wide at this point. On the other hand, if Smith was following the southern shoreline, the observation that no inhabitants were seen for the first 48 kilometers (30 mi) assumes additional importance. Apparently no native villages were visible to the Englishmen along that stretch of Potomac River shoreline.

Although not specifically mentioned in the accounts of the first exploration of the mouth of the Potomac River, the Wicocomocos were also visited by Smith's party (not to be confused with another Indian

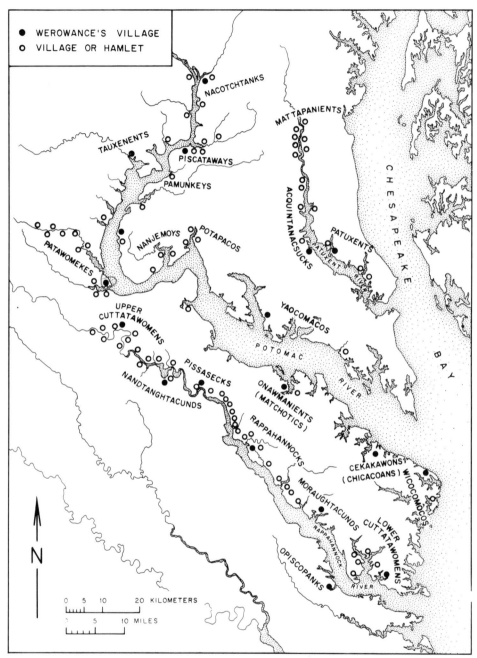

1. Native groups and villages on the lower Patuxent, Potomac, and Rappahannock rivers, ca. 1608. (Map by G. Robert Lewis)

group of the same name on Maryland's Eastern Shore). It was at their village that Smith and his men met Mosco, "a lusty Salvage of Wighcocomoco," whom they believed was "some French mans sonne, because he had a thicke blacke bush beard" (Smith 1986c:173). This meeting probably took place after the ambush near Nomini Bay but before Smith went to the village of Patawomeke, which suggests that he may have backtracked downriver after learning the whereabouts of the Chicacoans and Wicocomocos from the Matchotics.

Aided by Mosco and "divers of his Countrymen" who helped the Englishmen tow their barge "against winde or tyde from place to place," Smith's party finally reached Patawomeke (Smith 1986c:173). There Mosco stayed to rest while Smith and his men proceeded upriver. In contrast to the initial hostility of the Chicacoans, Matchotics, and Patawomekes, Smith was welcomed at the villages of Tauxenent, Moyaone, and Nacotchtank (Smith 1986b:227). The latter two villages, and possibly all three, were the principal towns of groups belonging to the Conoy chiefdom, a polity composed of at least six groups living mainly along the Potomac River's left bank in what is now southern Maryland (Feest 1978b:240–41).

Restricting themselves principally to those places where their barge could carry them, Captain Smith's company traveled only a short distance beyond the villages of Tauxenent and Nacotchtank before they were stopped by the Great Falls of the Potomac River. Still seeking the source of the "glistering mettal," the Englishmen returned to Patawomeke where the chief, or werowance, provided guides who took them to an aboriginal mine. Hoping for silver, they found antimony. Though the Patawomeke's mine "proved of no value" to the English, the party of explorers could console themselves with the realization that they had met most of their goals—"to search what furres, metals, rivers, Rockes, nations, woods, fishings, victuals and other commodities the land afforded" (Smith 1986b:227–28).

Of great value to modern archaeologists, historians, and ethnographers is the information Smith and others left about the eleven different Indian "nations" or groups living along the lower Potomac River, from the falls to its mouth. Starting below the falls and going east, the groups on the left bank, or Maryland shore, were the Nacotchtanks, Piscataways, Pamunkeys, Nanjemoys, Potapacos, and Yaocomacos. Groups living on the right bank, or Virginia shore, were the Tauxenents, Patawomekes, Matchotics, Chicacoans, and Wicocomocos (see Feest 1978a:268–69, 1978b:249–50, for a detailed synonymy of Algonquian group and place names).

The Language They Spoke

Most of the native peoples of the tidal Potomac in the early seventeenth century probably spoke dialects of an Eastern Algonquian language (Rountree 1989:7–8; Cissna 1986:41–46; Goddard 1978: 73–74). Although the only direct evidence for their linguistic placement is a 1633 Jesuit priest's Conoy translation of the Lord's Prayer and the Ten Commandments (Cissna 1986:42; Goddard 1978:73), there are three indirect lines of evidence: the accounts of John Smith, Henry Spelman, and Henry Fleet.

When John Smith first arrived in Virginia in the spring of 1607, he was armed with only a few words of Carolina Algonquian gleaned from Richard Hakluyt's *Principal Navigations* (1598–1600), the last volume of which contained Thomas Hariot's account of the Roanoke colony (Barbour 1972:22). Over the next year frequent interaction with various members of Powhatan's chiefdom—mostly groups living near Jamestown—increased his knowledge of Algonquian (Smith 1986b:217). Although Smith was by no means fluent in Algonquian, he did know enough to serve as interpreter during the explorations of the Chesapeake in 1608 (Rountree 1989:8). Whenever he encountered natives who could not "speake the language of Powhatan," Smith (1986b:231) noted it.

Smith needed interpreters to converse with the Iroquoian-speaking Susquehannocks, the Siouan-speaking Manahoacs, and the Tockwoghs, who apparently spoke a dialect of Algonquian that was unintelligible to Smith (1986b:190 n.8, 231, 1986c:175–76). As for the Iroquoian-speaking Massawomecks, the Englishmen "understood them nothing at all but by signes" (Smith 1986b:231). Neither Smith nor any of the men who accompanied him during the "discoverie of the bay" mentioned the need for an interpreter other than Smith to talk with any of the native groups living in the lower Potomac Valley (Smith 1986b:227–28, 1986c:168–73).

Four years after his voyages around Chesapeake Bay, Smith summed up his observations concerning the native languages of the region in his *Map of Virginia*. "Amongst those people," wrote Smith (1986b:150), "are thus many severall nations of sundry languages, that environ Powhatans Territories. The Chawonokes, the Mangoags, the Monacans, the Mannahokes, the Masawomekes, the Powhatans, the Sasquesahannocks, the Atquanachukes, the Tockwoghes, and the Kuscarawaokes. Al those not any one understandeth another but by Interpreters."

Henry Spelman, "the best linguist of the Indian Tongue of this Countrys" (Kingsbury 1935:4:89), began his education in Algonquian when Captain John Smith left the fourteen-year-old boy with the Powhatans in August 1609 as a sign of trust. Tired of being a pawn in intercultural diplomacy, Spelman escaped the following March from the paramount chief, Powhatan (Fausz 1987:45–48). Recounting his adventures, Spelman (1910:ciii–civ) wrote, "I shifted for my self and gott to the Patomeckes cuntry, With this Kinge of Patomecke I lived a year and more at a towne of his called Pasptanzie, untill such time as an worthy gentelman named Capt: Argall arived . . . [and] gave the Kinge copper for me, which he receyved Thus was I sett at libertye and brought into England." While in England, Spelman put his experiences among the Powhatans and Patawomekes on paper, titling his manuscript account simply "Relation of Virginia." Nowhere in that work did Spelman mention that the Patawomekes and Powhatans spoke different languages.

In 1619 Spelman returned to Virginia as an interpreter and trader, restricting himself to dealing with the Indians of tidewater Virginia and Maryland. Not only were they the native groups he knew best from personal experience, but they probably spoke mutually understandable variants of Algonquian, the native language Spelman knew so well. Unfortunately, Spelman's familiarity with the Indians may have been his undoing. In March 1623 Henry Spelman and nineteen other Englishmen were killed by the Nacotchtanks while on a trading expedition to the Potomac River, perhaps, as John Smith (1986c:320) concluded, because "hee presumed to much upon his acquaintance amongst them."

Miraculously, one member of Spelman's trading party survived. "Taken prisoner and detained five years" by the Nacotchtanks, Henry Fleet (1956:482, 489), like Spelman before him, emerged from captivity "better proficient in the Indian language than mine own." Fleet's observations contained in his "Brief Journal of a Voyage in the Barque Warwick" indicate that language was Algonquian. Although Fleet could converse fluently with all of the Indian groups living in the lower Potomac Valley and elsewhere in tidewater Virginia and Maryland, he required interpreters to talk with the Iroquoian-speaking Massawomecks and their enemies, the Susquehannocks (Hall 1925: 41, 55–56, 72; Fleet 1956:482, 484–87; Fausz 1988:60, 69, 74, 81; Pendergast 191:41–46).

The works of Smith, Spelman, and Fleet, as well as other accounts by their contemporaries, indicate that the groups living along the Po-

tomac below the falls probably spoke dialects of the same language—
Eastern Algonquian. Whenever Smith, Spelman, or Fleet came in
contact with Iroquoian or Siouan speakers, and on occasion some
Algonquian-speakers, they spoke through interpreters or by signs.
Spelman, who lived with the Powhatans and Patawomekes for almost
two years, and Fleet, who lived with the Nacotchtanks for five years,
were used as interpreters by the colonial governments of Virginia and
Maryland because they "spake the Countrey language very well" (Hall
1925:72). The "Countrey language" was a generic term, probably
used in much the same fashion as Smith's "the language of Powhatan"
to denote any of the mutually intelligible variants of Eastern Algonquian language spoken around the Chesapeake region.

Political Organization in the Virginia-Maryland Tidewater

In 1608 the largest centralized polity in tidewater Virginia was the
Powhatan chiefdom. The apical status position of paramount chief,
or *mamanatowick,* meaning great king, was occupied by Powhatan, or
Wahunsenacawh, from late in the sixteenth century until shortly before his death in 1618 (Smith 1986c:265; Strachey 1953;56; Feest
1978a:254). Subordinate to Powhatan were the district chiefs, male
(werowances) or female (*weroansquas*), who ruled the local chiefdoms
(Smith 1986b:173; Rountree 1989:103–4)). Beneath the district
chiefs were the subchiefs, or "lesser werowances," who governed the
villages where the werowances did not reside (Strachey 1953:64). Cus-
tomarily, chiefly positions were inherited through the female line
(Smith 1986b:174).

The hierarchical nature of Powhatan's political organization is reflected on John Smith's 1612 map of Virginia (fig. 2). On the map
some villages are designated as "Kings howses," while others are
marked "Ordinary howses." The symbol of a king's house represented
the village where the werowance of a local chiefdom resided. These
have been likened to territorial, or district, capitals. With the exception of the Chickahominies, ordinary houses represent villages or
hamlets within a werowance's territory ruled by lesser werowances.
The Chickahominies were the only group of Virginia Algonquians not
governed by a werowance. They were ruled by a council of eight great
men, or *munguys,* and, consequently, no symbol for a "Kings howse" is
shown in Chickahominy territory (Feest 1973:67–68, 1978a:261).

Important nonchiefly positions included advisers or *cronoccoes* (an-

2. *Detail from John Smith's Map of Virginia, 1612, showing native groups and villages along the Potomac River. Longhouses represent villages where a district werowance lived, and circles with a dot in the center represent "ordinary villages," where a district werowance did not reside. (Photograph by Victor E. Krantz)*

glicized to "cockarouse"), priests, and conjurers or shamans. Advisers were usually distinguished warriors picked by the chiefs from the ranks of the common people to serve as counselors to their rulers (Rountree 1989:101). Priests and shamans acted as healers and diviners, performed various weather ceremonies, served as counselors, and frequented the mortuary temples. However, the priests alone were considered sacred, and they were viewed as being superior in rank to the shamans. Priests were also in charge of maintaining the mortuary temples (Turner 1972:119–20; Rountree 1989:100–101, 131–33).

Thus, the social and political structure of the Powhatan chiefdom can be summarized at several levels. At the paramount chief's level there was the position of mamanatowick, the occupant's family (including his brothers who would succeed him, his wives and children, and other matrilineal relatives), his seven chief priests who maintained the principal mortuary temples at Uttamussack, his cronoccoes, and his personal bodyguard. Below the paramount chief there were the district chiefs—werowances or weroansquas—their families and relatives, lesser werowances and their families, priests, cronoccoes, and shamans. The bottom two rungs of the status ladder were occupied by commoners and war captives.

In order to understand the relationships between the various social and political positions within Powhatan society, it is appropriate to define what is meant by status, power, and authority. Status is a ranked position conferring unequal privileges within the cultural system (Sahlins 1958:x). As defined by Paul Bohannan (1963:268), "Power is . . . the ability to produce intended effects on oneself, on other human beings, and on things." Consequently, an individual is powerful in so far as he or she can produce intended results. When these power relationships are considered legitimate, right, and natural, as rules for maintaining the society successfully, then a change in the quality of the power has occurred, and the product of this transformation is called authority (Bohannan 1963:269).

As paramount chief Powhatan had extensive powers of punishment over his subjects and was viewed by those of lower status as possessing a certain degree of divinity (Smith 1986b:174). Werowances, likewise, held similar power but were subordinate to the authority of Powhatan (Strachey 1953:77). The only major limitation to the authority of the paramount and other chiefs was in declaring war. The priests advised the paramount and his chiefs concerning war and commonly had the final word (Strachey 1953:104).

Other chiefly privileges included having attendants and bodyguards and receiving deference shown through the performance of elaborate obeisance by those of lower status (Smith 1986c:201; Percy 1967:16; Spelman 1910:cxiii). According to Spelman (1910:cxii), the paramount chief—and possibly the other chiefs, as well—did not participate in the planting and harvesting of his fields. It was also among the chiefs that the practice of polygyny was common, primarily because they could most readily afford it. While a commoner could have more than one wife, certain economically restrictive practices were enforced by the chiefs and their advisers which served to limit the amount of wealth and level of status a commoner could achieve through war deeds and economic ventures. Chiefs had as many wives as they could afford, and Powhatan supposedly had more than one hundred (Smith 1986a:61; Strachey 1953:61).

Although the position of werowance was inherited or ascribed, social ranking was based on the accumulation of wealth. Indeed, the Algonquian word *werowance* has been variously interpreted as meaning "he is rich," "he is of influence," or "he is wise" (Gerard 1905:229–30; Barbour 1972:46–47; Tooker 1905:525). The primary means of wealth acquisition by the paramount chief and the chiefs of the local chiefdoms was through a hierarchical system of tribute collection. Items received by Powhatan as tribute from his petty chiefs included "skinnes, beades, copper, pearle, deare, turkies, wild beasts, and corne" (Smith 1986b:174). William Strachey (1953:87), one of the early Jamestown chroniclers, discussed tribute collection in some detail in a frequently cited passage:

> Every Weroance knowes his owne Meeres and lymitts to fish fowle or hunt in (as before said) but they hold all of their great Weroance Powhatan, unto whome they paie 8. parts of 10. tribute of all the Commodities which their Countrey yeildeth, as of wheat, pease, beanes, 8. measures of 10. (and these measured out in little Cades or Basketts which the great king appoints) of the dying roots 8. measures of ten; of all sorts of skyns and furrs 8. of tenne, and so he robbes the poore in effect of al they have even to the deares Skyn wherewith they cover them from Could, in so much as they dare not dresse yt and put yt on untill he have seene yt and refused yt; for what he Comaundeth they dare not disobey in the least thing.

As John Haynes (1984:100) has noted, Powhatan's assessment of eight parts out of every ten was probably made against the total tribute collected by each district chief and was not an assessment made against all the economic yields and goods produced by each chiefdom. The goods collected usually were stored in or near the house of each chief, although in 1607 Powhatan's main storehouse was not near his principal residence but was located 1.6 kilometers (1 mi) from the village of Orapaks, near the fall line (Smith 1986b:173–74; Strachey 1953:62). Tribute items were used to support the chiefs, their families, and the priests. The chiefs used luxury items such as beads, pearls, and copper to reward warriors for bravery, to repay those individuals who aided in planting and harvesting their fields, and, possibly, to dispense to needy people after certain funeral rites. In addition, the paramount and district chiefs used tribute goods for entertaining important guests, supporting communal feasts and religious activities, and paying other chiefdoms for their assistance in warfare (Feest 1978a:261; Binford 1964:94; Turner 1976:108).

In egalitarian societies, Robert S. Grumet (1980:48) has stated that leaders "depended upon the power of persuasion rather than the persuasion of power." The reverse situation is true in chiefdoms where "leadership," observed Elman R. Service (1975:74), "is centralized, statuses are arranged hierarchically, and there is to some degree a hereditary aristocratic ethos." Thus, the political organization of the Powhatans was that of a ranked, kin-oriented society in which the number of status positions was limited and the status and administrative structure was arranged in a hierarchy of major and minor leaders governing major and minor subdivisions of the group (Sahlins 1968:26).

Sometime during the latter part of the sixteenth century, Powhatan inherited a number of small chiefdoms along the James and York rivers. According to John Smith (1986b:173), these chiefdoms were the Powhatans proper, Arrohatecks, Appamatucks, Pamunkeys, Youghtanunds, and Mattaponis. Strachey (1953:43, 57) mentioned all of the groups listed by Smith and added three more: the Orapaks, Kiskiacks, and Werowocomocos. The territory inhabited by these groups formed a large crescent from the south bank of the James River, near the fall line, north-northeast to the upper and middle reaches of the York River (see frontispiece).

Driven by "certayne Prophesies" related by his priests "that from the Chesapeack Bay a Nation should arise, which should dissolve and give end to his empier," Powhatan expanded his chiefdom eastward to the coast (Strachey 1953:104). In a series of attacks initiated between the late 1500s and 1608, Powhatan conquered the coastal chiefdoms of Kecoughtan, Chesapeake, and Payankatank (Strachey 1953:43–44, 67–68, 104; Potter 1976:21–22; Rountree 1989:118–23). By the end of 1608, through intimidation and warfare, Powhatan controlled all but one of the groups living between the falls of the James and York rivers and Chesapeake Bay. The exception to Powhatan's conquests were his neighbors the Chickahominies, who thwarted his efforts to appoint a werowance to rule them (Rountree 1989:8–9).

Beyond the York and James rivers, Powhatan's authority diminished as the distance from the heartland of his chiefdom increased. The groups of the Rappahannock River, the Wicocomocos, Chicacoans, and Matchotics of the Potomac River, and the Accomacs and Occohannocks of Virginia's Eastern Shore were part of what Helen Rountree (1989:14) has called Powhatan's "ethnic fringe"—peripheral chiefdoms strongly influenced, though not absolutely dominated, by Powhatan. Other groups with lands along the right bank of the Potomac River—the Patawomekes and Tauxenents—probably were not part of Powhatan's ethnic fringe. Apparently, at the time of Smith's explorations, the Patawomekes were attempting to maintain their autonomy, while the Tauxenents were influenced by the Conoy chiefdom (see chapter 5).

North across the Potomac River there were a number of Algonquian-speaking groups living in what is now the tidewater portion of southern Maryland. Excluding the Indians of the Patuxent River, all remaining groups were part of a chiefdom called the Conoys by their Iroquoian-speaking enemies (Feest 1978b:240; Cissna 1986:88–89). The composition and extent of the Conoys' territory was described in the Jesuits' annual letter of 1639 (Hall 1925:125): "Their kingdoms are generally circumscribed by the narrow confines of a single village and the adjacent country; though the Tayac has a much more extensive dominion, stretching about one hundred and thirty miles [209 km], to whose empire also other inferior chieftains are subject." In modern terms, the "dominion" of the *tayac*, or paramount chief, went from St. Marys County, Maryland, at the mouth of the Potomac River, to Washington, D.C., and the falls, possibly including lands on the Virginia side of the Potomac River from opposite Washington to below Mount Vernon (Cissna 1986:63, 1990:25–27).

The individual "kingdoms" or groups of the Conoys in 1608 were the Nacotchtanks, Piscataways, Pamunkeys (not to be confused with the Virginia Pamunkeys), Nanjemoys, Potapacos, Yaocomacos, and, perhaps, the Tauxenents (Feest 1978b:240–43; MacLeod 1926:302). The anonymous author of *A Relation of Maryland, 1635,* noted that with the exception of the Piscataways, each of these groups was governed by an "inferior chieftain" who "is called the Werowance, and is assisted by some that consult with him of the common affaires, who are called Wisoes. . . . The Wisoes are chosen at the pleasure of the Werowances, yet commonly they are chosen of the same family, if they be of yeeres capable. . . . They have also Cockorooses [advisers] that are their Captains in time of war, to whom they are very obedient" (Hall 1925:84). Like the Powhatans of Virginia, the Conoy chiefs and their advisers formed an elite stratum of society distinguished from the common people by their wealth, distinctive dress, and the respect accorded them (Cissna 1986:62–75; Feest 1978b:245).

The Piscataways were the largest and most politically powerful group of the Conoys. It was from among the Piscataways that the position of tayac was inherited through matrilineal succession. And it was from "the metropolis of Pascatoa [Piscataway]" that the tayac ruled both the Piscataways and the larger polity that they were a part (Hall 1925:124; Feest 1978b:240–45).

Three different Algonquian-speaking groups inhabited the Patuxent Valley: the Acquintanacsucks, Patuxents, and Mattapanients. Although they lacked a strong central leadership, the Patuxent River groups were, nonetheless, largely independent of the Conoys. Evidence from Smith's map suggests that each group was lead by a chief who held sway over adjacent villages (Steponaitis 1986:32–33; Feest 1978b:242).

Across Chesapeake Bay, on the Eastern Shore, there were a number of Algonquian-speaking groups living in what is now Maryland and portions of Delaware, the major ones being the Pocomokes, Assateagues, Nanticokes, and Choptanks. In some of those groups, centralized political authority existed in the form of a paramount chief and subordinate chiefs, while in others it was weakly developed. Near the head of the bay lived several little-known groups like the Wicomisses of the Chester River and the Tockwoghs of the Sassafras River (Feest 1978b:240–45).

Demography

Population estimates for the Virginia and Maryland Algonquians are based upon censuslike figures drawn up by John Smith (1986b:146–48, 1986c:103–5) and William Strachey (1953:45–47, 63–69). Smith's figures come from his personal observations during exploration of the Virginia-Maryland tidewater and Chesapeake Bay in 1607–8. Because he was most familiar with the James and York rivers, Smith's figures for these areas are probably more reliable. However, none of his figures should be accepted uncritically. Smith was not fluent in the Algonquian dialect spoken by the Powhatans, and he was forced to make most of his observations under the peculiar circumstances surrounding the establishment of Anglo-Indian relations, sometimes in hostile settings (Feest 1973:66). Strachey copied Smith in some instances, while in others he supplemented Smith's figures with data collected from native informants and his own limited firsthand observations. Also, it must be kept in mind that Smith's and Strachey's figures are useful only for approximating the size of early seventeenth-century Algonquian populations; they cannot be considered estimates of aboriginal populations before their contact with Europeans in the sixteenth century.

Both Smith's and Strachey's population estimates are of "bowmen" or "warriors" only. To arrive at the total population of a specific group, a ratio of warriors to total population has to be calculated. This is usually derived from a statement of John Smith's (1986b:160): "Within 60 miles [97 km] of James Towne there are about 5000 people, but of able men fit for their warres scarse 1500." Using this information, James Mooney (1907) and Maurice Mook (1944) assumed a 3:10 ratio of warriors to total population. In a later work Mooney (1928) did not use a fixed ratio. Rather, his population estimates were computed by multiplying Smith's warrior counts by figures of 3.5 to 5 (Turner 1973:58).

Research by Douglas Ubelaker (1974, 1976), Christian Feest (1973), and E. Randolph Turner (1973, 1976, 1982) indicates that earlier population estimates for the Virginia-Maryland Algonquians were much too conservative. Feest (1973:67) has suggested that a ratio of 1:4 is preferable to a 3:10 ratio, in part because warriors were probably overrepresented in Smith's own ratio. Turner (1982:50) used a ratio of 1:4.25, derived by averaging the warrior to overall population ratios for ossuaries I and II (pits containing mass reburials) from the Late Woodland period Juhle Farm site (18CH89) on Nanjemoy Creek in southern Maryland (Ubelaker 1974:69). Although they used a fixed ratio, Feest (1973) and Turner (1982) made some adjustments in their population estimates when there were discrepancies between the estimates and other historic data that may indicate a group's size, such as houses per village or villages per group.

Population estimates for the chiefdoms along the south side of the Potomac River are presented in table 1. The columns under Smith's and Strachey's names represent their estimates for the number of warriors per chiefdom. All the figures are the same, except for the Patawomekes. Smith (1986c:104–5) revised his 1624 count for Patawomeke warriors upward from his earlier estimate. Feest (1973:67) considered this revision and others made in 1624 as an attempt by

Table 1. Population estimates for chiefdoms along the south side (right bank) of the Potomac River

| Chiefdom | "Bowmen" or "warrior" estimates | | | Total population estimates | | | |
	Smith 1612	Smith 1624	Strachey 1610/1611	3:10 ratio	1:4 ratio	1:4.25 ratio	Turner 1976
Wicocomoco	130	130	130	435	520	552	550
Chicacoan	30	30	30	100	120	127	130
Matchotic	100	100	100	335	400	425	425
Patawomeke	160	>200	160	535	640	680	850
Tauxenent	40	40	40	135	160	170	170

Smith to improve the accuracy of his earlier report. The other columns represent total population estimates for each chiefdom, computed on the basis of three different fixed ratios: 3:10, 1:4, and 1:4.25. A column of population figures based upon Turner's (1982:54–56) calculations is also presented.

Population estimates for individual groups of the Conoy chiefdom ca. 1608 are more difficult to calculate, mainly due to John Smith's (1986b:148) description: "On the north side of this river [Potomac] is Secowocomoco [Yaocomaco] with 40 men. Some what further Potapaco with 20. In the East part of the bought of the river, is Pamacacack with 60 men, After Moyowances [Piscataway] with 100. and lastly Nacotchtanke with 80 able men." Because two of the names Smith mentioned—Potapaco and Pamacacack—are the names of "ordinary" or common villages, some researchers have assumed Smith's estimates were of individual villages, rather than groups (Ubelaker 1974:68–69; Cissna 1986:49). This assumption is contrary to all the interpretations of Smith's and Strachey's warrior counts for the Virginia Algonquians (Rountree 1989; Turner 1982; Feest 1973; Binford 1964). Further confusion has resulted from different scholars' interpretations of the number of groups included in the Conoy chiefdom (see Cissna 1986:49–51; Ubelaker 1974:67–68). Even more confusion is created by the disparity between the number of werowances' villages (four) shown on Smith's map along the north side of the Potomac River and the number of individual ethnic groups (at least six) estimated to have lived there. Therefore, only an approximation of the Conoys' total population is offered.

Estimates for the Conoys' total population have ranged from

Feest's (1978b:242) low of one thousand to Ubelaker's (1974:69) high of at least seven thousand. Reality probably lies somewhere in between. Feest's estimate was based on John Smith's warrior counts, using Smith's own ratio of 3:10; but he included only the Yaocomacos, Potapacos, Pamunkeys, Piscataways, and Nacotchtanks (Anacostanks) in his estimate, even though he showed the Nanjemoys (Nangemeicks) as one of the six Conoy groups in 1608 (Feest 1978b:241, fig. 1). Ubelaker (1974:67) included all the villages on the north side of the Potomac, as well as all those on the west side of the Patuxent River, in his interpretation of "the area occupied historically by the Conoy" (this gives a total of twenty-nine villages, not Ubelaker's total of twenty-eight; see fig. 2). Calculating a population estimate of 1,440 for the size of the group that contributed to Ossuary II at the Juhle site (18CH89), Ubelaker assumed that the remaining Conoy groups were of equal size. In 1624 John Smith (1986c:297) wrote that "these wilde naked natives live not in great numbers together, but dispersed, commonly in thirtie, fortie, fiftie, or sixtie in a company. Some places have two hundred, few places more, but many lesse." This remark and Smith's earlier observation on the great disparity between the number of Conoy warriors living close to the mouth of the Potomac compared to those living close to the falls make Ubelaker's estimate of 1,440 people too high as an average figure for each Conoy group. Nevertheless, Ubelaker (1974:69) arrived at a "prehistoric Conoy population of 7,200" by multiplying 1,440 times five werowance's villages (four along the Potomac and one from the Patuxent's west side).

If Turner's population estimates for the groups on the south side of the Potomac River are totaled, the sum equals 2,125 persons. Dividing that figure by the total number of individual chiefdoms results in a quotient of 425 people per chiefdom. Using this as an average figure for the number of people per Potomac River chiefdom, then a conservative approximation of the Conoys' total population is 2,550 people.

Feest (1973:73) suggested that the "true early seventeenth-century population" of the Algonquian Indians on the Virginia side of the Potomac River may have been between twenty-five hundred and five thousand. If so, then the Conoys' total population would be somewhere between three and six thousand. This conforms with Paul Cissna's (1986:53) estimate of approximately 3,600 people for the Conoy ca. 1608.

The sole source of the number of Virginia Algonquians per household comes from John Smith, who stated that from six to twenty people lived in a longhouse (Smith 1986b:162). In 1699 the Piscataways' village on Conoy Island had a total population of just above three hundred people (eighty or ninety warriors) living in twenty-seven longhouses, or an average of eleven people, or slightly more, per household (Feest 1973:68). In arriving at conservative estimates for various villages, Feest (1973:69) assumed a mean house size of eight, while Turner (1976:144) used an average of ten persons.

Features of Settlement

INDIVIDUAL STRUCTURES

The basic structure common to all places of Algonquian settlement in Virginia and Maryland was the longhouse. Smith (1986b:161) noted that "their houses are built like our Arbors of small young springs [saplings] bowed and tyed, and so close covered with mats or the barkes of trees very handsomely, that notwithstanding either winde raine or weather, they are as warme as stooves, but very smoaky; yet at the toppe of the house there is a hole made for the smoake to goe into right over the fire." Entrance was gained through two doors, hung with mats, located at each end of the longhouse. Inside, the walls were lined with sleeping platforms built a foot or more off the ground. Hearths apparently were located in the center of the dwelling. A commoner's longhouse consisted of a single room, with no interior divisions. Storage scaffolds made of saplings and reeds usually were found adjacent to the longhouse (Strachey 1953:78–79; Smith 1986b:162; Spelman 1910:cvi).

Andrew White (Hall 1925:43–44), a Jesuit priest, wrote a brief description of Conoy longhouses in 1634 that is similar to Smith's but added information about their size: "Their houses are built in an halfe ovall forme 20 foot [6 m] long, and 9 or 10 foot [2.7–3.0 m] high with a place open in the top, halfe a yard square, whereby they admit light, and let forth the smoake, for they build their fire . . . in the middle of the house, about which they lie to sleep upon mats spread on a low scaffold hafe a yard from the ground." A year later, an anonymous observer wrote that in length Conoy houses were "30. others 40. some a 100. foote; and in breadth about 12. foote" (Hall 1925:86).

No early seventeenth-century Virginia accounts provide measurements for the longhouses of common people. However, recent archaeological excavations at several sites in tidewater Virginia revealed over twenty-five late prehistoric or early historic house patterns (fig. 3). At

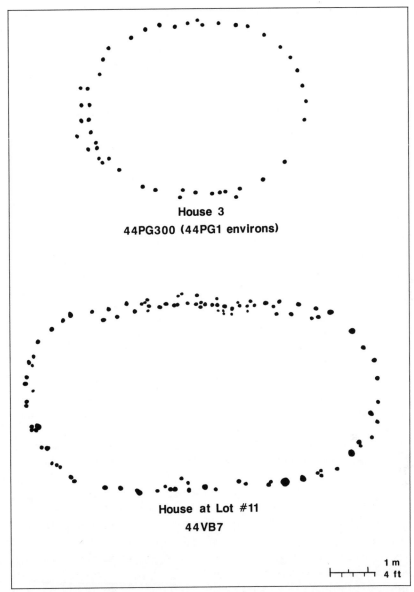

House 3
44PG300 (44PG1 environs)

House at Lot #11
44VB7

1 m
4 ft

3. Plans of two house patterns from sites 44PG300 (44PG1 environs) and 44VB7. (Redrawn courtesy of the Virginia Department of Historic Resources)

the Great Neck site (44VB7) in Virginia Beach, "the best preserved longhouse," according to Turner (in press), "was 6.5 meters [21 ft] in width and extended over 12 meters [39 ft] before excavations had to be terminated." In slight contrast to the Great Neck longhouses, the twenty house patterns from Jordan's Point (44PG1 environs) on the James River in Prince George County are smaller and more oval in shape (Turner in press). Dimensions range from 4 to 5 meters (13–16 ft) in width and 5.5–9 meters (18–30 ft) in length. An additional thirty-five whole or partial house patterns recently have been uncovered at site 44JC308, located on the east bank of the Chickahominy River near its confluence with the James at Governor's Land at Two Rivers (Mary Ellen N. Hodges, personal communication 1992).

While the general form of the chief's, or werowance's, house was the same as those of the commoners, it was much larger. The paramount chief, Powhatan, had longhouses 27–38 meters (30–40 yds) in length (Smith 1986b:173). Spelman (1910:cvi) related that the king's house had "many darke windinges and turnings before any cum wher the Kinge is," indicating the werowance's longhouses had interior partitions, unlike the commoner's dwellings.

Also located in or near the werowance's village of each local chiefdom was a mortuary temple. Here the prepared remains of deceased werowances were kept. These arborlike structures were from 18 to 30 meters (60–100 ft) long and about 6 meters (20 ft) wide, with one door opening to the east. Inside, at the western end of the mortuary temple, was a raised platform upon which the remains of the werowances and their burial goods were placed. The remainder of the mortuary temple served as a storehouse for goods received through tribute. These items included corn, animal skins, copper, beads, pearls, and dyes (Smith 1986b:173; Spelman 1910:civ–cv; Rountree 1989:133–34). Various carved posts with images of their gods were set inside and outside the structure. Generally, the temples were maintained by two or three priests, although Powhatan's three mortuary temples at Uttamussak, in the heartland of the chiefdom, were cared for by seven chief priests. John White's late sixteenth-century watercolor drawings of the North Carolina Algonquians show mortuary temples located within the villages, while reports on some of the Virginia Algonquians place them away from the villages, out of the sight of commoners. Only priests and werowances could enter the temples (Smith 1986b:169, 1986c:122; Strachey 1953:88–89).

Additional structures associated with Algonquian villages were sweathouses and menstrual huts. The sweathouses, located on riverbanks, were small structures, probably oval in ground plan with a domed roof, able to hold six or eight people (Turner 1972:67–68; Rountree 1989:62–63). Strachey (1953:74) briefly mentioned the existence of menstrual huts but did not give a description of their form. During the communal winter deer hunts, small huts covered with mats were erected by the women (Smith 1986b:164). Other small, round, and conical structures probably existed in the villages as well (Turner 1972:66).

THE VILLAGES

The size of villages varied greatly according to contemporary documents. Smith's (1986b:162) first estimate for the number of houses in a village was from two to one hundred. Later, he modified his original estimate to read from two to fifty houses (Smith 1986c:116). Strachey (1953:77–78) wrote that "their howses are not manie in one towne, and those that are stand dissite [set apart] and scattered, without forme of a street, far and wyde asunder."

Gabriel Archer's (1969:103) account provides one of the earliest descriptions of Virginia Algonquian villages along the James River: "They dwell as I guesse by families of kindred and allyance some 40tie or 50tie in a Hatto or small village; w'ch townes are not past a myle or half a myle asunder in most places." Henry Spelman (1910:cvi), who lived with members of the Patawomeke chiefdom for approximately one year, stated that "places of Habitation they have but feaw for ye greatest toune have not above 20 or 30 houses in it." Archaeological excavations at a protohistoric village of the Patawomekes revealed that the site was surrounded by palisades (Schmitt 1965:68). For this reason, Feest (1973:67) noted that Spelman's account might refer to palisaded villages.

The basic distinction to be drawn concerning the Algonquian villages of the Virginia-Maryland tidewater is whether or not a district chief, or werowance, resided in the village. If he or she did, then such a village consisted of the werowance's longhouse, the werowance's mortuary temple and "treasury," and the houses and associated structures of kinfolk, other elite supporters, and some common people. If a village was not the seat of the district chief, it lacked all of the foregoing except the commoners' residences. Functionally specific structures such as household storage units, sweathouses, and menstrual huts were common to all places of settlement. The distinction between the village of a werowance and an "ordinary" village or hamlet is nowhere more apparent than on John Smith's map of Virginia.

Lewis R. Binford (1964:85) incorporated the attribute of size in his definitions of village and hamlet, the two settlement types he proposed as being characteristic of the Powhatan chiefdom. Reduced to its essentials, Binford's lengthy definition of a village is a settlement where the werowance lived, with from twelve to forty houses. A hamlet lacked the werowance's longhouse and the mortuary temple / storehouse found in a village and contained two to ten longhouses (Binford 1964:85). Problems exist with both definitions. There are no ethnohistorical data to support the proposition that a district chief's, or werowance's, village always had twelve or more houses. Nor are there data which indicate that ten was the maximum number of houses ever found in settlements lacking a resident district chief (Feest 1973:68).

Turner (1976:138) equated the term *village* with John Smith's "Kings howses" and *hamlet* with Smith's "Ordinary howses." As long as the distinction drawn by these two terms serves to define settlements where a werowance did and did not live, they are useful in reducing Smith's descriptive phrases to two concise words. However, these terms, so defined, can be considered only relative indicators of small and large settlements. Because of the potential overlap in the number of houses found in the two settlement types, hamlets and villages are regarded "as the small and large ends of a size continuum" (Flannery 1976:164).

Several criteria were used by the Virginia Algonquians in selecting a village location (Turner 1976:137–38; Rountree n.d.). As Smith (1986b:161) noted, "Their buildings and habitations are for the most part by the rivers or not farre distant from some fresh spring." Strachey (1953:77) added another criterion to Smith's observations: "Theire habitations or Townes, are for the most parte by the Rivers; or not far distant from fresh Springes comonly upon the Rice [rise] of a hill, that they maie overlooke the River and take every smale thing into view which sturrs upon the same." Gabriel Archer (1910:xliii), in his description of the village of Powhatan, near the falls of the James River, wrote: "It is scituat upon a highe Hill by the water syde, a playne between it and the water."

Another determinant of village location was nearness to marshlands. Smith's (1986a:39–40) passage describing the Chickahominy village of Manosquosick illustrates the interplay of four criteria for village location: "This place is called Manosquosick, a quarter of a mile from the river, conteining thirtie or fortie houses, upon an exceeding high land: at the foote of the hill towards the river is a plaine wood, watered with many springes, which fall twentie yardes right downe into the river: right against the same is a great marsh, of 4. or 5. miles circuit, devided in 2 ilands, by the parting of the river, abounding with fish and foule of all sorts."

The final determinant of village location mentioned in the historical sources is proximity to land suitable for slash-and-burn subsistence cultivation. A good example comes from Smith's (1986a:81) account of the discovery of Nansemond: "The river divideth in two, the neck a plaine high Corne field, the wester bought a high plaine likewise, the Northeast answerable in all respects. In these plaines are planted aboundance of houses and people. They may containe 1000. Acres of most excellent fertill ground."

In summarizing the discussion of villages, a number of points need to be made. The ethnohistorical data indicate that the houses of most villages (at least in the outer coastal plain) probably were dispersed (fig. 4). As Smith (1986c:116) stated: "Their houses are in the midst of their fields or gardens, which are small plots of ground. Some 20 acres, some 40, some 100. some 200. some more, some lesse. In some places from 2 to 50 of those houses together, or but a little separated by groves of trees."

One would expect most of the native villages in the coastal plain, near the Chesapeake Bay to have been situated on broad necklands, along the smaller estuaries. Smith's passage concerning the settlements of the Nansemonds vividly illustrates this. An examination of Smith's map of Virginia shows that many of the coastal villages were located on the tributaries of the major rivers, not along the banks of the mouths of the major rivers. All of the four major tidewater rivers are quite broad at their mouths. Any village situated directly on the banks of those rivers, along the lower reaches near their mouths, would have been more exposed to storms and wind and would have experienced colder temperatures in the winter. It is probably for those reasons that no Indians, or Indian villages, were visible to John Smith and his men for the first 48 kilometers (30 mi) of Potomac River shoreline. Therefore, it is unlikely that a major Late Woodland or historic period village in the Chicacoan locality would have been located along the Potomac River nearshore environment.

Curiously, only two palisaded villages (fig. 5) are mentioned in the early seventeenth-century documentary sources, even though archaeologists have uncovered six protohistoric or early historic palisaded villages in the Virginia-Maryland tidewater (Turner in press; Clark and Hughes 1983; Schmitt 1965:6–8; Stephenson et al. 1963:52–53).

Their rype corne

Their greene corne

Their newly sprong

The place of Solemne

Prayer

The hougé wherin the Tombe of their Herounds standeth

Their sitting at meate

SECOTON

A Cerémony in their prayers w strange testures and songes danfing about postes carued of the toppé lyke mens faces .

4. *John White watercolor of the North Carolina Algonquian village of Secoton, 1585, showing the dispersed houses of an open village. (Photograph by Victor E. Krantz; reproduced by permission of the University of North Carolina Press and the British Museum)*

*The towne of Pomeiock and true forme of their howses, covered
and enclosed some wth matts, and some wth barcks of trees. All compassed
abowt wth smale poles stuck thick together in steadd of a wall.*

5. *John White watercolor of the North Carolina Algonquian village of
Pomeiooc, 1585, showing houses enclosed by a circular palisade. (Photograph
by Victor E. Krantz; reproduced by permission of the University of North
Carolina Press and the British Museum)*

Nathaniell Powell and Anas Todkill (Smith 1986b:231) described the
fortified village of the Tockwoghs on the Eastern Shore near the head
of Chesapeake Bay as a "pallizadoed towne, mantelled with the barkes
of trees, with Scaffolds like mounts, brested about with Barks very for-
mally." In August or September 1609, the Jamestown colonists purchased the village of Powhatan and surrounding lands (Smith
1986b:221–23). Smith (1986c:223) described it as a "Salvage Fort,
readie built, and prettily fortified with poles and barkes of trees, sufficient to have defended them from all the Salvages in Virginia, dry
houses for lodgings and neere two hundred acres of ground ready to
be planted."

The Problem of Village Movement

Just as important as the factors involved in village selection were those factors involved in village movement. No early seventeenth-century sources describe the process of relocating a Virginia or Maryland Algonquian village to a new site. Nonetheless, it is likely that villages did shift from time to time to new locations.

One of the factors which may have necessitated village relocation was soil exhaustion. According to Smith (1986d:291), overworn fields were few because the ground was very fertile for the most part. However, using extant data on grass and weed growth, insect infestation, and natural soil fertility, E. Randolph Turner (1976:192–95) has calculated that agricultural soils in the tidewater would have required a slash-and-burn cycle with fallow periods of twenty-one to forty-two years if used for two to three consecutive years of planting.

Another problem, in conjunction with soil exhaustion, was weed control. The difficulty of keeping the agricultural plots free from weeds was related by Strachey (1953:114) and Smith (1986b:145, 151). The distance one would have to walk to gather wood for fuel or building is a third factor. Smith (1986c:116) observed that "neare their habitations is little small wood or old trees on the ground by reason of their burning them for fire." Other conditions which might have prompted a village to move, discussed by Conrad Heidenreich (1971:213–16) in his study of the Hurons, are fear of enemy attack, social tension arising from too large a village populace, and/or increases in the number of village pests, such as insects and rodents.

It should be noted that all of these factors are relative and must be weighed differently in each case. How they might have affected the relocation of a particular Algonquian village would have depended, among other things, upon the frequency and intensity of warfare, the village's total population, whether or not a district chief was resident, its storage capabilities, the degree of dispersion or nucleation of the village's longhouses, and the extent of the village's potential agricultural lands within its catchment area—the resource zone around a settlement that is within convenient walking or canoeing distance.

Subsistence

Cultivation, Soils, and Corn Estimates

In 1607 the subsistence economy of the Algonquian chiefdoms of the Virginia-Maryland tidewater was based, in part, on slash-and-burn or swidden cultivation. Varieties of maize, beans, squash, pumpkins, gourds, sunflower, and tobacco were grown by the natives, with the greatest emphasis on maize production (Feest 1978a:258; Strachey 1953:118–21). The best land for plant husbandry was "knowne by the vesture it beareth, as by the greatnesse of trees or abundance of weedes, etc." (Smith 1986a:145).

The Algonquians prepared their fields by girdling the trees near the roots and then scorching the trunks with fire to prevent any further growth (Smith 1986b:157). Once dead, many large trees were cut down (Spelman 1910:cxi), but some were left standing, as Smith observed (1986d:291): "Betwixt those trees they plant their corne, whose great bodies doe defend it from extreme gusts, and heat of the Sunne; where that in the plaines, where the trees by time they have consumed, is subject to both; and this is the most easie way to have pasture and corne fields, which is much more fertile than the other."

It is doubtful the low-intensity, controlled firing of the plots being prepared for cultivation caused more than superficial destruction of the humic material and soil microorganisms. Any burning of the humus which did occur contributed to the immediate availability of nutrients, and the death of microorganisms resulted in the release of their materials as nutrients and humic resources (Limbrey 1975:118–19). Erosion was retarded not only by allowing some dead trees to stand but by leaving all the stumps in place. The roots and stumps decaying in the soil provided a longer period of reserve nutrients, being released slowly into the soil over a number of years and compensating for the losses due to forest clearance and cropping (Limbrey 1975:124).

After a year the men worked up the area around the dead trees and stumps with a wooden hoelike tool (Smith 1986b:157). Then, using a dibble, or digging stick, the women made holes in the prepared ground in each of which they dropped four maize kernels and two bean seeds (Smith 1986b:157). This practice of planting beans and maize together aided in replenishing the nitrogen content of the soil. Hans Jenny (1941:257) noted that "continuous cropping of corn has a destructive effect on soil fertility, whereas the intensive use of legumes will preserve the original nitrogen content or may even increase it." The Virginia Algonquians never manured their overworn fields, which were few because the ground was so fertile for the most part (Smith 1986d:291).

Two types of fields were maintained for plant husbandry. The larger fields ranged from 8 to 81 hectares (20–200 a) per community, according to Smith (1986b:162, 1986c:116). In these fields were planted maize and some beans. The small plots, or household gardens, were from 30 to 61 meters (100–200 ft) on a side and contained the other cultigens grown by the Indians (Strachey 1953:79). These gardens were commonly interspersed between the individual dwellings.

The Algonquians' heavy dependence on maize production makes it of interest to examine the soil characteristics most suitable to its growth. Although maize can grow in soil with a pH from 5.0 to 8.0, yields are usually adversely affected by acidity below a pH of 5.5 (USDA 1938:757–58). In terms of natural fertility, moderately heavy clay loam, silt loam, or fine sandy loam is best suited for maize agriculture in most areas (Wilson 1955:647). Clayey soils would not have been suitable for digging stick and hoe cultivation. Nor would extremely light, sandy soils have been conducive to aboriginal maize production because of the necessity of adding fertilizers and their low capacity to retain water (Ward 1965:43).

It has been proposed that the soils most suited for late prehistoric agriculture within the Virginia coastal plain were the Class I soils (Turner 1976:31). These are currently the best agricultural soils in the region. The Class I soils have few limitations that restrict their use and are moderately deep, well-drained, and nearly level. In addition, they are easily worked and have a moderately high capacity to hold moisture. The soils are medium to low in organic matter and can be maintained at high productivity under continuous cultivation if adequate fertilization and good management are followed (Elder et al. 1963:24). Good management practices include crop rotation and the application of fertilizer and lime, none of which were practiced by the Virginia Algonquians (the addition of wood ash to the soil as a byproduct of slash-and-burn techniques may have increased the alkalinity, but this was not a conscious management practice and the ash was not spread over the plots).

Turner (1976:31) postulated that the distribution of Class I soils, currently restricted "to a very large extent to narrow strips bordering the major rivers and streams of the region," confined the late prehistoric settlements of the tidewater to these areas. In Northumberland and Lancaster counties, Virginia, the Class I soils are the Kempsville fine sandy loam, nearly level (1.4% of the total soil in Northumberland County), Matapeake silt loam, nearly level (5.9% of the total soil), and Sassafras fine sandy loam, nearly level (10% of the total soil; Elder et al. 1963:5, 24). Most of the class I Kempsville and Sassafras soils occur in the uplands (the area above the 50-foot contour interval) and not in the necklands containing the first and second terraces bordering the streams and rivers. It would seem, therefore, that in some instances the use of soil class as a predictive device for late prehistoric settlement locations is too general. On the other hand, the soil type, in most instances, is too specific.

However, the concept of soil association appears to be of some value in predicting late prehistoric site locations. A soil association is a group of defined and named soil units, containing a few major soil types and several minor ones, which occur together in a characteristic, though not strictly uniform, pattern. The soil associations are named for the major soil types within them. The major soil type for one soil association may also be present in other areas, but in a different pattern and proportion (Elder et al. 1963:18).

Using John Smith's map of Virginia, the approximate locations of historic Algonquian village sites were correlated with the soil associations on the general soil map for Northumberland and Lancaster counties. Three soil associations containing soils favorable to slash-and-burn maize cultivation are found in the vicinity of the general village locales in significantly higher proportions relative to their overall distributions within the two-county area. These associations are the Mattapex-Bertie, Matapeake-Mattapex, and Woodstown-Dragston (fig. 6).

The Mattapex-Bertie association covers 10 percent of Northumberland County and 7.5 percent of Lancaster County. It is made up of the following soil types: 35% Mattapex, 25% Bertie, 15% Woodstown, 10% steep and sloping lands, and 15% other soil types. The Matapeake-Mattapex association covers 7.5 percent of Northumberland and a few small areas in the southeastern part of Lancaster County. This association includes 60% Matapeake, 25% Mattapex, 5% Bertie, 5% steep and sloping lands, and 5% other soils. The Woodstown-Dragston association covers 10 percent of Northumberland County and 15 percent of Lancaster County and is composed of 35% Woodstown, 20% Dragston, 15% Mattapex, 10% steep and sloping lands, and 20% other soils (Elder et al. 1963:20–21).

The approximate location of the Chicacoan village, near or east of the L-shaped bend in the Coan River, is in an area of the Mattapex-Bertie association (see fig. 6). Situated near the head of the Little Wicomico River, the village of Wicocomoco was surrounded by soils of the Matapeake-Mattapex association, while its satellite village, Cinquack, was located along Cockrell Creek in an area of Mattapex-

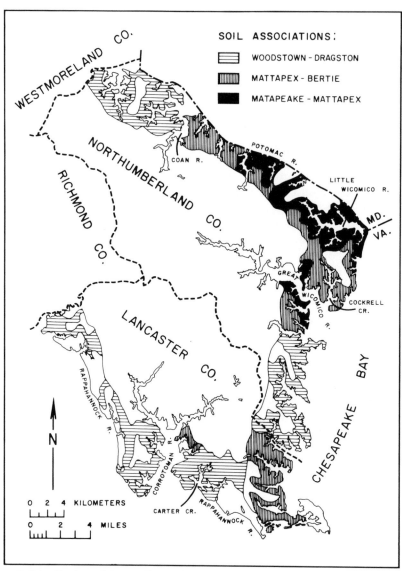

6. *Distribution of three soil associations in Northumberland and Lancaster counties, Va., most favorable to slash-and-burn cultivation. (Map by G. Robert Lewis)*

Bertie soils. The five villages of the lower Cuttatawomen apparently were distributed along the banks of the lower half of the Corrotoman River and along Carter Creek and its coves and branches. That area consists mainly of Woodstown-Dragston and Mattapex-Bertie associations.

In Northumberland and Lancaster counties, the soils that occur with the greatest frequency in the necklands, on the first and second terraces bordering the rivers and streams, are the Class II soils. Such soil types as the Mattapex silt loam, Woodstown fine sandy loam, and local alluvial land (all Class II soils) occur exclusively in the necklands, along with the Class I Matapeake silt loam soil. The remaining Class I soils occur in the uplands (Elder et al. 1963:24).

Relatively speaking, most Class I soils, taken as a whole, are more productive than most Class II soils; but the category of soil Class is so broad that it masks important similarities and differences. Reference to table 2 reveals that for Northumberland and Lancaster counties the three best Class II soils match the corn yields for the three best Class I soils, regardless of land management. An important difference between certain Class II and Class I soils is in their productivity during periods of drought. In the lower Northern Neck, the Class II Mattapex and Woodstown soils "are among the best soils in the area, and they may be cropped intensively" (Elder et al. 1963:25). Although they are slightly less well drained than the Sassafras and Kempsville Class I soils, in dry years the Mattapex and Woodstown soils are more productive of corn and soybeans. They are medium in natural fertil-

Table 2. Estimated productivity ratings of corn for the three best Class I and Class II soils (data from Elder et al. 1963:table 6)

Soils	Corn (bushels per acre)	
	Ordinary land management	Improved land management
Class I		
Kempsville fine sandy loam, nearly level	60	85
Matapeake silt loam, nearly level	65	100
Sassafras fine sandy loam, nearly level	60	90
Class II		
Mattapex silt loam	60	90
Woodstown fine sandy loam	60	85
Local alluvial land	65	100

ity, easy to cultivate, and slightly to strongly acid, with the Mattapex soil having a higher pH that is more suitable for optimum corn growth. Similarly, the Matapeake Class I soil is particularly favorable for corn because it has a greater capacity to supply the moisture that corn needs during the growing season (Elder et al. 1963:24–25).

Periods of deficient rainfall in the summer and fall cause droughts that damage crops about one out of every three years (Rice 1963:2). Such droughts seldom last long enough to affect all the crops grown in a particular season. Yet there are occasional periods when several dry years occur in succession, resulting in serious crop loss. Excessive periods of precipitation also occur, but these are less of a threat than drought (Bailey 1974:122; Rice 1963:2).

Historically, a number of droughts were recorded for the Virginia-Maryland tidewater several decades before and after permanent English settlement. During the late 1560s to about 1570, a six-year drought in tidewater Virginia forced native populations to disperse (Lewis and Loomie 1953:39–41, 89). In 1615 the Powhatans' harvest was so poor that John Rolfe (1971:6) noted that "som of their petty Kinges have borrowed this last yere, 4. or 500, bushelles of wheate [corn], for payment whereof this harvest, they have mortgaged their wholl Countries." Things had not improved by 1617, judging from Samuel Argall's remark: "Indians so poor cant pay their debts & tribute" (Kingsbury 1933:3:92). Another "great drought" was recorded by Samuel Argall and John Rolfe the following year (Smith 1986c:263). In 1632 a summer-long drought caused such a scarcity of corn that it probably helped to end the Second Anglo-Powhatan War (McCartney 1985:5). And "when famine prevailed among the Indians, on account of the excessive drought of this past summer," wrote the Maryland Jesuits in their annual letter of 1640 (Hall 1925:132), ". . . though corn was sold at a great price, nevertheless we considered it necessary to relieve their want of bread by assisting them."

As anthropologist Marvin Harris (1975:239) points out, "A basic principle of ecological analysis states that communities of organisms adapt to the minimum life-sustaining conditions in their habitats rather than to average conditions." If droughts occurred one out of every three years during protohistoric and early historic times, as they do today, then the Indians would have had to adapt to such agriculturally limiting environmental conditions. One means of doing so would have been to locate the majority of their agricultural plots on necklands containing the greatest percentage of easily tilled loams that are more productive of corn during periods of drought. Therefore, it seems likely that the agricultural fields and villages of the Chicacoans, Wicocomocos, and lower Cuttatawomens were located mainly on the broad terraces of the necklands, in catchment areas containing relatively high percentages of the Mattapex-Bertie, Matapeake-Mattapex, and Woodstown-Dragston soil associations (taking into consideration other determinants of village location).

As one moves up the Potomac River, toward the fall line, the soil associations and topography change. However, soil associations having properties similar to those in Northumberland and Lancaster counties probably were chosen for slash-and-burn maize cultivation for the same reasons. On the Virginia side of the river, the Nansemond-Tetotum-State, Tetotum-Bojac-Pamunkey, Tetotum-Bladen-Bertie, Galestown-Sassafras-Woodstown, and Matapeake-Mattapex-Woodstown soil associations would have been best (John C. Nicholson, personal communication 1979; Porter et al. 1963; Isgrig and Strobel 1974; Nicholson 1981). In Maryland soil associations like the Matapeake-Mattapex-Sassafras, Elkton-Othello-Keyport, Sassafras-Keyport-Elkton, and Collington-Matapeake-Galestown would probably have been most favorable for slash-and-burn subsistence cultivation (Kirby et al. 1967; Hall and Matthews 1974; Gibson 1978). However, as Francine Bromberg (1987:195) points out, geological maps may be more useful for predicting Algonquian village locations in the inner coastal plain, since these soil associations coincide with the Pleistocene and Holocene terraces near the river and its tributaries.

Using data gleaned from the observations of John Smith and William Strachey, Turner (1976:182–87) estimated Algonquian maize yields. A figure of 0.3 hectare (0.75 a) of land under cultivation per person per year seemed to him the most reasonable approximation when compared to Smith's (1986c:267) comment that "an industrious man not other waies imploied, may well tend foure akers of Corne, and 1000. plants of Tobacco" (Turner 1976:182–84; Smith 1986b:162). Smith (1986b:157) also mentioned that one stalk of corn averaged two ears, bearing between two and five hundred grains. Strachey (1953:118) wrote that the corn plants were spaced 1 to 1.5 meters (4–5 ft) apart. Furnished with this information, Turner (1976:184–85) assumed each maize plant was spaced slightly more than one meter (about 4 ft) apart, produced two ears, and yielded three hundred kernels per ear (this is a conservative estimate, since four kernels were planted per hole and more than one corn plant can grow in the same hole). This results in 705 liters (20 bu) of shelled maize per acre, or 529 liters (15 bu) of maize per person per year. In turn, this accords well with Smith's (1986c:267) estimate of 423 to 1,128 liters (12–32 bu) of maize per acre, which averages out to 775 liters (22 bu) per acre.

It is clear from Turner's (1976:182–87) analysis that maize contributed 50 percent or more to the yearly subsistence of the Virginia Algonquians. Conservatively, it at least can be said that Algonquians in Virginia's coastal plain were observed consuming maize, in various forms, throughout most of the year, although those partaking may have been only the chiefs and other high-status individuals (Turner 1976:179–82; Rountree 1989:46). In addition, when the English could not get all the maize they wanted from the Powhatans, they found it easier to get it from groups outside the core area of the Powhatan chiefdom, such as the chiefdoms along the Potomac River or the Accomacs and Occohannocks of the Eastern Shore (Fausz 1985:241; Feest 1966:74–75).

The scarcity of maize among the Powhatans during late winter and spring observed by the English may have resulted from several factors. Although the most obvious one would appear to be insufficient crop yields, perhaps the effects of heavy tribute payments to the chiefs drained off any surpluses from the commoners, leaving them with no extra maize to trade with the English and still sustain themselves (Feest 1966:80). Another possibility is that commoners put less effort into maize production for their own families, supplying the deficit with low-status foods that the paramount chief did not want (Rountree 1989:110). Or, as Turner (1976:181) has suggested, member groups of the Powhatan chiefdom "may have, on occasion, intentionally misled the English about the availability of maize and other domesticates since they may have had enough for year-round consumption though not sufficient for extensive trade with the English."

THE YEARLY ROUND

The Virginia Algonquians divided the year into five seasons. The winter was called Popanow, the spring was Cattapeuk, the summer was Cohattayough, the "earing" of the maize was Nepinough, and the harvest and fall of the leaf was Taquitock (Smith 1986b:156).

In late fall and winter the major deer hunts took place, usually inland, near the fall line, since deer were less plentiful in the coastal areas (Smith 1986b:154, 164). Once a favorable hunting spot was chosen, the women followed after the men and set up the base camp. According to William Strachey (1953:82), and corroborated by John

Smith (1986b:164), "Their hunting howses are not so laboured, sub-stancill nor arteficiall as their other, but are like our Soldiers Cabyns the frame sett up in twoo or three howres, cast over head with Matts, which the women beare after them, as they carry likewise Corne, Acorns, Mortars, and all bag and baggage to use." Sometimes as many as two or three hundred men from different local chiefdoms partici-pated in communal deer hunts. Drives and fire surrounds were the most common techniques employed (Smith 1986c:118).

Other animals taken during late fall and winter were rabbits, bears, turkeys, and a multitude of waterfowl, such as swans, cranes, geese, ducks, and mallards (Smith 1986a:43, 1986b:245, 1986c:194; Turner 1972:71). Strachey (1953:128) noted that oysters were smoked for year-round consumption. Similarly, Smith (1986b:158, 163) men-tioned the smoking or drying of fish, which preserved it a month or more. The consumption of oysters, both fresh and dried, is docu-mented for December, January, and February, while fish were served at feasts during December and January (Smith 1986c:194).

Walnuts, chestnuts, acorns, and chinquapins harvested during the fall were dried to keep and served as staples through the winter and into spring (Smith 1986b:152, 162; Archer 1910:xlviii). Bread made from the flour of maize was served to the English on occasions in De-cember and January (Smith 1986b:245, 1986c:112–13, 194). English expeditions throughout the territories of the tidewater Algonquians acquired corn, either by trade or force, during November, December, January, February, and even into early March (Smith 1986a:39–40, 79, 1986b:217, 250, 256–57, 1986c:155–57, 195, 198, 268).

"In March and Aprill they live much upon their fishing weares, and feed on fish, Turkies and squirrels" (Smith 1986b:162). Solitary deer were also taken (Smith 1986a:77). In the latter part of April and into May and June, strawberries, raspberries, blackberries, and huck-leberries were gathered (Smith 1986b:153, 162; Strachey 1953:121). Herbs were also collected during this time (Smith 1986b:153).

George Percy (1967:89) wrote that on April 27, 1607, "we came to a place where they [the Indians] had made a great fire, and had been newly roasting oysters. When they perceived our coming, they fled away to the mountains, and left many of the oysters in the fire. We ate some of the oysters, which were very large and delicate in taste."

April and May were the peak months for catching anadromous fish—fish that live in saltwater but spawn in freshwater—and consid-erable numbers were mentioned for June (Smith 1986b:228). They remained an important dietary item through August, with sturgeon runs noted until mid-September (Smith 1986b:162; Turner 1972:73). Marine fish would have been most abundant from March through September (Binford 1964:42–44).

"In Aprill they begin to plant, but their chiefe plantation is in May, and so they continue till the midst of June" (Smith 1986b:157). During the month of May, Archer (1910:xlii, xlviii, xlix) noted, the Indians served to the English walnuts, mulberries, strawberries, raspberries, parched maize, "sodd" beans, "wheate [maize], beanes and mulberyes sodd together," dried oysters, tortoises, fish, and deer. The walnuts, maize, and beans were stored items harvested the previous year, since walnuts were gathered in the fall and the maize and bean crops were planted in May (Smith 1986b:157; Archer 1969:100).

Smith (1986b:162) wrote: "In May and June they plant their fieldes, and live most of Acornes, walnuts, and fish. But to mend their diet, some disperse themselves in small companies and live upon fish, beasts, crabs, oysters, land Torteyses, strawberries, mulberries, and such like." Edible wild roots, called tuckahoe, were gathered in the marshlands from June through August. Green maize, considered a delicacy by the Indians, was also eaten during this time (Smith 1986b:162, 1986c:116). As the summer months wore on, more plant domesticates were gathered. By the end of July, squashes, gourds, and beans were available and continued so through August and into September, along with pumpkins (Smith 1986b:158; Strachey 1953:79; Archer 1969:100).

"From September untill the midst of November are the chiefe Feasts and sacrifice. Then have they plenty of fruits as well planted as naturall, as corne, greene and ripe, fish, fowle, and wilde beastes exceeding fat" (Smith 1986b:156–57). Mature maize was harvested in September and October. Acorns, chestnuts, hickory nuts, walnuts, and other nuts were gathered and stored for the winter. By late October and November, waterfowl, deer, turkeys, rabbits, and bear once again were taken in greater numbers (Smith 1986a:41–43, 1986b:152; Turner 1972:71).

Thus, the village was the center of most social and cultural activities from September through the middle of November. In the latter half of November the village population broke up, with mainly old men, women, and children staying in the village, while the men, with some women and children, established hunting base camps in the interiors of the peninsulas, near the fall line. Such winter hunts among the Powhatans involved men from several local chiefdoms. When John Smith was taken captive by Opechancanough in December 1607, the

latter was leading a hunting party of two hundred men from Paspah-
egh, Chickahominy, Youghtanund, Pamunkey, Mattaponi, and Kis-
kiack (Smith 1986a:45–47, 89–91).

Although the major hunts occurred primarily during the late fall
and winter months, hunting parties from particular villages went out
during other times of the year. Percy (1967:17) recorded on May 19,
1607, that "at length we came to a savage town, where we found but
few people. They told us the rest were gone a hunting with the Werowance of Paspiha [Paspahegh]." In a similar vein, several of the
Jamestown colonists noted during late August or early September
1608 that the people of Payankatank, a coastal chiefdom of the Middle
Peninsula, "were most a hunting, save a few old men, women, and
children, that were tending their corne" (Smith 1986c:178). Several
days later, but before September 7, the same party of Englishmen
went to a village of the Nansemonds where they were told by a native
that most of the people were away hunting. It is possible this was
a ruse on the Indians' part, since shortly afterward the English were
attacked by a large party of Indians farther upriver (Smith 1986c:
178–79).

By late winter or early spring, the majority of the people returned
to the villages. The agricultural fields and garden plots were worked
up, and the men probably cleared any new agricultural lands at this
time. Once most of the planting was under way, part of the village
populace broke up into smaller groups, to subsist upon fishing and
gathering oysters, berries, and chance quarry such as terrapins and
tortoises. The English accounts note that some group hunting was
conducted during late spring and late summer. If the hunting, fishing,
or gathering activities took place farther than a convenient day's journey to and from the village or were going to last awhile, camps were
established. Most of the village populace was resident again by the latter half of September.

The Chicacoans, 1608

Thomas Jefferson (1972:94–95) was the first person to suggest a location for the Chicacoan (Cekekawwon or Sekacawoni) village shown on
John Smith's map of 1612. He proposed that it was located somewhere
along the Coan River. Following Jefferson's lead, John Swanton
(1952:69) and Ben McCary (1957:6) placed the werowance's village on
the Coan River. Philip Barbour (1971:299), however, put Chicacoan
on Cherry Point Neck, which is west of the Coan River. He offered no

explanation for this departure from the preceding interpretations, but it can be refuted on two counts. First, comparing Smith's map of Virginia to a modern map (fig. 7), the Chicacoan village was located east of the first major drainage upriver from the mouth of the Poto-

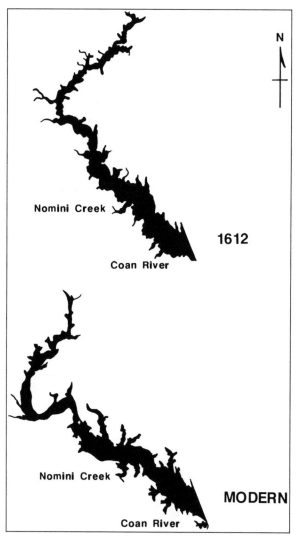

7. *Silhouettes of a 1612 map and a modern map of the lower Potomac River, showing the location of the Coan River and Nomini Creek*

mac, which is the Coan River. Or, one can use Nomini Creek and Bay as a point of reference, for their distinctive outline is readily recognizable on Smith's map. The werowance's village for the Matchotic (Onawmanient) was located along the west bank of Nomini Creek, which Barbour (1971:294) also agreed was the site of this village. Counting Nomini Creek as the first drainage and then proceeding down the Potomac to the fourth drainage, one is, again, at the Coan River. Also, historical accounts indicate that the first permanent English settler in Northumberland County settled along the east bank of the Coan River, on land he bought from the chief of the Chicacoan Indians (Potter 1976:40).

Chicacoan political organization was based on kinship. The major status position was that of chief, or werowance, which was inherited matrilineally. The nonchiefly status positions were advisers, or cronoccoes, priests, and shamans. A system of tribute collection supported the werowance, his or her family, other elites, and the priests. The tribute also provided for communal feasts, religious activities, entertaining distinguished guests, and sealing alliances with other groups. Commoners and war captives occupied the lowest two positions within the social and political hierarchy.

Like most of the Northern Neck groups, the Chicacoans were living on the "fringe" of a new ethnic identity Powhatan was shaping to fit the expanding bounds of his chiefdom (Rountree 1989:13–14). The Chicacoans apparently dealt with neighboring groups on an individual and independent basis. There is no evidence to indicate that they were involved in interchiefdom hostilities. Political relationships across the Potomac River, with the Yaocomacos of the Conoy chiefdom, were probably peaceful; at least, historical records for the 1640s and early 1650s indicate amicable cultural relationships. Indeed, the only groups with whom the Chicacoans may have had hostile dealings were the Iroquoian-speaking Susquehannocks and Massawomecks. Even though both groups lived some distance away, to the north and northwest, during the early 1600s they were raiding the Algonquians of southern Maryland and the Potomac River (see chapter 5).

The total number of Chicacoan warriors was put at thirty by both John Smith and William Strachey. This suggests an overall population of 120 to 130 people. Average household size was most likely between eight and ten individuals, or about eleven to sixteen households living in as many longhouses. Add to this the werowance's longhouse and at least one mortuary temple / storehouse for the werowance, and there were probably a total of between fifteen to eighteen longhouse structures. Ancillary storage units, sweathouses, and menstrual huts were also part of the village makeup.

Probably not all of the village structures were clustered. Rather, most of the longhouses were dispersed, with maybe a few clustering around the werowance's longhouse and storehouse. Any longhouses clustered near the werowance's house may have represented an overt display of close matrilineal kinship to the chief. Thus, the areal extent of the village was large because the village population was dispersed. Occasional raids by the Susquehannocks or Massawomecks probably would not have caused a major alteration in the village layout, but they might have led to the construction of a palisade around the werowance's longhouse, a few other structures, and perhaps the mortuary temple / storehouse. The preponderance of the longhouses would have remained dispersed outside this "fortified core" (Binford 1964:144; cf. Beverley 1968:177).

The Chicacoan village was probably located near the Coan River, along its eastern bank. It may have been situated on a rise adjacent to or within the terraced necklands. Freshwater springs also would have been nearby. The village's catchment area probably contained some marshlands, as well as high proportions of Mattapex-Bertie, Matapeake-Mattapex, and/or Woodstown-Dragston soil associations. The village would not have been located along the Potomac River shoreline, where it would have been more exposed to storms and colder winter temperatures due to the great breadth of the river.

To support the village population, about 36 to 41 hectares (90–100 a) of maize would have to have been under cultivation per year. That would have resulted in 63,428 to 70,476 liters (1,800–2,000 bu) of maize per year, or 529 liters (15 bu) per person. Such data, plus the historical records on the Virginia Algonquians, indicate that 50 percent or more of the total subsistence needs of the Chicacoans may have come from maize alone.

The ethnohistorical information makes it likely that the archaeological remains of the early seventeenth-century Chicacoans would be somewhat sparse, because they consist of the accumulated debris of a small population spread out over a relatively large area. The werowance's village should be visible as a horizontally extensive but vertically shallow midden, created by sustained human occupation of the site. Midden soil discoloration and artifact density should vary considerably within the village site. If a clustered area or a "fortified core" existed, this should appear as an area of dark midden whose outward perimeter approximates the periphery of the cluster or the palisade line. A high artifact density might also be expected within the dark midden. Other small midden stains and artifact clusters, representing the dispersion of longhouses outside any possible core area, may lie scattered over an extensive area.

Chicacoan gathering and hunting sites present a different set of problems in archaeological identification. Shell middens are the most obvious of gathering sites. If an oyster bar was within a convenient day's journey of the village, then the main activities conducted at the site probably were extractive. Consequently, the archaeological remains should reflect those activities associated with gathering and consuming mollusks and, perhaps, other aquatic resources, as well as limited hunting and gathering of resources within the immediate site environment. George Percy (1967:89) described visiting such a site on April 27, 1607. If, on the other hand, people were living on a site, in addition to gathering and consuming mollusks, then archaeological evidence of both extractive activities and camping should be present. Sites of this nature would have been created when some of the village population dispersed into small kin groups to live off marine resources, as was common in May and June. In consequence, such a shell midden should yield a greater diversity of archaeological remains, as opposed to a shell midden that served primarily as an extractive site.

Archaeological evidence of late fall and winter hunting base camps should be found quite some distance outside the village's catchment area, in the interior uplands. Other limited activity sites may be recognizable archaeologically, depending upon the nature and number of different activities which took place there and how often the site was revisited. With the ethnohistory of the Chicacoans thus predicting some of the archaeological possibilities, the search for Chicacoan began.

CHAPTER 2

The
Chicacoan
Locality

Introduction

TODAY THE AREA THAT WAS ONCE PART of the Chicacoan's heartland is defined by the Potomac River on the north and a ridge in the interior uplands which marks the head of the Coan, Presley, and Hull drainages on the south. This ridge corresponds roughly to Virginia State Highway Route 360. The neck of land along the east (right) bank of Hull Creek marks the eastern boundary, and the western boundary is the neck of land adjacent to the west (left) bank of the Coan River. This locality, encompassing approximately 65 square kilometers (25 mi²), was the area of intense archaeological study (fig. 8).

Systematic archaeological investigations in the Chicacoan locality began in the spring of 1976 with a three-day reconnaissance and low-altitude aerial flights. During the summer of the same year, nine weeks of archaeological survey and test excavations were conducted. In 1978 brief on-the-ground surveys were done periodically throughout the year, along with low-altitude aerial survey. From May 17 to August 16, 1978, excavations took place at three sites: Blue Fish Beach (44NB147 on fig. 9), Boathouse Pond (44NB111), and Plum Nelly (44NB128). The next year, a low-altitude aerial survey, with on-the-ground confirmation, was done in the spring.

In addition to the archaeological research within the Chicacoan locality, on-the-ground survey was done at selected spots along the Yeocomico River and the Little and Great Wicomico rivers in Northumberland County, Farnham Creek in Richmond County, and the Corrotoman River in Lancaster County (see fig. 8). Low-altitude aerial surveys were flown throughout the four counties of Westmoreland,

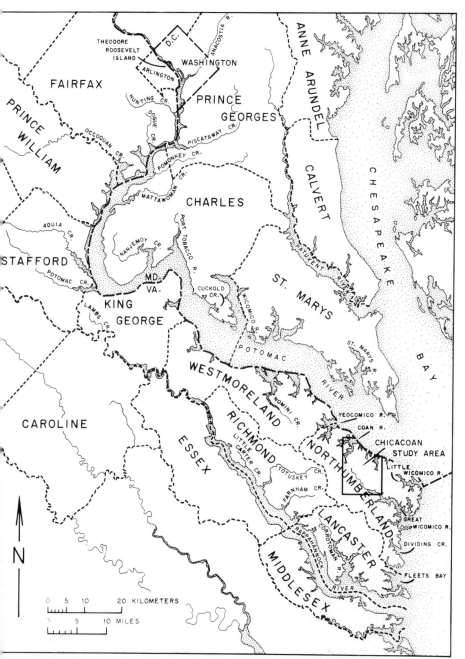

8. *Modern map showing the relationship of the Chicacoan study area to
counties and streams in the lower Patuxent, Potomac, and Rappahannock
river basins. (Map by G. Robert Lewis)*

Northumberland, Richmond, and Lancaster. Flight coverage was most intense over the area from the Yeocomico River to the Chesapeake Bay and from the Potomac River south to the interior uplands around the headwaters of the Great Wicomico River. A flight was also made along the north bank of the Rappahannock River, starting around Little Carter Creek and heading eastward to the east (left) bank of the Corrotoman River.

At the conclusion of the archaeological field investigations, 181 archaeological sites were recorded. These sites are the result of human occupation from as early as 8,000 B.C., during the Dalton subphase of the Paleo-Indian period, up to the middle of the nineteenth century A.D. However, because the purpose of the research was to examine locational changes in Indian occupations from A.D. 200 through the seventeenth century, only archaeological sites containing evidence of these occupations were analyzed—a total of fifty-six sites, of which fifty were recorded in the Chicacoan study area (fig. 9).

The Archaeological Survey and Excavations

EARLIER INVESTIGATIONS IN THE LOCALITY

In 1891 and 1892 William Dinwiddie and occasionally W. H. Holmes and Gerard Fowke of the Smithsonian Institution surveyed sections of the Northern Neck, principally along the shorelines of the lower Potomac River, Chesapeake Bay, and the lower Rappahannock River (Holmes et al. 1891). Their intent was to record the locations of Native American archaeological sites and to collect representative samples of artifacts from the region. Site locations were plotted on maps, but no system of site designation was used. Therefore, only in some cases can the artifact collections be correlated with specific archaeological sites. Most commonly, stream or creek drainages were named as the proveniences of the artifact collections.

Several points need to be made concerning the Smithsonian's survey. First, Holmes and his assistants were very familiar with the accounts of the historic Algonquians contained in John Bozman's 1837 *History of Maryland* and the 1884 edition by Edward Arber of *Capt. John Smith, Works, 1608–1631*. Second, although Holmes (1907:114) believed some of the oyster-shell middens of the south Atlantic coast were of "considerable age," indicating the "lapse of many centuries," he thought the shell middens along the middle and northern Atlantic were "so nearly homogeneous throughout their mass as to be re-

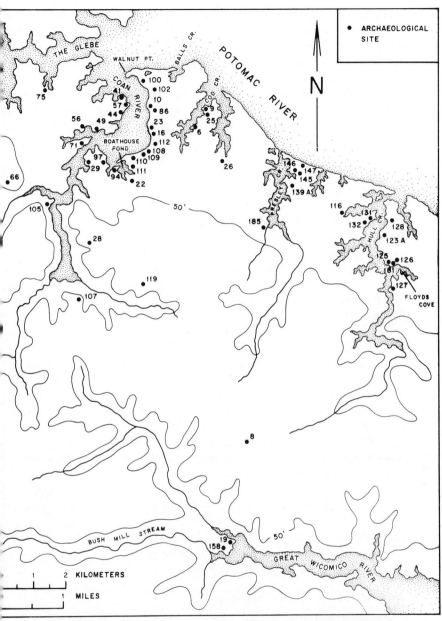

9. Archaeological sites in the Chicacoan study area with Native American components dating from ca. A.D. 200 to the mid-seventeenth century. (Map by G. Robert Lewis)

garded as representing a rather limited and not seriously interrupted period of occupancy." Therefore, all of the oyster-shell middens discovered during Holmes and Dinwiddie's survey of the Northern Neck were thought to be the result of occupations by the historic Virginia Algonquians or their immediate ancestors. However, subsequent archaeological research has revealed that some of the shell middens found throughout the lower Potomac River valley accumulated as a result of intermittent native occupations from at least the Late Archaic period to the historic period, a range of about 5,000 years. Consequently, it cannot be assumed, as Dinwiddie did, that the sites he located were contemporaneous (Holmes et al. 1891).

Dinwiddie jotted down some of his ideas on archaeological site locations, a few of which deserve to be mentioned. For Dinwiddie, the main determinants of "good aboriginal town sites" were: (1) spring water, (2) ease of access to lodges, (3) shallow oyster bars, and (4) quiet navigable water for small boats. He found that all of those factors prevailed on the small creeks, where most of the archaeological sites were located. Few of those conditions were present along the shoreline of the Potomac River, and Dinwiddie did not find many sites there (Holmes et al. 1891). However, he failed to consider the dynamic nature of the Potomac River shoreline over time and the possible loss of archaeological sites to shoreline erosion.

Even more interesting is Dinwiddie's explanation for why he found so few archaeological sites along the creeks and rivers that empty into the Chesapeake Bay between the Potomac and Rappahannock rivers. With the exception of the Great Wicomico River, Dinwiddie noted that all of the creeks were quite short and emptied into the wide and turbulent Chesapeake, and there were few oyster bars with only very light production (in 1891). Although the Great Wicomico River was much longer, he thought that "the depth of water in the Wicomico itself was too great to have admitted of aboriginal oystering, even if bars had existed, but the oyster seems to have found only a limited natural footing here, and the more extensive bars are mostly of artificial propagation" (Holmes et al. 1891). According to Dinwiddie, such conditions made it unlikely that any native villages were located on these creeks on the Chesapeake Bay (Holmes et al. 1891).

SURVEY STRATEGY AND TECHNIQUES

The main objective of the survey was to identify and isolate prehistoric and historic Indian occupations dating from about A.D. 200 through the seventeenth century. There were three corollary objectives: (1) to

identify the protohistoric and historic period archaeological components and to trace the historically documented Chicacoans back in
prehistory; (2) to locate sites with buried archaeological deposits in
order to increase the chance of recovering environmental data and to
provide data on the local sequence of archaeological cultures; and (3)
to test a hypothesis of William Dunwiddie's concerning the location of
the early seventeenth-century Chicacoan village.

Most of the survey was done during nine weeks in the summer of
1976 by a field crew of two people. Total on-the-ground coverage of
the 65 square kilometers (25 mi²) of the study area was not feasible
given the limited time and resources. While random selection of sampling units within the Chicacoan locality would have provided an accurate basis for estimating the number and diversity of archaeological
sites by environmental variables (Flannery 1976:159–60), it would not
have increased the probability of discovering protohistoric or historic
Chicacoan occupations, nor would it have been particularly feasible in
an area broken up into hundreds of privately owned parcels of land
(Wilke and Thompson 1977:62). A survey strategy was needed which
would increase the probability of discovering protohistoric and historic Chicacoan components, crosscut the lesser physiographic zones
of necklands, slopes, and uplands, and provide a basis for accurately
estimating the location of various types of sites during the 1,450 years
under study.

Prior analysis of the historical sources indicated that the Chicacoans were most likely living along the east (right) bank of the Coan
River in the early seventeenth century. It seemed reasonable to assume that there would be a higher probability of discovering protohistoric and historic Chicacoan components here than elsewhere in the
study area. Therefore, the land adjacent to the east bank of the Coan
River, as well as portions of the west bank, was purposely selected for
complete coverage as a sampling unit within the Chicacoan study
area.

The sampling unit was defined as the land along the east bank of
the Coan River drained by streams flowing into the Coan River or Cod
Creek. Its physiographic bounds were the Potomac River, Cod Creek,
the interior uplands drained by the easternmost heads of streams
flowing into the Coan River, and the western bank of the Coan (the
boundary is shown as the heavy solid line in fig. 10). Those bounds
encompassed roughly 22.3 square kilometers (8.6 mi²), or about 33
percent of the total study area. The sampling unit had the following
characteristics: (1) it incorporated the area thought to have been oc-

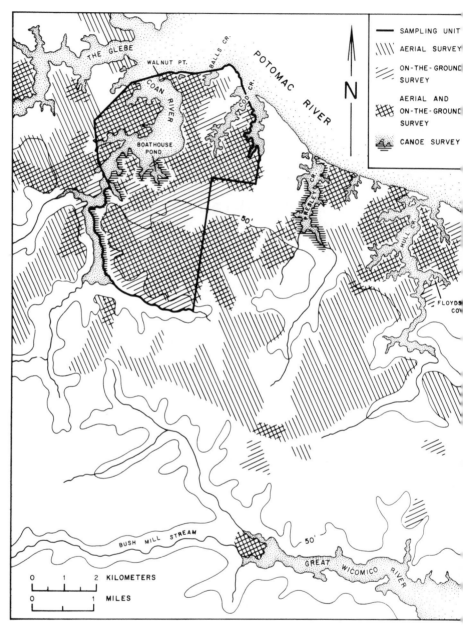

10. The Chicacoan study area showing sampling unit, lands surveyed, and methods used. (Map by G. Robert Lewis; redrawn by permission of the Smithsonian Institution Press)

cupied by an early seventeenth-century Chicacoan village; (2) it was defined according to physiographic boundaries; (3) it included a complete physiographic cross section of uplands, slopes, and necklands, with 45 percent of the unit being uplands (the land above the 50-foot contour interval); (4) there was a high percentage of large tracts of land with single owners, making it easier to survey; and (5) complete coverage would provide an accurate basis for estimating the types of archaeological components within the study area. Although complete coverage of the sampling unit was planned, only 85 percent of the area could be surveyed (see fig. 10). The remaining 15 percent consisted of properties where access was not obtained. Fortunately, of the 85 percent of the sampling unit surveyed, the proportion of upland to neckland was the same as the proportion for the entire unit. Thus, given the state of land ownership at the time of the fieldwork, the sampling unit was surveyed as completely as possible.

Along the west (left) bank of the Coan River, 65 percent of the necklands were walked. The remainder could not be surveyed due to crop cover, such as wheat, or owner refusal. Other widely dispersed land tracts in the uplands of the west bank and head of the Coan River were selected for survey as a basis for hypothesis formulation or testing. Additional land tracts farther in the interior uplands of the Chicacoan locality were surveyed with the same purpose in mind.

Approximately one-third of the west bank of Presley Creek could not be surveyed, because of a cottage and recreational community. The remainder of the creek's shoreline was completely surveyed by foot and canoe, in addition to on-the-ground coverage of two large tracts of land adjacent to the creek. One tract was selected near the western head of Presley Creek, which transected the necklands, slopes, and uplands. The second tract was selected near the eastern side and mouth of the creek, to sample this area as well as the Potomac River shorefront. The two tracts were of equivalent size.

The lower half of the east bank of Hull Creek was surveyed in order to test a hypothesis proposed by William Dinwiddie. In 1891 Dinwiddie observed:

> It is more than probable that the large and extensive sites found here are the ancient remains of the village or "King's Howse" known to John Smith as Cekakawon. . . .
> The largest settlement was apparently in the right a little more than a mile above the mouth, on a farm now owned by Mr. T. R. Cole, and originally in Colonial times formed a portion of the Cralle estate. [Holmes et al. 1891]

Since Dinwiddie's hypothesis on the location of the 1608 Chicacoan village was at variance with the generally accepted historical location, it was decided that the area mentioned by Dinwiddie, as well as the opposing west bank of Hull Creek, should be reexamined by a thorough walkover.

There were three means of surveying: by foot, canoe, and air (see fig. 10). In cultivated fields the on-the-ground survey consisted of team members walking approximately 9.5 meters (about 30 ft) apart. Each person looked for artifacts, faunal remains (mollusk shells or animal bones), surface indications of features, or soil textural or color differences. Soil probes were used to determine the nature of the soil profile and to detect subsurface features or midden deposits. In wooded areas random shovel tests and soil probes were relied upon, as well as the examination of eroded areas, tree falls, and banks.

The canoe was used to gain access to thickly wooded shoreline properties or to examine the shoreline for archaeological sites. The latter procedure required the team to paddle close to the shoreline, looking for artifacts, faunal remains (especially mollusk shells), features, or soil discolorations. The canoe proved most useful in surveying shorelines along shallow waters.

Aerial survey was done using several different light aircraft, mainly Cessnas. Flights were made at low altitudes, usually between 152 and 305 meters (500–1,000 ft). Experimentation at various seasons during a three-year period proved that the optimum times for spotting archaeological sites from the air were late winter and early spring. If a small-grained winter cover crop, such as wheat, was growing over an archaeological midden, the wheat would be denser, greener, and thicker than in surrounding areas, especially when the soils began to warm up in late winter. On the other hand, in plowed fields the damp soil marks of archaeological middens showed up most clearly about two days after disc-harrowing for spring planting. During times of severe drought, such as the summer of 1976, green crop marks, similar to those observed in late winter, were sometimes visible in small-grained crops like wheat or rye.

The best photographic results were attained at oblique angles to the suspected archaeological site, at between 152 and 213 meters (500–700 ft) altitude. The plane usually made one complete circle around the site before any photographs were taken. This was done to determine the best photographic angle, taking into consideration the height and angle of the plane, the angle of the sun, the direction of cultivation, and the size and nature of the archaeological site. Both color and black-and-white shots were taken, using a hand-held 35-mm camera.

A dozen flights were made over the Chicacoan locality during a three-year period. At least once during these flights all cultivated fields in the study area were observed under damp soil conditions shortly after spring cultivation. No large or intermediate-size prehistoric or historic Indian sites with either dark-earth or shell midden were observed in the interior uplands, above the 50-foot contour interval. All tracts of land containing suspected archaeological sites observed from the air were completely surveyed on the ground.

Once a site was located and its limits were ascertained, one of three procedures was used to make the surface collection: (1) the entire site was completely walked, using cultivation rows or survey flags as markers, and all visible archaeological material was collected; (2) the investigators spaced themselves about 4 meters (approximately 13 ft) apart and collected all cultural debris in their path; and (3) a controlled surface collection was made of the entire site using grid units 20 meters square (about 65 ft on a side), with everything of potential archaeological significance picked up.

The first procedure was used on small and intermediate-size sites with concentrations of cultural debris. The second procedure was utilized on sites of intermediate size with diffuse artifact scatters and on some large sites. When this procedure was applied to a large site, the site would be divided into collection units based on observable physiographic features, such as knolls, slopes, or swales. The third procedure was used on one large and one intermediate-size, multicomponent site. The first two procedures were employed in the summer of 1976, when the survey team consisted of two members. The third procedure was applied in the summer of 1978, when survey crews of four or more people were available.

EXCAVATION TECHNIQUES

When the decision was made to excavate a particular site, a grid system of either 1.5- or 2.0-meter (5- or 6.56-ft) squares was laid out; the size of the square depended on the extent of the archaeological site and the nature and depth of the deposits. Squares were designated by reference to the southeast corner.

Since most archaeological sites in the Chicacoan locality either were under cultivation or had been plowed sometime during the past three hundred years, the plow zone was shoveled off, followed by the removal of plow scars and plow ridges. All soil was screened through

6-millimeter (1/4-in) wire mesh. If there were no archaeological deposits below the base of the plow zone, the top of the subsoil was troweled in the hope of identifying subsurface features, such as post-molds, storage pits, trash pits, or rock-hearth clusters. On the other hand, if there were archaeological deposits beneath the plow zone, the site was excavated either by natural and cultural zones of deposition or by 5-centimeter (2.0-in) arbitrary levels, whichever was most appropriate to the conditions at that site.

All soil and oyster-shell midden was removed by trowels or three-tine hand forks and screened through 6-millimeter (1/4-in) wire mesh. Material from each zone or level was bagged and recorded separately by zone and unit. Artifacts recovered in situ were plotted by horizontal and vertical coordinates and bagged separately from the general finds recorded by zone and unit. Horizontal plans were drawn and photographed for each cultural zone within each unit, and the profiles of the units were drawn and photographed (black-and-white prints and color slides).

Similarly, all features were mapped and photographed before and after excavation. Cross sections of features were drawn when appropriate. In most instances two samples of fill were taken from the features, one for flotation and the other for soil analysis. If a feature contained mollusk shell, a sample of shell also was taken.

Feature fill was floated using rectangular stainless steel frame baskets lined with 1-millimeter wire mesh. The fill was placed in the baskets that were carried to the shallow waters along the shoreline adjacent to the sites where they were partially immersed. With gentle agitation, the soil particles were suspended in the water, the heavy, noncharred material stayed in the bottom of the basket, and the light, carbonized plant remains (e.g., seeds and nut fragments) floated to the surface, where they were gathered using a strainer of 1-millimeter wire mesh. The carbonized plant remains were air-dried and then placed in plastic bags labeled with the appropriate provenience information.

SITE DESIGNATION AND CLASSIFICATION

The sites were recorded following the Smithsonian Institution's River Basin Survey system, in use by the Virginia Department of Historic Resources and the Maryland Historical Trust. Each archaeological site is given a three-part designation consisting of codes for the state and county, followed by a unique number. For example, 44NB111 stands for Virginia (44), Northumberland County (NB), and site number

111. In addition, certain sites were assigned descriptive names, by which they were known in the field; site 44NB111 is also known as the Boathouse Pond site. Detailed information pertaining to sites from the Chicacoan locality is available to researchers on the site survey forms in the Virginia Department of Historic Resources' Archaeological Inventory Archives (hereafter referred to as VDHR Archaeological Inventory Archives), or in the author's "Analysis of Chicacoan Settlement Patterns" (Ph.D. diss., 1982).

The method of site classification employed in the descriptions is modified from a classification system devised by John Cottier and Gregory Waselkov (Waselkov 1980:137–41). The main feature of the system is that it distinguishes units of observation from units of systemic interpretation (table 3). Site size, integrity, and predominant midden composition were chosen as the most significant attributes for site classification. Sites with more than 50 percent of the midden volume composed of dark earth (the remainder being mollusk shell) are termed "midden" sites. Sites consisting of 50 percent or more mollusk shell (the remainder being dark-earth midden) are termed "shell midden" sites. Those sites lacking dark-earth and/or shell midden are called "decomposed" (after Waselkov 1980:139). These three varieties are further subdivided into three arbitrarily chosen size grades: (1) large—1 hectare (2.47 a) or larger; (2) intermediate—between 1 hectare and 1,000 square meters (2.47 a and 10,800 ft^2); and (3) small—1,000 square meters (10,800 ft^2) or less.

This system allows one to classify sites readily based on attributes observable during intensive survey. In the case of shallow, multicomponent sites, "if the limits of different components can be identified by controlled surface collections, then an archaeologist can assign each component to a class and need not assume site homogeneity" (Waselkov 1980:139–40).

Finally, the archaeological site classification is not to be confused with a settlement typology. The former is not based on an interpretation of the cultural system, while the latter is. Although relationships between site observation and systemic interpretation are suggested, in most instances additional excavations are needed to confirm the interpretations.

DESCRIPTIVE CLASSIFICATION FOR LITHIC ARTIFACTS

The description of stone artifacts found during the archaeological investigations is modified from lithic typologies developed by William Fitzhugh (1972:71–72), Jefferson Chapman (1977:85–96), and John

Table 3. Archaeological survey site classification

Class	Description	Observable characteristics
1	Large midden site	1 ha or larger with more than 50% of the midden composed of dark earth
2	Intermediate midden site	Between 1 ha and 1,000 m² in size with more than 50% of the midden composed of dark earth
3	Small midden site	1,000 m² or less in size with more than 50% of the midden composed of dark earth
4	Large shell midden site	1 ha or larger with 50% or more of the midden composed of mollusk shell
5	Intermediate shell midden site	Between 1 ha and 1,000 m² in size with 50% or more of the midden composed of mollusk shell
6	Small shell midden site	1,000 m² or less size with 50% or more of the midden composed of mollusk shell
7	Large decomposed site	1 ha or larger without dark-earth midden and/or shell midden
8	Intermediate decomposed site	Between 1 ha and 1,000 m² in size without dark-earth midden and/or shell midden
9	Small decomposed site	1,000 m² or less in size without dark-earth midden and/or shell midden

House and Ronald Wogaman (1978:58–61). Classes of lithic artifacts not defined below are described and/or illustrated in the text using generally accepted terms.

Core: Any mass of stone from which one or more flakes have been removed (leaving primary flake scars) that exhibits no evidence of prepared tool edges or edge damage indicative of use as a tool.

Chunk: An angular piece of lithic debris, shatter, or core fragment considered to be the by-product of lithic reduction in the early stages of stone tool manufacture.

Hammerstone: Usually a fist-size, roughly spherical or oblong cobble, with edge wear indicative of battering. Most specimens in the lower Northern Neck are made from quartzite.

Flake: Usually a thin piece of chipped stone debris which, if complete, has an observable striking platform, dorsal and ventral faces, and no original exterior surface or cortex.

Decortication flake: A thin piece of chipped stone with cortex on the dorsal face.

Utilized flake: A tool made from a flake, exhibiting intentional, secondary flake scars along the flake edge(s). Utilized flakes were made without a standard form of production, the flake itself being a by-product of other manufacturing processes. Only slightly modified, they were used casually and discarded.

Point: A morphologically defined class of bifacially chipped stone tools generally having basal modification for hafting, symmetrical working edges, and relatively sharp tips. The class may include some tools used to tip projectiles, as well as those which were used as knives or for multiple functions.

Biface: A tool class which includes artifacts with bifacial flaking that cannot be grouped functionally as points or blanks. Artifacts in the biface category actually may have served as projectile points, knives, or blanks, but the attributes of the specimens do not indicate the kind of use.

Blank: A bifacial or unifacial chipped stone artifact in uncompleted form, generally intended for use as either a projectile point or knife. It is recognized by its sinuous edges, lack of retouch, large flake scars, and thick body. The artifact outline approximates the length-width ratio of the completed form.

Scraper: A unifacial or bifacial chipped stone artifact with steep working edges, generally greater than 40°. This class of artifacts consists of tools made specifically for scraping and does not include casual tools like utilized flakes.

Ground stone axe: A large, thick bifacial tool, shaped by flaking or pecking followed by grinding and, in some instances, polishing. The tool possesses a single, bifacial, transversely oriented working edge on one end. In outline, the tool can be trianguloid, or rectanguloid, and without grooves for hafting (celts) or rectanguloid with a groove completely around the tool (full-grooved axe) or a groove only three-quarters of the way around the tool (three-quarter-grooved axe).

ARTIFACT TYPES AND CHRONOLOGY

Artifact types are analytical units created by an archaeologist as a means of arranging data to solve a particular research problem. The nature of the problem defines the cluster of attributes used in constructing a type (Griffith 1977:32–35). Because the purpose of the survey was to locate and document changes in Chicacoan settlement location over time, artifact types were needed as chronological indicators. Hence, of primary interest were temporal or historical types, which are types defined by clusters of temporally sensitive attributes. For the period of time under consideration, pottery vessels are the most sensitive temporal indicators, and therefore, much of this volume's discussion revolves around this class of artifacts. Ceramic types dating to approximately the same time and having similar temper or paste are grouped into wares (Griffith and Artusy 1977:11–12).

To order the sites and components from the Chicacoan locality in time, four temporal units were defined on the basis of time-sensitive artifact types. These temporal units are: (1) the late Middle Woodland period, which dates from about A.D. 200 to perhaps as late as A.D. 900; the Late Woodland period, which is subdivided into (2) Late Woodland I, dating from A.D. 900 to approximately 1300, and (3) Late Woodland II, which dates from roughly A.D. 1300 to about 1500; and (4) the protohistoric and early historic period, dating from A.D. 1500 to the 1650s. Using the data from an analysis of the trends and variations in archaeological component location, size, integrity, predominant midden composition, and proposed function, settlement patterns are described and interpreted for each temporal unit.

Late Middle Woodland Period, A.D. 200–900

DIAGNOSTIC ARTIFACTS

The pottery characteristic of the latter half of the Middle Woodland period, from around A.D. 200, or somewhat earlier, until about A.D. 800 or 900, is a coarse, thick, shell-tempered ceramic known as Mockley ware (fig. 11). This ware, defined by Robert Stephenson (et al. 1963:105–9), consists of three types: Mockley Cord-marked, Mockley Net-impressed, and Mockley Plain. Radiocarbon dates from southern Delaware to the lower James River, Virginia, confirm the temporal placement of Mockley ware (table 4).

Mockley ware vessels are medium to large coil-constructed jars with direct rims and rounded or semiconical bottoms. Rims are usually straight, although inverted and everted forms occur occasionally (Stephenson et al. 1963:105). Depending upon the clay source used and how well the clay was prepared, varying amounts of sand, limon-

11. Mockley Net-impressed (a, b, and d) and Cord-marked (c) pottery from Blue Fish Beach (44NB147) and Nomini Cord-marked (e and g) and Fabric-impressed (f and h) pottery from White Oak Point (44WM119). (Photograph by Victor E. Krantz)

Table 4. Radiocarbon dates associated with ceramics from the Chesapeake coastal plain

Associated ceramic ware	Uncorrected date, years A.D.	Laboratory no.	State	Reference
Mockley	20 ± 70	Beta-25913	VA	Edwards et al. 1989:63
	40 ± 80	Beta-25914	VA	Edwards et al. 1989:63
	175 ± 65	SI-3669	MD	Curry and Kavanagh 1991:19
	200 ± 90	SI-449	MD	Curry and Kavanagh 1991:20
	200 ± 90	I-5817	DE	Custer 1984:181
	210 ± 260	AA-321	MD	Custer 1989:355
	240 ± 70	UGa-1762	DE	Custer 1984:181
	250 ± 60	Not given	VA	Gleach 1988:94
	280 ± 60	Not given	VA	Gleach 1988:94
	300 ± 70	Beta-25915	VA	Edwards et al. 1989:63
	300 ± 110	I-6060	DE	Custer 1984:181
	325 ± 160	UGa-1273b	DE	Custer 1984:181
	330 ± 65	UGa-1273a	DE	Custer 1984:181
	340 ± 60	Not given	VA	Gleach 1988:94
	410 ± 60	Not given	VA	Gleach 1988:94
	445 ± 90	Not given	VA	Opperman 1980:4
	450 ± 60	Not given	VA	Gleach 1988:94
	460 ± 90	Not given	VA	Gleach 1988:94
	480 ± 60	Not given	VA	Gleach 1988:94
	580 ± 120	M-1608	MD	Curry and Kavanagh 1991:18
	700 ± 90	SI-3670	MD	Curry and Kavanagh 1991:19
	775 ± 75	SI-4942	DE	Custer 1984:181
	815 ± 95	I-5246	MD	Curry and Kavanagh 1991:20
	860 ± 60	DIC-1763	VA	Waselkov 1982:247
	875 ± 90	Not given	VA	Opperman 1980:4
	880 ± 60	DIC-1769	VA	Waselkov 1982:237
Nomini	860 ± 60	DIC-1763	VA	Waselkov 1982:247
	880 ± 60	DIC-1769	VA	Waselkov 1982:237
Currioman	1340 ± 55	DIC-1768	VA	Waselkov 1982:243
Sullivan	1040 ± 60	SI-3666	MD	Curry and Kavanagh 1991:18
	1330 ± 50	Beta-13050	MD	Curry and Kavanagh 1991:19
	1385 ± 55	SI-3665	MD	Curry and Kavanagh 1991:18
	1420 ± 70	Beta-13051	MD	Curry and Kavanagh 1991:19
Townsend	880 ± 70	Beta-27073	MD	Curry and Kavanagh 1991:19

Table 4. (continued)

Associated ceramic ware	Uncorrected date, years A.D.	Laboratory no.	State	Reference
	945 ± 65	UGa-1460	VA	Outlaw 1990:85
	970 ± 80	Beta-27069	MD	Curry and Kavanagh 1991:19
	975 ± 60	SI-4946	DE	Custer 1984:181
	1000 ± 60	SI-2686	MD	Custer 1984:183
	1005 ± 70	SI-4374	VA	Waselkov 1982:241
	1015 ± 55	UGa-1760	DE	Custer 1984:181
	1030 ± 110	Beta-11638	MD	Curry and Kavanagh 1991:18
	1045 ± 60	SI-2684	MD	Custer 1984:183
	1070 ± 50	Beta-27074	MD	Curry and Kavanagh 1991:20
	1085 ± 75	UGa-923	DE	Custer 1984:180
	1100 ± 55	UGa-1440	DE	Custer 1984:180
	1125 ± 65	SI-4230	VA	Potter 1982:241–42
	1140 ± 80	Beta-11639	MD	Curry and Kavanagh 1991:18
	1225 ± 75	SI-4232	VA	Potter 1982:241–42
	1235 ± 60	SI-2188	MD	Custer 1984:183
	1245 ± 125	UGa-1547	VA	Outlaw 1990:85
	1260 ± 50	UGa-1461	VA	Outlaw 1990:85
	1285 ± 75	UGa-925	DE	Custer 1984:180
	1310 ± 50	DIC-1764	VA	Waselkov 1982:240
	1340 ± 55	DIC-1768	VA	Waselkov 1982:243
	1345 ± 60	SI-4943	DE	Custer 1984:180
	1370 ± 60	UGa-924	DE	Custer 1984:180
	1460 ± 45	DIC-1766	VA	Waselkov 1982:240
	1590 ± 120	SI-137	VA	MacCord 1965:102
Yeocomico	1510 ± 75	DIC-1765	VA	Waselkov 1982:252
	1540 ± 55	DIC-1770	VA	Waselkov 1982:252
	1575 ± 65	UGa-4571	MD	Boyce and Frye 1986:9
	1575 ± 90	DATA-13560	MD	Boyce and Frye 1986:9
	1605 ± 70	SI-4231	VA	Potter 1982:241–42
	1630 ± 55	DIC-1767	VA	Waselkov 1982:252
	1645 ± 70	SI-4372	VA	Potter 1982:241–42
	1690 ± 55	DIC-1762	VA	Waselkov 1982:252
Potomac Creek	1200 ± 55	UGa-1761	DE	Custer 1984:180
	1520 ± 90	Beta-34804	VA	Moore 1990a:35
	1575 ± 90	DATA-13560	MD	Boyce and Frye 1986:9; Barse 1985:155–56
Moyaone	1310 ± 50	DIC-1764	VA	Waselkov 1982:240
	1460 ± 45	DIC-1766	VA	Waselkov 1982:240

ite, and organic matter are found in the plastic as natural inclusions. Typically, the paste is clayey and poorly paddled. Approximately 20 to 30 percent of the paste is composed of coarse, unburned, crushed shell, usually oyster or, occasionally, freshwater mussel. Vessel walls are thick. The interior of the vessel is usually smoothed, although a minority show signs of having been scraped. A small percentage of Mockley vessels were smoothed below the rims' exterior and then decorated with crude, broadline-incised chevrons, diamonds, or cross-hatched or parallel lines, some filled with punctations (Opperman 1980:23–25; Stephenson et al. 1963:107–8). The interior of the rim is often marked with finger impressions from pinching that created a notched or scalloped effect. In summary, the diagnostic attributes for Mockley ware are: (1) thick vessel walls; (2) coarse shell temper; (3) cord-marked or net-impressed surfaces; and (4) simple, conical jar forms with direct rims, wide mouths, and semiconical or rounded bottoms.

A previously unidentified ceramic, which is contemporaneous with the terminal manufacture of Mockley ware, was found in situ at the White Oak Point site (44WM119) in Westmoreland County, Virginia. The pottery, named Nomini ware, is made from compact paste tempered with medium-size, rounded quartz particles (see fig. 11). Vessels were large jars, with rounded bases, direct rims, and cord-marked or fabric-impressed exterior surfaces. Nomini ware occurs in Virginia's lower Northern Neck as a minority ware in ceramic assemblages dating between A.D. 700 and 900 (Waselkov 1982a:286, 291–93; Egloff and Potter 1982:104–6).

The points associated with Mockley ware occupations are varied (fig. 12). Selby Bay points are either weakly stemmed or side-notched, with elongated blades and straight to slightly excurvate edges. They exhibit little evidence of secondary flaking or retouch, especially around the base or hafting element (Thomas et al. 1974:56; Bastian 1974). Large, lanceolate blanks from which the stemmed and side-notched points were made are also found (Wright 1973:21). Selby Bay points from the Northern Neck frequently are made of rhyolite and occasionally from siltstone, chert, and quartz. Rhyolite is nonlocal, whereas siltstone, chert, and quartz are available locally as cobbles. The lengths of specimens from the Northern Neck range from 30 to 70 millimeters (1.2–2.8 in).

Fox Creek points (formerly called Steubenville points) are also found with Mockley pottery. These points are either broad-stemmed or lanceolate and, proportionately, rather wide relative to their length,

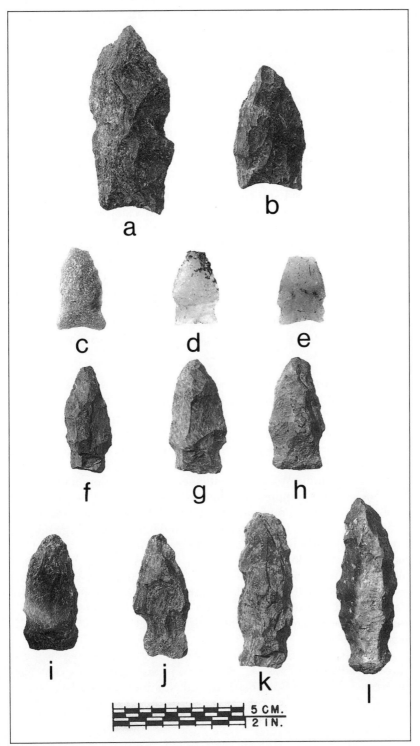

12. Fox Creek Lanceolate (a) *and Stemmed* (b), *Nomini* (c–e), *and Selby Bay Stemmed* (f–h) *and Side-notched* (i–l) *projectile points. Provenience: a, 44NB111C; b, 44NB19; c–e, 44WM119; f–k, 44NB128S; and l, 44RD48. (Photography by Victor E. Krantz)*

with excurvate edges and slightly concave bases (see fig. 12*a, b*). The lengths range from 26 to 80 millimeters (1.0–3.2 in). The shoulders of the broad, stemmed forms are so slight in some instances as to be almost nonexistent (Ritchie 1961:50–52; Ritchie and Funk 1973:120; Stephenson et al. 1963:140–41). In the lower Potomac Valley, Fox Creek points are made of rhyolite or sometimes argillite. Generally, Fox Creek points tend to be better made and exhibit more secondary retouch than Selby Bay points, which are cruder and show less evidence of retouch, especially around the hafting element.

Small, shallow side-notched points with broad blades and straight or slightly concave bases were found in the Mockley ware occupations at the White Oak Point site (fig. 12*c–e*). Named Nomini points, they range in length from 21 to 41 millimeters (0.8–1.6 in) and were made from locally available materials, such as quartz and quartzite, as well as from an occasional flake of nonlocal stone like rhyolite or green jasper (Waselkov 1982a:297). While the shape or morphology of the point is somewhat like the Potts point of the lower York and James river basins (McCary 1953), there is a minimum of secondary flaking confined mainly to the lateral edges—a trait similar to that found on Selby Bay points.

COMPONENT DISTRIBUTION, DESCRIPTION, AND INTERPRETATION

The archaeological survey in the Chicacoan study area identified twenty-two components containing diagnostic artifacts indicative of late Middle Woodland occupations (fig. 13). The majority of these components are located along the east bank of the Coan River in the vicinity of Boathouse Pond.

The late Middle Woodland settlement pattern is dominated by the Boathouse Pond component, which covers about 5.26 hectares (12.9 a) of the Boathouse Pond site (Potter 1982:245–70). This is the largest of all the sites in the Chicacoan locality, and it is the only large midden site (table 5). Clearly visible as a gray-black midden stain against the lighter, natural-colored soils, the site includes 7.29 hectares (18 a) along the east side of Boathouse Pond, not far from the L-shaped bend in the Coan River (fig. 14). The refuse midden is composed mainly of dark-colored earth and some oyster shell and blankets the tops of three headlands and an extensive area of flat neckland east of the headlands.

Artifacts from the late Middle Woodland are scattered over the three headlands (areas A, B, and C). Sherds of Mockley Net-impressed, Mockley Cord-marked, and Nomini Cord-marked pottery

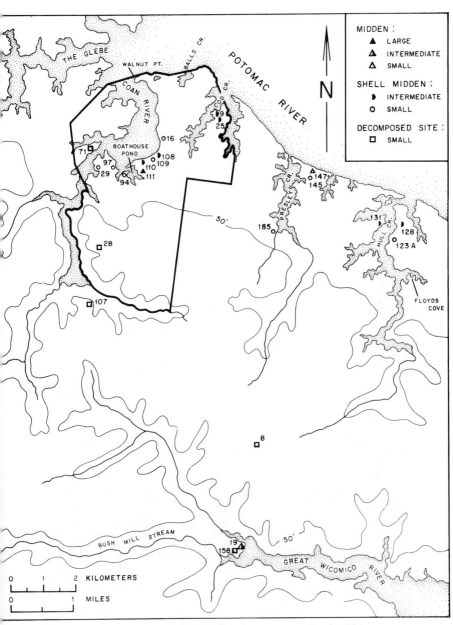

13. Distribution of late Middle Woodland components in the Chicacoan study area. (Map by G. Robert Lewis)

Table 5. Components in the Chicacoan locality by site class and size

Archaeological time period	Midden			Shell midden			De-composed			Total number of components per time period
	L	I	S	L	I	S	L	I	S	
Protohistoric-historic A.D. 1500 to 1650	1	—	—	—	4	6	—	—	4	15
Late Woodland II A.D. 1300 to 1500	1	—	1	—	5	4	—	—	1	12
Late Woodland I A.D. 900 to 1300	—	1	1	—	5	8	—	—	1	16
Late Middle Woodland A.D. 200 to 900	1	1	1	—	6	8	—	—	5	22

Symbols of site size: L = Large; I = Intermediate; S = Small. See table 3 for archaeological survey site classification.

14. Aerial view of the Boathouse Pond site (44NB111), looking southwest. The village midden is visible across the middle of the photograph as areas of dark wheat and soil.

were found, with 64 percent of the Mockley ware being net-impressed. Antony Opperman's study (1980:26, 29–30) of Mockley ware from the Maycock's Point site, Virginia, demonstrated that over time cord marking decreased in popularity as net impressing increased. Given Opperman's findings, the high percentage of Mockley Net-impressed sherds and the presence of Nomini ware probably indicate occupations during the latter half of the late Middle Woodland period, perhaps as late as A.D. 700–900 (Potter 1982:252, table 12).

A variety of Fox Creek and Selby Bay points were also found at the Boathouse Pond component, with 94 percent of them made from rhyolite, a nonlocal stone. The closest source for this exotic lithic material is the Catoctin formation of the Blue Ridge province in western Maryland (Stewart 1980:157–58). Some of the rhyolite points are heavily reworked, and others appear to be made from old bifaces and flakes. Just as interesting, no decortication flakes, cores, or chunks of rhyolite were discovered—only rhyolite flakes. All of this suggests several things. Rhyolite points and knives were not used casually and then discarded but were kept until they were worn-out and could no longer be resharpened. And, most of the rhyolite was being brought into the lower Northern Neck as blanks or preforms, probably from sources up the Potomac River in western Maryland (Potter 1982:261–64, tables 13–14).

Excavation of a trench consisting of five 1.5-meter (5-ft) squares in the central headland (area B) uncovered five postmolds. Four of the five occurred as two pairs, as though they were part of a pole-supported structure, with the poles placed in pairs separated by about one meter. Two of the four postmolds contained sherds belonging to three Mockley Net-impressed vessels. The limited surface area exposed during the test excavations makes it impossible to say little more than that some type of pole-supported structure was erected in this area, probably during the late Middle Woodland occupation (Potter 1982:267–69).

Given the horizontally extensive (5.26 ha or 12.9 a) but vertically shallow (20 cm or 8 in) midden, composed of mainly gray-black soil and some oyster shell, the Boathouse Pond component appears to have been a village site where a local or regional band gathered as a complete unit for several months during a particular season(s), with part of the group, perhaps, resident during most of the year. The occupations probably date between A.D. 550 and 900 and, due to the presence of Nomini ware, may even date closer to A.D. 700–900.

Seven intermediate-size sites were investigated, and all but one are coastal shell middens (see table 5). The exception is Betz Landing (44NB19), a midden site at the head of the Great Wicomico River in the interior uplands. Two of the shell middens, 44NB9 and 44NB25, appear to be single-component sites. The shell on these sites is dense, but the deposits are shallow. Following Opperman's (1980:26, 29–30) observation on the temporal change in the popularity of cord-marked versus net-impressed Mockley ware, it appears that site 44NB9 dates between A.D. 200 and 550, and site 44NB25 dates between A.D. 550 and 900. On the whole, sites of intermediate size seem to have been either places that were repeatedly visited by small kin groups or base camps used by bands.

Plum Nelly (44NB128) is the only intermediate-size shell midden site (class 5) where a variety of subsistence and functional data were recovered (Potter 1982:276–331). Situated in the broad necklands along the east bank of Hull Creek (see fig. 13), the site is about 14.5 kilometers (9 mi) west of the confluence of the Potomac River and Chesapeake Bay. The total area covered by the shell and dark-earth midden is slightly under 1 hectare (2.47 a). The site was divided into three areas based upon the topography: the northern rise, center swale, and southern rise. Deposits of shell and dark-earth midden are deepest in the swale, attaining a maximum depth of 84 centimeters (35 in), or 59 centimeters (23 in) below the base of the plow zone.

Ten 1.5-meter (5-ft) units, laid out in two adjacent rows of five units each, were excavated in the center swale (fig. 15). The stratigraphy of this portion of the Plum Nelly site consists of four zones: zone I, the plowed soil; zone II, midden refuse from the late Middle Woodland; and zones III and IV, dating to the Late Archaic period. A total of seven features assignable to the late Middle Woodland period were excavated (Potter 1982:287–88, 311–16).

Slightly more than three thousand animal bones were found during the excavations, with about two-thirds coming from late Middle Woodland contexts. These bones represent a variety of animals including the painted turtle, box turtle, copperhead, wild turkey, passenger pigeon, raccoon, gray fox, bobcat, gray and fox squirrels, muskrat, cottontail, and white-tailed deer. Apparently the late Middle Woodland occupants relied mainly upon wild turkey, raccoon, and the ubiquitous white-tailed deer for their meat (Waselkov 1982b). A minimum of nine deer are represented by the late Middle Woodland sample. Their estimated ages show that most of the individuals were the more vulnerable very young and older deer. These data may indicate that the late Middle Woodland hunters relied upon a stalking

15. *Excavations at Plum Nelly (44NB128)*

technique, rather than some method of mass capture such as deer drives and surrounds (Waselkov 1978a, 1982b:387).

Oysters, soft-shelled clams, ribbed mussels, and periwinkles were also part of the diet, with oysters being the most heavily gathered mollusk. The oysters and other mollusks were roasted in large, oval-shaped pits. The empty shells were tossed either into the roasting pits or into heaps adjacent to the pits. Remains from hickory nuts and acorns were found in the features, along with seeds from the hackberry, pokeweed, holly, and the genus *Prunus*, which includes cherry and plum (Potter 1982:326–27). Together, the paleobotanical and faunal remains indicate fall-winter occupations, with most of the diet composed of white-tailed deer, oysters, raccoon, wild turkey, hickory nuts, and acorns.

The lithic artifacts consist of Selby Bay points, bifaces, and a ground celt. A rhyolite Selby Bay Side-notched point was found in situ in zone II, along with sherds of Mockley ware. Four other Selby Bay Side-notched points and two Selby Bay Stemmed points, also made from rhyolite, were recovered in the surface collections from the southern rise. Three oval-shaped bifaces, made from locally obtainable quartzite and quartz, were also found in late Middle Woodland contexts. The midsection of a greenstone celt was associated with a thick deposit of oyster shell that was part of the midden refuse comprising zone II (Potter 1982:293–307).

Bone and antler artifacts found in the late Middle Woodland zone and features include bone awls, an antler awl, an antler projectile point, a fragment of a bone needle, the fragment of a bone spatula-shaped awl, and miscellaneous worked bone and antler. The bone spatula fragment is very thin and highly polished, with a tapered end, which perhaps indicates that it was used as a tool in basketmaking (Potter 1982:307–11).

The technological subsystem of the late Middle Woodland occupants of Plum Nelly included (but was not limited to) Mockley Net-impressed and Cord-marked pottery, Selby Bay points made from rhyolite, bifaces made from local stones, and celts of greenstone. Bone and antler awls, bone needles, bone spatulas, and antler projectile points were also used. The artifacts represent tools that functioned in a variety of activities including hunting, generalized cutting, perforating, woodworking, boneworking, short-term containment for cooking and storage, and stone heating for roasting mollusks and, perhaps, pot boiling. From the foregoing information, the late Middle Woodland occupation of Plum Nelly is interpreted as a fall-winter base camp.

Betz Landing (44NB19) is unique for an intermediate-size site because of its location in the interior uplands at the headwaters of the Great Wicomico River (see fig. 13). A light-gray soil discoloration marks the site, which occupies a 6-meter (20-ft) rise along the water. Three features were observed on top of the freshly cultivated surface, along with scattered oyster shell. The frequency and distribution of the diagnostic artifacts demonstrate that the major occupation of this site occurred during the late Middle Woodland period (Potter 1982:159–66).

Both Mockley Net-impressed and Cord-marked sherds were found, with the majority of the sherds being net-impressed (56%). Chipped stone artifacts associated with the Mockley ceramics are varied. Most of the Fox Creek Stemmed, Selby Bay Side-notched, and Selby Bay Stemmed points were manufactured from rhyolite (80%). In contrast, four small, shallow side-notched points made from quartz were found; they are similar to Nomini Side-notched points discovered at the White Oak Point site, associated with Mockley and Nomini wares in components radiocarbon-dated to A.D. 860 ± 60 and A.D. 880 ± 60 (Waselkov 1982a:297). The larger percentage of Mockley Net-impressed sherds and the presence of Nomini Side-notched points make it likely that the Betz Landing site was occupied between A.D. 550 and 900 (Potter 1982:160–63, 339–49).

The location of the site relative to extant soils and marshlands is interesting. The soil within a 2-kilometer (1.24-mi) catchment radius of the site is 60 percent Sassafras–sandy land association and 40 percent sandy-land–Sassafras–mixed alluvial land association. Of the former, only about 19 percent is available for tilth, with the remainder being excessively drained soils or soils on moderately steep to steep slopes. The latter soil association consists of excessively drained soils on steep side slopes, well-drained soils on narrow ridgetops, and poorly drained alluvial deposits along streams. This soil association is best suited for forest (Elder et al. 1963:18–19). Of all the intermediate-size sites dating to the late Middle Woodland, Betz Landing's catchment area has the lowest percentage of soils most favorable for plant tending or plant husbandry.

On the other hand, within a 2-kilometer (1.24-mi) catchment radius of Betz Landing are 34.6 hectares (85 a) of marshland. Indeed, the largest marshes of the Great Wicomico River system are located within this catchment area. Two of the four marshes are pocket marshes, one is a fringing marsh, and one a creek marsh. These marshes are made up of three plant communities: saltmarsh cordgrass, big cordgrass, and cattail. Such marsh plant communities serve as habitats for muskrats and various nesting birds, provide food for waterfowl, and are associated with fish spawning and nursery areas (Silberhorn 1975:4–7, 35, 41–44). If such extensive marshlands existed during late Middle Woodland times as well, then the Betz Landing site may have been occupied in order to exploit the resources of the nearby marshlands and, possibly, other resources of the interior uplands.

Fourteen small sites are attributed to late Middle Woodland occupations, of which eight are shell middens, five are decomposed sites, and one is a midden site (see table 5). Although no mollusk remains were found associated with the Mockley ware midden excavated at the Blue Fish Beach site (44NB147), it is probable that such remains existed just north of the present site. Most likely, the shell middens represent sites occupied by small groups, perhaps family-size units, for relatively brief periods.

Although classified as a small shell midden, site 44NB185 is unique and deserves further description (Potter 1982:186–90). The site is located on a small headland (less than 0.20 ha or 0.5 a) along the west side of Presley Creek, near the juncture of the necklands and uplands (see fig. 13). Shortly before the survey team discovered the site, trees and brush had been cleared from the headland in preparation for putting the land in cultivation. The clearing had proceeded with a minimum of soil removal, since the farmer wanted to leave as much of the topsoil as possible. The land had then been plowed, apparently for the first time. This resulted in the exposure of six discrete features, four of them (areas A, C, D, and E) dating to the late Middle Woodland period.

Area A is an oval cluster of oyster shell, 2 meters (6.5 ft) north-south by 8 meters (26 ft) east-west. Artifacts found include one quartz decortication flake and one lower-body sherd of Mockley Net-impressed pottery.

Area C is a half-moon-shaped cluster of densely packed oyster shell, 2 meters (6.5 ft) north-south by 3 meters (10 ft) east-west. Artifacts from the feature include one chert side-notched point, one quartz chunk, one quartz decortication flake, and one body sherd and one basal sherd from a Mockley Cord-marked vessel. The chert side-notched point is similar to other chert points found at the Boathouse Pond site (44NB111) and at the Woodbury Farm site no. 1 (44RD48) in adjacent Richmond County. Both of these sites have major Mockley occupations.

Area D is an elongated feature of dense oyster shell, 6 meters (20 ft) north-south by 13 meters (43 ft) east-west. The lithics collected from the feature consist of one red jasper core, one quartzite flake, two quartz decortication flakes, and one quartz flake. The ceramics found include one body sherd and one basal sherd to a Mockley Net-impressed vessel, three body sherds and one rimsherd to a Mockley Cord-marked vessel, two smoothed, shell-tempered body sherds, and two eroded, shell-tempered body sherds.

Area E is an elongated, thin cluster of oyster shell, 3 meters (10 ft) north-south by 12 meters (40 ft) east-west. Lithic artifacts found include three quartz chunks, one quartz decortication flake, one quartzite flake, one yellow jasper core, and one quartzite biface. The pottery collected from the feature consists of eight Mockley Cord-marked body sherds, one smoothed, shell-tempered sherd, and one smoothed sherd made of a fine paste with stray quartz-grain inclusions.

Site 44NB185 is quite informative because it provides spatial data on a series of discrete features, each one probably representing the activities of a small group of people on a single occasion. It also gives archaeologists an insight into one way shell middens are formed. As discovered, the "site" is actually six separate features, created at various intervals over a total span of perhaps twelve hundred years. If this headland had been used more frequently during this time, the discreteness of the features would have begun to blur as each group of oyster harvesters used a different spot on the headland. The end result would have been a seemingly continuous and homogeneous sheet of oyster-shell midden across the headland.

The five small decomposed sites are all found in the interior uplands, with the exception of 44NB71 (see fig. 13). These seem to have been specialized procurement sites or temporary camps designed primarily to exploit the resources of the interior uplands.

Late Woodland I Period, A.D. 900–1300

DIAGNOSTIC ARTIFACTS

Near the end of the late Middle Woodland Period, the local prehistoric cultures began to modify their pottery and projectile points until by the tenth century A.D. distinctive new types had replaced earlier ones. Throughout much of the Chesapeake Bay coastal plain the pottery characteristic of the Late Woodland period, in general, is Townsend ware (fig. 16). This shell-tempered pottery probably developed from the earlier Mockley ceramics, although this origin has by no means been demonstrated to every archaeologist's satisfaction (Custer 1984:88; Curry and Kavanagh 1991:24; Steponaitis 1986; Potter 1982; McLearen and Mouer 1989:16).

Townsend ware vessels are small to large wide-mouthed jars with direct rims, conoidal bodies, and rounded or semiconical bases. Exterior surfaces are fabric-impressed, and decoration, when present, occurs in a number of incised and cord-impressed varieties. The most common type of Townsend pottery, Rappahannock Fabric-impressed, was made from A.D. 900 till the early seventeenth century. Due to this long period of popularity, Rappahannock Fabric-impressed pottery by itself cannot be used to date components to particular temporal phases during the seven hundred years following A.D. 900. On the other hand, varieties of complex geometric motifs on another Townsend pottery type, Rappahannock Incised, are characteristic of the Late Woodland I period (Griffith 1980:29–33; Egloff and Potter 1982:107–9).

A local Northern Neck ceramic confined mainly to the Late Wood-

16. *Rappahannock Fabric-impressed* (a, b) *and Complex Geometric Incised* (c) *and Currioman Fabric–impressed* (d–h) *pottery from White Oak Point (44WM119). (Photograph by Victor E. Krantz)*

land I period is Currioman Fabric-impressed pottery (see fig. 16). This ware is tempered with rounded quartz particles and finely crushed oyster shell that constitute 30 to 50 percent of the paste. Vessels are large, open-mouthed jars and shallow bowls impressed with a rigid warp fabric on their exterior surfaces. Currioman Fabric-impressed pottery was found in situ at the White Oak Point site, mainly in components dating ca. A.D. 1100–1350 (Waselkov 1982a:239, 243, 293–94).

The other artifact diagnostic of Late Woodland I components in the Chicacoan locality is the Levanna Large Triangular point (fig. 17). These points are pressure-flaked equilateral forms greater than 32 millimeters (1.3 in) long and 22 millimeters (0.9 in) wide, with straight or concave bases. Their greatest popularity was from about A.D. 900 to 1300. In the Northern Neck, as elsewhere, large Levanna points decreased in size over time, until smaller triangular points predominated after ca. A.D. 1300. Over 75 percent of the points are made from local quartz cobbles, with the remainder made from local cobbles of quartzite, chert, and jasper, in that order.

Although large triangular points have been found in late Middle Woodland contexts in southeastern Virginia, the Richmond area, and southern Delaware (Gleach 1987a:96; Geier 1983:193–94; Custer 1984:83), no Levanna or Levanna-like points have been found in situ in coeval components from Maryland's western shore to the Rappahannock River in Virginia. In the latter area, unlike the other areas, the heavy importation of rhyolite for the manufacture of Fox Creek and Selby Bay points continued until A.D. 800–900, perhaps decreasing the likelihood that other point forms would be adopted. However, it is probable that in southern Maryland and Virginia's Northern Neck, large triangular points eventually will be found in contexts dated to ca. A.D. 700–900, associated with Mockley and Nomini pottery and the Potts-like Nomini projectile point.

COMPONENT DISTRIBUTION, DESCRIPTION, AND INTERPRETATION

The distribution of archaeological components containing artifacts diagnostic of the Late Woodland I period is shown in figure 18. When the distribution and classification of components dating to this period are compared to the previous late Middle Woodland period, a number of differences are apparent (tables 5 and 6). There are no large sites in the sampling unit or study area during Late Woodland I times. Also, the number of sites of intermediate size increased by 33 percent and the number of small sites decreased by 43 percent. Finally, during

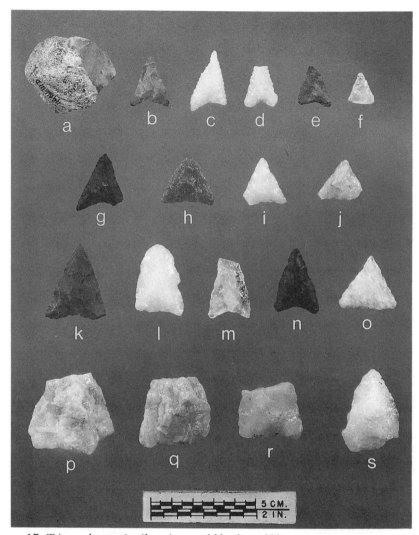

17. *Triangular projectile points and blanks: cobble core and Levanna
Small Triangular point of yellow jasper* (a, b); *Levanna Small Triangular
points* (c–e); *Holland's type A* (f); *reworked Levanna Large Triangular
points* (g, h, m–o); *reworked Levanna Small Triangular points* (i, j);
Levanna Large Triangular points (k, l); *Triangular blanks* (p–s).
Provenience: a–d, *44NB111D;* e, *44NB111B;* f, *44NB66;* g and i,
44NB19; h and j, *44RD48;* k–s, *44NB16. (Photograph by Victor E.
Krantz)*

Table 6. Components in the sampling unit by site class and size

Archaeological time period	Midden			Shell midden			Decomposed			Total number of components per time period
	L	I	S	L	I	S	L	I	S	
Protohistoric-historic A.D. 1500 to 1650	1	—	—	—	4	2	—	—	2	9
Late Woodland II A.D. 1300 to 1500	1	—	—	—	4	2	—	—	—	7
Late Woodland I A.D. 900 to 1300	—	1	—	—	5	3	—	—	1	10
Late Middle Woodland A.D. 200 to 900	1	—	—	—	4	5	—	—	2	12

Symbols of site size: *L* = Large; *I* = Intermediate; *S* = Small. See table 3 for archaeological survey site classification.

the late Middle Woodland period the east bank of the Coan River was used almost to the total exclusion of the west bank, whereas both banks of the river were occupied during the Late Woodland I period (see figs. 13 and 18).

Occupation of the large Boathouse Pond site was reduced to only portions of areas B and D, totaling not more than 0.81 hectare (2.0 a). Other components of intermediate size, like the Last Resort (44NB16) on the east bank, show greater use than in the preceding period. On the Coan's west bank, a series of intermediate-size shell middens were occupied at this time (see fig. 18).

It appears that the pattern of Late Woodland I components in the Chicacoan locality reflects a dispersal of the population within the necklands along both banks of the Coan River. Intermediate-size shell middens, such as the Last Resort (44NB16) or the Forest Kitchen site (44NB44), are interpreted as small, semipermanent villages or hamlets. All components found away from the Coan River are small shell middens, with the exception of one small midden (44NB147). Most of these components were probably oyster-gathering camps.

Late Woodland II Period, A.D. 1300–1500

DIAGNOSTIC ARTIFACTS

Diagnostic artifacts used to discriminate Late Woodland II components include a wider variety of ceramics than in the preceding Late Woodland I phase (fig. 19). By at least A.D 1300, complex geometric

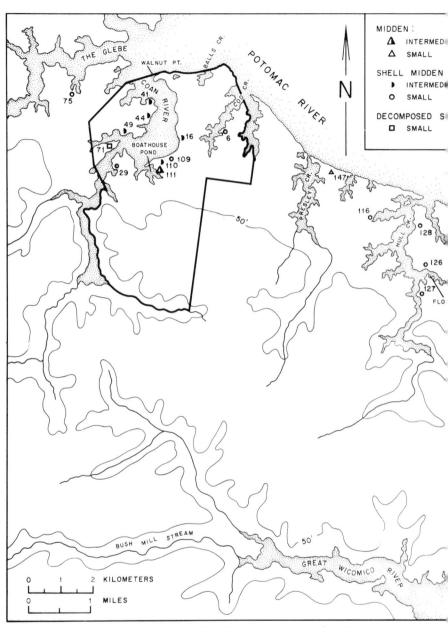

18. Distribution of Late Woodland I components in the Chicacoan study
area. (Map by G. Robert Lewis)

motifs on Rappahannock Incised pottery decreased in popularity as simple, broad-line incised motifs became more popular. Another Townsend ware pottery type, Townsend Corded, also occurs during this period. Various geometric motifs were impressed onto the fabric-marked exterior using a twisted cord, cord-wrapped stick, or the edge of a fabric-wrapped paddle (Egloff and Potter 1982:107–8; Stephenson et al. 1963: plate 11; Griffith 1980:29–30).

Other shell-tempered pottery made during this time is Sullivan ware (ongoing research may demonstrate that this ware was also made earlier). It is a thin-walled, lightly shell-tempered pottery with smoothed-over, fine cord marking. Vessels have constricted necks and conoidal bases (Wright 1973:22). This ware is found in greater quantities along Maryland's western shore north of the Patuxent River drainage (Steponaitis 1986:162–63; Wright 1973). Its occurrence in small quantities (up to 9% of the total ceramic assemblage) at components in Northumberland County, Virginia, suggests cultural interaction across the Potomac River with groups in southern Maryland.

Additional minority ceramics that occur in the lower Northern Neck during the Late Woodland II period apparently derive from interaction with cultural groups living farther up the Potomac River on the inner coastal plain, between the brackish water zone and the fall line. These minority wares consist of trade vessels, as well as vessels manufactured locally by women who may have been exchanged as marriage partners between groups living on the outer and inner coastal plain of the Potomac River. Such pottery includes specimens identical to Potomac Creek Cord-marked pottery found at components of the Potomac Creek complex on the inner coastal plain, as well as variants made from local clays and tempers. Potomac Creek pottery is characterized by sand- and quartz-tempered pastes, large- to medium-size globular vessel forms, and cord-marked exteriors, often decorated with a variety of cord-impressed designs just below the exterior of the rim (Stephenson 1963:113–19; Egloff and Potter 1982:112). A similar pottery type, called Moyaone Cord-impressed, consists of small-to-medium vessels with shoulders and constricted necks made from clay tempered with fine micaceous sand. Vessel exteriors were finished with a cord-wrapped paddle and decorated with cord-impressed motifs below the exterior rim (Stephenson 1963:120–23; Egloff and Potter 1982:112).

After about A.D. 1300, triangular projectile points became generally smaller (equal to or less than 32 mm or 1.3 in long and 22 mm or 0.9 in wide) than earlier ones (see fig. 17). In the Potomac Valley small,

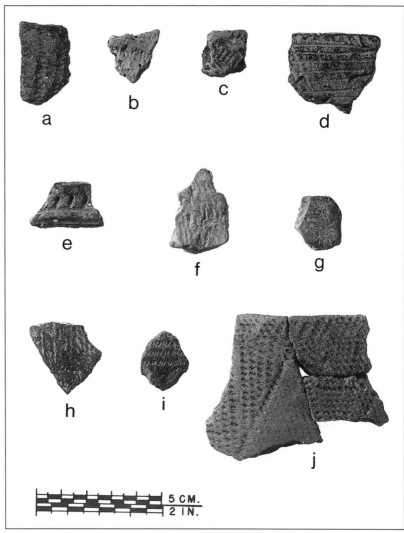

19. *Late Woodland II pottery: Townsend Corded* (a–c); *Rappahannock Incised* (d, e); *Sullivan Cord-marked* (f, g); *Potomac Creek Cord-marked* (h); *Potomac Creek Cord-impressed* (i); *Moyaone Cord-impressed* (j). *Provenience: a, e, and i, 44RD49; b and d, 44NB19; c, 44RD48; f, g, 44NB111C; h, 44NB111B; j, 44WM119. (Photograph by Victor E. Krantz)*

equilateral triangular points are sometimes referred to as Potomac points, even though they are equivalent to small Levanna points—a fact recognized by Robert Stephenson (et al. 1963:145–46), the archaeologist who first described Potomac points. "The only substantial difference between the two is that the latter [Levanna points] appear to be made predominantly of the flinty rocks while the Potomac Point is 91 per cent quartz, in the Accokeek Creek site collections. This may be only local variation and combining the two named types under Ritchie's term [Levanna point] should cause no trouble" (Stephenson et al. 1963:195). As Stephenson surmised, the differences in the stone used to make the Levanna points from New York State (cf. Ritchie 1961:31) and those from the Accokeek Creek site in Maryland merely reflect differences in the local geology of the two areas. For this reason, the name Levanna Small Triangular point is used here to refer to the smaller, equilateral triangular points characteristic of the Late Woodland II period.

COMPONENT DISTRIBUTION, DESCRIPTION, AND INTERPRETATION

Archaeological components for this period are shown on figure 20. Several differences are evident when the distribution and classification of Late Woodland II components within the sampling unit are compared to the Late Woodland I components. First, a large midden component was created at Boathouse Pond (44NB111) during the Late Woodland II period. Second, most of the Late Woodland II components are found within a 2-kilometer (1.24-mi) stretch of necklands along the east bank of the Coan River, whereas the Late Woodland I components were dispersed along the necklands adjacent to both banks of the river. And third, intermediate-size sites decreased in number from Late Woodland I to Late Woodland II times by 33 percent (see table 6).

The area covered by post–A.D. 1300 occupations at the Boathouse Pond site (44NB111) is approximately 4.45 hectares (11 a). This large midden is interpreted as the remains of a Late Woodland II village. All but one of the intermediate-size shell middens are located along the Coan River, within 2 kilometers (1.24 mi) of the Boathouse Pond site. The intermediate-size shell middens probably represent small house clusters or favored spots near the main village where mollusks were gathered and consumed. The reduction in the number of intermediate-size components along the Coan River and the appearance of a single, large midden component suggest the coalescence of most of the local population into one village, with some of the population perhaps scattered in outlying clusters composed of a few houses.

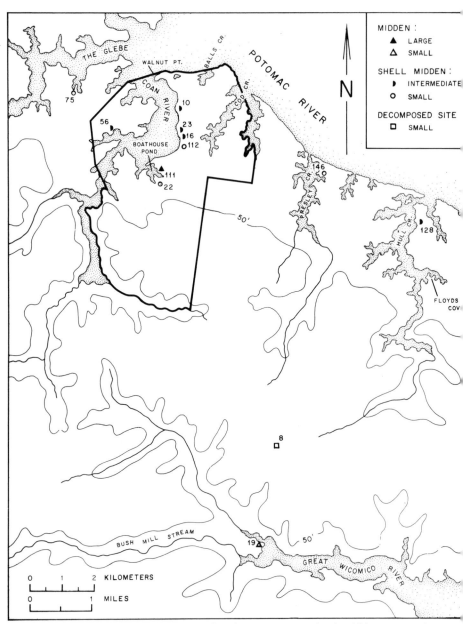

20. Distribution of Late Woodland II components in the Chicacoan study area. (Map by G. Robert Lewis)

All but one of the components beyond a 2-kilometer (1.24-mi) radius of Boathouse Pond are small sites classified as decomposed sites, middens, or shell middens. Such components probably represent the remains of periodic forays by small groups of people into the interior uplands for gathering and hunting or the fission of part of the population into smaller groups in order to collect estuarine resources. Indeed, the observed areal pattern of Late Woodland II components is similar to that of the succeeding protohistoric and early historic period.

Protohistoric and Historic Period, A.D. 1500– 1650s

DIAGNOSTIC ARTIFACTS

The protohistoric period is the harbinger of permanent European settlement, when Spanish, French, and English explorers made brief incursions into the Chesapeake Bay region, ca. A.D. 1500–1607. Although the protohistoric is not usually distinguished in the regional chronology, at least one aboriginal ceramic ware in the lower Potomac Valley has been identified as being specifically protohistoric and historic (fig. 21). The pottery, named Yeocomico ware, developed from the Townsend ceramic tradition, is tempered with relatively fine, crushed shell, and has a plain exterior surface or, more rarely, a scraped exterior surface (Potter 1982:376–79; Waselkov 1982a:294–96; Egloff and Potter 1982:112–14). Interior surfaces were sometimes scraped on both plain and exterior-scraped vessels. Rims are either straight or excurvate, with lips commonly rounded or tapered. Both direct rims and slightly constricted necks occur. Vessel walls are thin and coil-constructed. Decoration, when present, consists of vertical or slightly oblique lines of punctations or horizontal cord impressions just below the exterior lip of the rim. Vessel forms range from a small cup to medium-size bowls to globular jars with rounded bottoms. Eight radiocarbon dates place this ware between A.D. 1510 and 1690 (see table 4).

Potomac Creek and Moyaone Plain pottery increased in frequency during this time. Other ceramics that continued from the Late Woodland II period into the protohistoric and early historic times include Rappahannock Fabric-impressed, at least the simple Rappahannock Incised varieties, Townsend Corded, Potomac Creek Cord-marked, and Moyaone Cord-marked pottery.

21. *Yecomico ware from Blue Fish Beach (44NB147):* a–e, *rimsherds and body sherds from Yeocomico Plain vessel decorated with a single line of punctations below the rim;* f, g, *rimsherd and body sherd from Yeocomico Scraped vessel;* h, i, *rimsherd and body sherd from Yeocomico Scraped vessel;* j–l, *rimsherd and body sherds from Yeocomico Scraped vessel;* m, *slight foot ring on basal sherds from a small cup of Yeocomico Plain pottery. (Photograph by Victor E. Krantz)*

Occasionally, hollow reed or cane punctations were used as part of the decorative motif on both the Rappahannock Incised and Townsend Corded types (Winfree 1967:9; MacCord 1965:101; Smith 1971:276–77). This is considered to be a late decorative attribute in tidewater Virginia, dating from the protohistoric and early historic periods. Evidence from the De Shazo site (44KG3) in King George County and the Hand site (44SN22) in Southampton County support such an interpretation (MacCord 1965:101–3; Smith 1971:276–77).

The triangular point most common during this time was the Levanna Small Triangular point. However, by the beginning of the early historic period, points similar to C. G. Holland's type A, Small Triangular (1955:166), were probably being manufactured (see fig. 17*f*). These diminutive isosceles or equilateral triangular points are usually 15–16 mm (0.6 in) long and 12–13 mm (0.5 in) wide. In the Northern Neck most of the points are made from quartz and are isosceles in shape, with serrated edges. Although some archaeologists might refer to such points as Clarksville Small Triangular ones, that name seems inappropriate for several reasons. Usually, Clarksville points are not isosceles or serrated, and they are most often found in the Virginia–North Carolina piedmont on late prehistoric or historic sites of known or suspected Siouan affiliation (Coe 1952:310–11, 1964:112). Therefore, Holland's descriptive and less culturally oriented terminology is used.

COMPONENT DISTRIBUTION, DESCRIPTION, AND INTERPRETATION

From an examination of the distribution of the protohistoric-historic components within the sampling unit (fig. 22), it appears that most of the occupation occurred in the necklands along the east bank of the Coan River. A similar situation was observed for the preceding Late Woodland II period. All but one of the protohistoric-historic intermediate-size and small components within 2 kilometers (1.24 mi) of the large Boathouse Pond site are in the neckland along the river's east bank. This is the predicted ethnohistoric settlement pattern, where swidden plots, secondary dwelling areas, and favored spots for mollusk gathering were within a convenient day's walk of the main village.

In order to measure the degree of similarity between the distribution of Late Woodland II to protohistoric-historic components, a coefficient of partial association (C'_{sa}) was calculated (Sorensen 1974:172–76). The coefficient of partial association is a pure number expressing the partial correspondence between two populations whose elements may be regarded as occupying points in space. The level of association

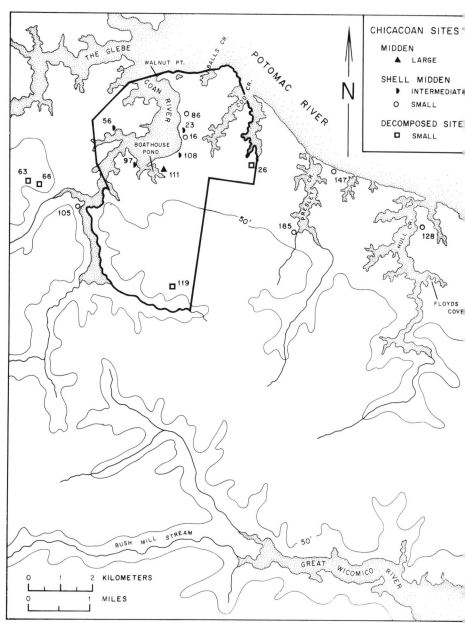

22. Distribution of protohistoric-historic components in the Chicacoan study area. (Map by G. Robert Lewis)

is calculated on the basis of the closest distances between the elements or points of one population to the nearest neighbors of a second population. In order to apply this method for measuring the spatial association between point patterns, it must be assumed that the components assigned to each period were contemporaneous. For the purpose of this analysis, the durations of the Late Woodland II and protohistoric-historic periods were considered brief enough segments of time that such an assumption could be made. The calculated coefficient of partial association (C'_{sa}) equals 0.63. Table 7 shows that a value of 0.63 for the coefficient of partial association indicates a high association of Late Woodland II to protohistoric-historic components.

On the other hand, if the distribution of protohistoric-historic components is compared to that of the Late Woodland II components, the calculated coefficient of partial association (C'_{sb}) equals 0.2. In table 7 a value of 0.2 for the coefficient of partial association indicate a moderate association of protohistoric-historic to Late Woodland II components. Thus, Late Woodland II components are more closely associated with protohistoric-historic components than the latter are to the former. This means that the settlement pattern established during Late Woodland II times served as the basis for the succeeding settlement pattern.

If, as is generally assumed, there is some correlation between population and the number and size of archaeological sites, then it is possible to get a crude measure of population change over time by computing component frequency and area (Steponaitis 1986:269–75). Using data from the sampling unit, component frequency was calculated for each time period. Because the four periods are of unequal length, component frequencies were standardized per 1,000 years per time period (table 8), following the method used by Laurie

Table 7. Analysis of C_s values

Crude C_s value	Transformed C_s value	Degree of association/disassociation
<⅓	< −0.5	High disassociation
⅓–⅔	−0.5– −0.2	Moderate disassociation
⅔–1.5	−0.2– +0.2	Indeterminate relationship
1.5–3.0	0.2–0.5	Moderate association
>3.0	>0.5	High association

Source: Reprinted, by permission of the Association of American Geographers, from Sorensen 1974:table 1

Table 8. Component frequency and average aggregate component area by period

Measure	Late Middle Woodland A.D. 200–900	Late Woodland I A.D. 900–1300	Late Woodland II A.D. 1300–1500	Protohistoric/ early historic A.D. 1500–1650
Component Frequency				
Number in sampling unit	12	10	7	9
Std. frequency per 1,000 yrs.	17.14	25	35	60
Average aggregate component area				
Average aggregate area	5.68	3.5	5.43	5.53
Std. average aggregate area	8.1	8.75	27.15	36.86

Steponaitis (1986:270–72) in her analysis of prehistoric settlement patterns along Maryland's lower Patuxent River. When the standardized component frequencies are plotted over time, a significant increase in component frequency is evident between the Late Woodland II and protohistoric-historic periods (fig. 23).

As Steponaitis (1986:273) has observed, however, "Two populations of similar size could generate two different patterns of component frequency: one producing many small components, the other producing fewer large ones." To offset any potential interpretive problems this might cause, a standardized average component area was also calculated. The site classification system was used to compute the average component area of all components within the sampling unit (see table 6). Once the average component area per time period was totaled, it was standardized by dividing the sum of the period's length in millennia (see table 8). When plotted, the resulting curve is similar to the one for component frequency (fig. 24). From these calculations, it is inferred that the population in the Chicacoan locality was increasing, particularly after A.D. 1300.

The large midden component (4.45 ha or 11 a) of the Boathouse Pond site (44NB111), situated beside Boathouse Pond on the east bank of the Coan River, continued to dominate the settlement pattern in the Chicacoan locality. To date, this is the most extensive protohistoric-historic component found. The historical data, limited though they are, point to the east bank of the Coan River as the location of the

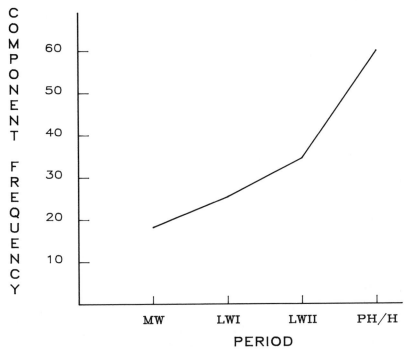

23. *Standardized component frequency plotted by period (based on table 8).*
Key: MW, *late Middle Woodland;* LWI, *Late Woodland I;* LWII, *Late Woodland II;* PH/H, *protohistoric-historic. (Graph by J. D. Ross)*

historic Chicacoan village, from its first documentation in A.D. 1608 till, perhaps, the relocation of the Chicacoans ca. 1655–56.

William Dinwiddie's hypothesis of 1891, that the early historic period Chicacoan village was located along the east bank of Hull Creek, was not supported by the survey. Most of the sites found there were small shell middens dating from A.D. 900 to 1300. Plum Nelly (44NB128) was the largest site discovered in the Hull Creek drainage, and its primary occupation occurred around 2000 B.C. Only a small protohistoric-historic component was found at Plum Nelly (see fig. 22).

The varying densities and clusters of protohistoric and early historic artifacts over the surface of the Boathouse Pond site probably reflect the dispersal of longhouses within the village area. However, part of the protohistoric and historic Chicacoan population may have occupied other spots around Boathouse Pond. During the survey,

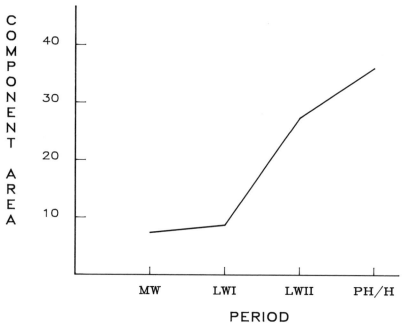

PERIOD

24. Standardized average, aggregate component area by period (based on table 8). Key: MW, late Middle Woodland; *LWI,* Late Woodland I; *LWII, Late Woodland II;* PH/H, *protohistoric-historic. (Graph by J. D. Ross)*

thin, dark, organic middens with some oyster shell were found on the tops of two wooded tongues of land south of the Boathouse Pond site. Unfortunately, no artifacts were found during the brief examination of these two loci. At the entrance to Boathouse Pond, site 44NB97 produced evidence of a protohistoric-historic component (see chapter 5). It remains to be demonstrated, however, whether or not the Chicacoan Indians occupied site 44NB97 and the Boathouse Pond site simultaneously.

The advantageous setting of the Boathouse Pond site becomes apparent when it is compared to the criteria used by the historic Virginia Algonquians in selecting a village site: (1) proximity to rivers and streams, (2) nearness to freshwater springs, (3) location upon the rise of a hill or ridge, (4) nearness to marshlands, and (5) proximity to sufficient land suitable for slash-and-burn cultivation. The Boathouse Pond site meets all of the criteria with the exception of item 3. It is beside a broad, shallow cove off from the main channel of the Coan

River, about one-third the length of the river from its confluence with the Potomac. Approximately 600 meters (2,000 ft) due south of the site is the base of the interior uplands. Near the juncture of the neck-lands and uplands there are several freshwater springs, as well as freshwater streams in the easily accessible interior uplands.

Currently, the Coan River system has the greatest number of hec-tares of marshland anywhere in Northumberland County, with three of the largest marshes within 4 kilometers (2.5 mi) of the Boathouse Pond site. As for mollusks, in 1891 Dinwiddie (Holmes et al. 1891) noted that the Coan River had "quite a reputation for fine oyster bars . . . [with] good oyster bars jutting out at every point." However, Din-widdie dismissed their prehistoric value because at low tide the oyster bars were below 1.5–2.4 meters (5–8 ft) of water and, therefore, too deep to be dredged by hand. At the time of his remarks, Dinwiddie was unaware of the consequences of sea-level rise on the Chesapeake and its estuaries. Although it is possible that four hundred years ago the Coan River experienced lower tides, there are no data available that would allow determination of the accessibility or extent of the Coan River oyster bars during the protohistoric or early historic peri-ods. And, even if the oyster bars were too deep for hand collecting at low tide, the Indians could have harvested the mollusks by dredging with wooden hand rakes and by diving (Waselkov 1982a:20–22).

The soil type of the northern part of the Boathouse Pond site is Matapeake silt loam, while the remainder of the site is Mattapex silt loam. The Matapeake and Mattapex soils can be cropped intensively using modern agricultural practices, and they are particularly favor-able for corn because of their capacity to supply the moisture that corn needs during the growing season (Elder et al. 1963:24–25). Both of these soil types are part of the Mattapex-Bertie association that blan-kets the necklands from the east bank of the Coan River to the west bank of Hull Creek, at its mouth (see fig. 6). In the lower Northern Neck, the Mattapex-Bertie soil association is one of three that are par-ticularly suitable for slash-and-burn maize cultivation.

If the ethnographic evidence presented by Michael Chisolm (1968:131) is correct and the maximum distance most agriculturalists are willing to walk to their fields is 2 kilometers (1.24 mi), then 51 percent of the land within a 2-kilometer catchment area of the Boathouse Pond site is soil of the Mattapex-Bertie association. The remainder of the land within a 2-kilometer radius is 6 percent Woodstown-Dragston association and 42 percent Sassafras–sandy land association. About one-third of the Sassafras–sandy land association is not fit for tilling because it is too steep. Although only 10 percent of the soils in Northumberland County are of the Mattapex-Bertie association (Elder et al. 1963:20), 51 percent of the soils within a 2-kilometer catchment radius of the Boathouse Pond site are part of this soil association.

Anthropologist Robert Carneiro (1960:229–34) has devised a formula to calculate the smallest area of arable soil necessary to permit a village to stay in the same locale. The formula is:

$$T = \frac{PA}{Y}(R + Y).$$

The variables are:

P is the population of the community.

A is the area of cultivated land (in acres) required to provide the average individual with the amount of food he ordinarily derives from cultivated plants per year.

Y is the number of years that a plot of land continues to produce before it has to be abandoned.

R is the number of years an abandoned plot must lie fallow before it can be recultivated.

T is the smallest area of cultivable land that will support a village of a given size in the same locale indefinitely.

For the Chicacoans, the following values (derived from the ethnohistorical subsistence data) are assigned to the variables: $P = 120$ to 130; $A = 0.75$; $Y = 2$ to 3; and $R = 21$ to 42. If we solve for the values at the lowest end of the range, a figure of 1,035 acres (419 ha) is computed. If the highest values are selected, a total of 1,463 acres (593 ha) is derived. Thus, if one considers only soil exhaustion as a factor in village movement, the Chicacoans could have stayed indefinitely in the same locale if 1,035 to 1,463 acres (419 to 593 ha) of arable soil favorable to maize growth were within the village's catchment area.

There are approximately 1,125 acres (456 ha) of arable land within a 2-kilometer (1.24-mi) catchment radius of the Boathouse Pond site. If the protohistoric-historic component of this site is the werowance's village of the Chicacoans, then there was enough arable land within a 2-kilometer catchment radius of the village to support a population of about 125 indefinitely. Perhaps that is why there is no apparent archaeological evidence of any relocation of major village sites in the Chicacoan locality during the protohistoric and early historic periods.

The dispersal of dwellings within the village area would have reduced the need to relocate the village as often. Wood supplies for fuel and building would have been depleted more slowly, and pests, such as field mice and termites, would have been less of a problem if the individual longhouses of a village were dispersed, rather than nucleated. When the houses of a village were dispersed over a large area, village movement probably was a slow, almost imperceptible process, since some factors contributing to the relocation of one house, such as pests, depleted wood supplies, or grass in the household gardens, would not have necessitated the movement of all the houses belonging to a village. Also, the dispersion of a village's houses would have caused greater disruption to the mature forests and increased the amount of edge areas. This, in turn, would have resulted in an increase in transition area wildlife, especially white-tailed deer (Allen 1962:136).

Beyond a 2-kilometer (1.24-mi) catchment radius of the Boathouse Pond site, all of the protohistoric-historic components are either small decomposed sites or small shell middens (see fig. 22). Small decomposed sites, such as 44NB66 and 44NB119, probably represent briefly occupied interior hunting and gathering sites, as evidenced by their assemblages, which consist of a triangular point, a scraper or biface, and a few flakes. Small shell middens, like the excavated component at Blue Fish Beach (44NB147), probably were created by "small companies," as John Smith (1986b:162) put it, dispersed over the landscape "to mend their diet . . . upon . . . oysters."

The site of Blue Fish Beach occupied a shallow depression along the edge of a cultivated field adjacent to the Potomac River shoreline, between Presley Creek on the east and Corbin Pond on the west. The so-called pond is actually the remnant of an old estuary that has been closed by a stable sandspit. When the shell midden was first discovered in the summer of 1976, the mouth of Presley Creek was just barely open, and now it, too, is closed like Corbin Pond. These nearby sealed estuaries are graphic illustrations of the ongoing process of shoreline evolution in the lower Potomac. Indeed, the shallow depression in which the site was deposited was the remnant of an old ravine once located at the head of a small, embayed tidal marsh that emptied into the Potomac River in the early 1600s.

A total of twenty-one 2-meter (6.56-ft) squares were excavated at Blue Fish Beach, laid out in three adjacent rows of seven units each (fig. 25). The severe annual erosion along this segment of the Potomac shore (1.16 m or 3.8 ft per year) and the small size of the midden led to the decision to excavate most of the site, leaving only a strip one-

25. Excavations at Blue Fish Beach (44NB147)

half-meter (20 in) wide along the shoreline. The stratigraphy of the site consisted of six zones: zone I, a recent layer of storm-deposited sand; zone IIA, a recent plow zone; zone IIB, an earlier plow zone; zone IIIA, a silt loam midden above the shell midden; zone IIIB, the lens of oyster shell; and zone IIIC, the silt loam beneath the shell midden (Potter 1982:204–44).

Potsherds, a few projectile points, and a shallow layer of dark-earth midden are all that remained of the earliest use of the site during the Late Archaic, late Middle Woodland, and Late Woodland I periods. The shell midden, however, was created by people temporarily living at the site sometime during the first half of the seventeenth century. This interpretation is based on several lines of evidence: (1) two radio-carbon dates of A.D. 1605 ± 70 and A.D. 1645 ± 70, derived from wood charcoal found in the shell midden; (2) the association of Yeocomico pottery, which has been consistently dated between A.D. 1510 and 1690, with zone IIIA, the silt loam midden, and zone IIIB, the shell midden; and (3), the vertical distribution of three European-made artifacts and two artifacts made from European materials—an iron knife blade fragment, two white pipestems with bore diameters of 7/64 of an inch, and a wasted core and flake of English flint (fig. 26)—which indicates their direct or probable association with the Yeo-comico occupation (see Potter 1982:231–35).

The absence of projectile points in the shell midden and the recovery of only eight calcined bone fragments may indicate the limited importance of hunting during the seventeenth-century occupation of the site. The primary activity appears to have been the gathering and eating of oysters, soft-shell clams, and other shellfish. Although about 56 percent of the site had eroded away, it is estimated that the original shell midden probably contained the remains of some 50,000 shell-

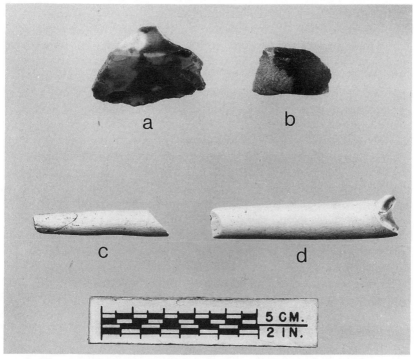

26. *Wasted core* (a) *and flake* (b) *of European flint and European-made white clay pipe fragments* (c, d) *from Blue Fish Beach (44NB147).* (*Photograph by Victor E. Krantz*)

fish, yielding about 250,000 grams of usable meat (Potter 1982:237–40; Waselkov 1982b:387–96). The uniformity and thinness of the shell deposit coupled with the limited number of artifacts is suggestive of a single occupancy of somewhat short duration by a small group of Indians.

Chicacoan Settlement Patterns

During the first half of the late Middle Woodland period (ca. A.D. 200–550), the settlement pattern in the Chicacoan locality was composed of small and intermediate-size estuarine shell middens and small interior sites. Family-size groups, perhaps belonging to a local band, were most likely responsible for creation of the small shell middens. The seasonal fusion of these smaller groups into larger, band-size groups resulted in the formation of some of the intermediate-size shell middens, like Plum Nelly (44NB128), which probably served as base camps during the fall and winter, and possibly into early spring.

Sometime after A.D. 550, perhaps between A.D. 700 and 900, very large midden sites were located in the necklands adjacent to coves or embayments of tributaries. Sites of this nature, such as the late Middle Woodland component of the Boathouse Pond site (44NB111), seem to have been villages where a local or regional band gathered during seasonally optimum times of the year, perhaps with some members of the band resident throughout most of the year. This change in settlement pattern occurred at the end of a period of environmental stress that characterized the transition from the Sub-Atlantic to the Scandic climatic episode, between A.D. 210 and 645, when temperatures were lower and there was less rain (Brush 1986:150–51; Carbone 1976:200). The pattern of small and intermediate-size shell middens continued to occur in essentially the same coastal locations as earlier Mockley occupations, while small and intermediate-size specialized procurement sites or temporary extractive camps were found in the interior uplands.

It is also interesting to note that some of the rhyolite points and knives from components probably dating to ca. A.D. 700–900, such as Boathouse Pond (44NB111), have been reworked or made from old bifaces and flakes. Apparently, as rhyolite became harder to get, people recycled old rhyolite tools. This reflects a disruption in the supply of rhyolite, from quarries in western Maryland to Virginia's Northern Neck, by the closing century of the late Middle Woodland period.

Around A.D. 900, the population within the Chicacoan locality dispersed. There were no large village sites. Rather, there was an increase in the number of intermediate-size sites along the banks of the Coan River and a decrease in the number of small sites throughout the area. Such a pattern suggests a shift away from one large village to several smaller villages, represented by some of the intermediate-size sites, such as Forest Kitchen (44NB44) and the Last Resort (44NB16). Small shell middens found farther than 2 kilometers (1.24 mi) from the Coan River probably were oyster-gathering camps occupied during lean times of the year.

The change in settlement pattern from one large residential base or village to several smaller villages or hamlets coincided with two major events, one natural and one cultural. Analysis of sediment cores taken from the Nanticoke and Magothy rivers, Maryland, and reconstructions of the paleoenvironment of the northern Shenandoah Valley in Virginia point to a pronounced dry period from A.D. 1000 to 1200 (Brush 1986:151; Carbone 1976:200). Pollen samples from this period contain high ratios of plants that prefer drier conditions (oak, hickory, and pine) to those which grow best under wet conditions (river birch, sweet gum, and black gum). Also, the amount of charcoal and metals found in a sediment core extracted from the Nanticoke River is similar to a more recent sedimentary horizon in the Magothy River associated with the Baltimore City fire of 1904. Using these data, Grace Brush (1986:151) hypothesized that the "dry period from 1000 to 1200 A.D. was characterized by intermittent fires, releasing metals from the soil and vegetation which were then deposited in the [Nanticoke] estuary."

About the time the dry period began, or shortly before, maize, beans, and squash gradually became part of the subsistence base. At the Reynolds-Alvis site (44HE470) in northern Henrico County, Virginia, squash and beans were found in a cooking basin which was radiocarbon-dated to A.D. 920 ± 75 (Gleach 1987b:221, 223). To the west, in piedmont Fluvanna County, a storage pit at the Spessard site (44FV134) containing maize and squash yielded a radiocarbon date of A.D. 1160 ± 80, while maize was found in a trash pit dated to A.D. 1030 ± 75 at the Point of Fork site (44FV19; Jeffrey L. Hantman, personal communication 1988; L. Daniel Mouer, personal communication 1988). Agriculture is also documented at the beginning of the Late Woodland period in piedmont Maryland and the northern Shenandoah Valley (Kavanagh 1982:70; Gardner and Carbone n.d.; Gardner 1986:77).

By A.D. 1300–1500, the areal settlement pattern was similar to the early seventeenth-century pattern observed by the English colonists. This is not unexpected, given the data from Virginia, Maryland, and adjacent regions that indicate an increased reliance upon plant domesticates after ca. A.D. 1300 (Green 1987:87–106; Ritchie and Funk 1973:359–68; Kinsey 1972:388). A single large, internally dispersed village, the Boathouse Pond site component, was located in the necklands along the east bank of the Coan River, with outlying intermediate-size and small shell middens within a 2-kilometer (1.24-mi) radius of the village. Some of the shell middens of intermediate size may represent the location of small clusters of houses, while others resulted from repeated visits to temporary collecting sites by people gathering and consuming mollusks. Beyond a 2-kilometer (1.24-mi) radius of the village were a number of small sites indicative of the exploitation of resources in the interior uplands, as well as the seasonal fission of the village population in order to live upon shellfish and other coastal resources.

Within a 2-kilometer (1.24-mi) catchment radius of the Boathouse Pond site, there was enough arable land to support a population of about 125 people indefinitely. This could explain, in part, why there was no archaeological evidence of any other major late prehistoric or early historic village sites in the Chicacoan locality. Also, when the longhouses of a village were dispersed over a large area, village movement probably would have been a slow process, since some of the factors contributing to the relocation of one or several houses, such as pests, would not have necessarily caused the movement of other houses in the village.

The main difference between the settlement pattern of the Late Woodland II period and that of the protohistoric-historic period was a substantial increase in the number of components (see fig. 23). This seems to represent an increase in the local population. By June 1608 John Smith noted that the Chicacoans had about thirty warriors, or a total population estimated to be between 120 and 130 people. Most of them probably lived in the werowance's village, which consisted of fifteen to eighteen arborlike structures, built of poles covered with cane mats or bark, spread out over a large area. Scattered among the structures were small household gardens containing squash, pumpkins, gourds, sunflowers, and tobacco. Larger fields of corn and some beans, as well as abandoned agricultural fields in varying stages of regrowth to forest, were located in the broad, flat expanses of land near the village. Part of this historic occupation is represented by the protohistoric-historic component of the Boathouse Pond site (44NB111) and other sites, such as 44NB97, rimming the banks of Boathouse Pond. Most likely, it was there that Captain Smith and his men first encountered the Chicacoans.

CHAPTER 3

The
Late Prehistory
of the Lower
Potomac River Basin

Introduction

THE CHICACOANS AND THEIR ANCESTORS did not live in cultural isolation. Their development was interwoven with the general pattern of late prehistoric cultural development in southern Maryland and northeastern Virginia. This chapter looks beyond the Chicacoan locality and examines other noteworthy components, dating between A.D. 200 and 1500, from sites and locales throughout the lower Potomac River basin and adjacent areas, interpreting them within the context of a regional chronological sequence.

The Mockley Phase

DEFINITION

The Mockley phase takes its name from the pottery that characterizes components of the late Middle Woodland period, ca. A.D. 200–900, throughout the lower Potomac River basin (McNett 1975:135; Handsman and McNett 1974:22–24). On Maryland's western shore the equivalent archaeological culture is referred to as the Selby Bay phase, named by Thomas Mayr after a large site on the South River, Maryland (Wright 1973:21; Curry and Kavanagh 1991:20). In the Potomac basin, where similar archaeological manifestations on the coastal plain of both Maryland and Virginia occur, the more inclusive name Mockley phase is used. The term *phase* is an archaeological construct (synonymous with archaeological culture) referring to components that share similar cultural remains, "spatially limited to . . . a locality or region, and chronologically limited to a relatively brief interval of time" (Willey and Phillips 1958:22). Mockley pottery and other artifacts diagnostic of this phase were described in chapter 2.

POTOMAC RIVER BASIN SITES AND LOCALES

Excavated components from the White Oak Point site (44WM119) in Westmoreland County, Virginia, provide comparative data on seasonal shellfish-gathering sites of the late Mockley phase (fig. 27). This large shell midden covers 6 hectares (14.8 a) on the east side of Nomini Creek, on the outer coastal plain. Intensive excavation by Gregory A. Waselkov (1982a) resulted in the identification of twenty-six archaeological components dating from ca. 2000 B.C. to A.D. 1700. Four of these components were dated by means of stratigraphic superposition and radiocarbon determinations to A.D. 700–900. The artifact assemblages (fig. 28) consisted of Mockley ware (dominant), Nomini ware, Nomini points (similar to Potts points), bone awls, ovoid bifaces, a beaver-tooth chisel, and an unfinished miniature platform pipe of chlorite schist (Waselkov 1982a: 235–37, 247).

Each of the four components consisted of a series of features created by people camping at White Oak Point between April and June for the sole purpose of collecting and processing oysters. The diversity of species found in the Mockley/Nomini components drops dramatically from earlier components at the site, indicating an increase in subsistence specialization. Furthermore, the average number of oysters per volume of midden sharply increases, with invertebrates providing most of the available meat (Waselkov 1982a:200–207).

Farther up the outer coastal plain, in the brackish water zone, a Mockley phase component was excavated at the multicomponent Loyola Retreat site (18CH58) on the Potomac River shore in Charles County, Maryland. Sherds of Mockley Cord-marked and Net-impressed pottery were found near the bottom of zone I, described by Charles McNett (1975:135) as "a midden with much black loam rather than the shell dumps from earlier periods. This means, unfortunately, that the cultural deposits were rather churned up and associations between the pottery and other artifacts are rather hard to come by." An antler-tine projectile point and a fossilized shark's tooth possibly were associated with the Mockley ceramics. The very bottom of zone I, the black loam and shell midden, was radiocarbon-dated to A.D. 815 ± 95 (Gardner and McNett 1971:45; Handsman and McNett 1974:22; Boyce and Frye 1986:11).

On the inner coastal plain of the Potomac River, small and inter-

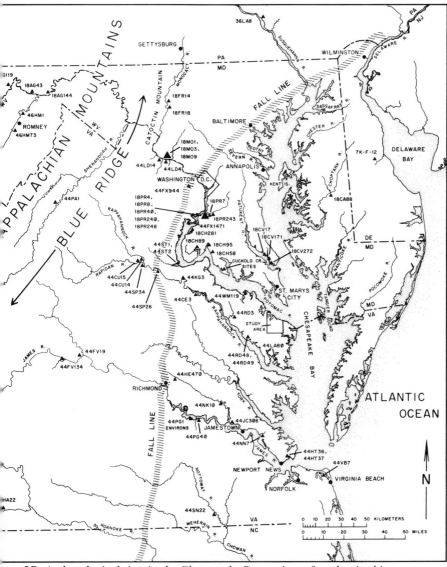

27. *Archaeological sites in the Chesapeake Bay region referred to in this volume. (Map by G. Robert Lewis)*

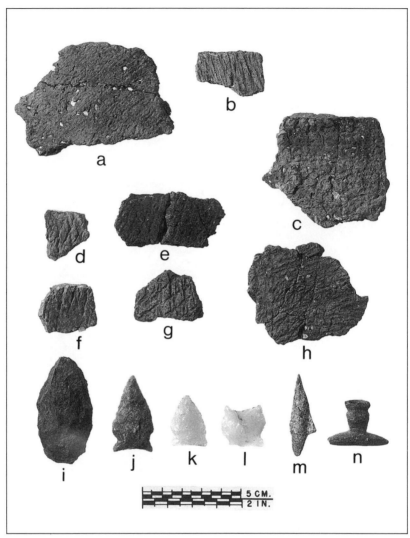

28. Late Mockley phase artifact assemblage from White Oak Point (44WM119): a, b, *Mockley Net–impressed pottery;* c *and* h, *Mockley Cord-marked pottery;* d *and* f, *Nomini Cord-marked pottery;* e *and* g, *Nomini Fabric-impressed pottery;* i, *ovoid biface of rhyolite;* j–l, *Nomini projectile points;* m, *stemmed projectile point of deer bone;* n, *chlorite schist, miniature platform pipe. (Photograph by Victor E. Krantz)*

mediate-size components containing Mockley ceramics and Fox Creek–Selby Bay points occur along the freshwater streams, with many small components lining the Potomac River and its tributaries below Great Falls (Johnson 1991; Inashima 1985; Potter 1980). During late winter and early spring, anadromous fish, like herring, leave the salt water of the Atlantic Ocean and Chesapeake Bay to spawn in fresh water (Lippson 1973:28, 34). This cycle has been repeated annually in the area below the Great Falls of the Potomac River since at least 1500 B.C. Prehistorically, the number and variety of anadromous fish making this journey was much greater and included the once ubiquitous sturgeon. Most likely, the small Mockley components represent fishing camps and processing sites occupied during the spring fish runs (Gardner 1982:60, 78).

Some of the intermediate-size components may have served as residential bases at various times during the year. The Mockley components of the Piscataway site (18PR7) and the type site of Mockley Point (18PR240), both in Prince Georges County, Maryland, contained evidence which is suggestive of reuse throughout the annual subsistence cycle. Storage pits were found at the Piscataway site, and the midden is described as "richly dark in refuse not unlike the appearance of Late Woodland midden" (Woodward and Phebus 1973). Both storage pits and burials apparently were associated with the late Middle Woodland occupation of Mockley Point (Stephenson et al. 1963:74–79). Several millennia of prehistoric activities and the manner in which both sites were excavated conspire against making more precise statements about the function and temporal and spatial extent of the Mockley components at the sites.

Evidence of Mockley phase activities in the interior uplands, some distance away from the Potomac River, recently has come to light in piedmont Fairfax County, Virginia. Archaeological survey and subsequent excavations at the Karell site (44FX944) revealed a small late Middle Woodland component containing Mockley ware and a Selby Bay point (Johnson 1986:3, 1991). The limited quantity and nature of the artifacts indicate a relatively brief stay by a few people. From this, it is inferred that the site was a temporary camp used by a party of collectors sent out from one of the residential bases near the Potomac River to exploit specific resources found in the interior uplands.

Task-specific groups of collectors were also ranging beyond the Great Falls of the Potomac into the piedmont of Virginia and Maryland and the Blue Ridge province of Maryland. They apparently came in search of rhyolite, which occurs in deposits from Gettysburg, Pennsylvania, to South Mountain, Maryland, and along the western side of Catoctin Mountain. Aboriginal rhyolite quarries were located on the west slope of Catoctin from Wolfsville to Fisher's Hollow, and also near Foxville, Maryland (Kavanagh 1982:68).

After the rhyolite was shaped into rough blanks at the quarry site, it was taken to base camps where the flint knappers probably stayed while quarrying the rhyolite. Additional processing of the rhyolite took place there, as well. Three such base camps were found in the nearby Monocacy River valley. Many small Mockley components, consisting of only Selby Bay points and other lithic artifacts, are also scattered throughout the valley. Seven components from three rock-shelters, three open riverine sites, and one base camp / rhyolite-processing station contained Mockley ceramics (Kavanagh 1982:66–68). The nature and distribution of the Mockley phase components in the western Piedmont and Blue Ridge provinces of Maryland probably resulted from periodic trips to the rhyolite quarries by groups of flint knappers from southern Maryland and northern Virginia (Stewart 1989:60; Curry and Kavanagh 1991:13–15).

The direct procurement of rhyolite by groups of coastal plain flint knappers does not negate the further movement of rhyolite blanks via broad-based trade networks. The extensive distribution of exotic lithics throughout the coastal plain of Maryland and Virginia is testament that such a network existed. It is also obvious that the major flow of rhyolite blanks was from the western interior to the coastal plain, and then south and north through the coastal areas (Stewart 1989:60, in press).

Hoarding, in the form of rhyolite blade caches, is evident below the Great Falls of the Potomac at Washington, D.C., and around Annapolis, Maryland (Holmes 1897:78–79; Wilson 1897:972; Wimsatt 1958:87–92). In addition to rhyolite, caches of argillite and green jasper have been found near Annapolis (Holmes 1897:78–79). Laurie Steponaitis (1986:283) has noted that argillite and green jasper are not as common in the lower Patuxent River basin as they are farther north, near Annapolis, and similar observations have been made along the Maryland shore of the lower Potomac River (Wanser 1982:150, 194). In the lower Northern Neck of Virginia, rhyolite is common in late Middle Woodland Mockley components, but argillite and green jasper are rare. Perhaps cultural groups in the Washington, D.C., and Annapolis areas occasionally manipulated the broad-based, down-the-line exchange networks by hoarding certain trade items within their home territories (Stewart 1989:65).

SITES AND LOCALES IN ADJACENT AREAS

Severn River, Maryland. The Mockley phase settlement pattern along the Severn River "is one of smaller shell heaps and middens . . . and larger shell heaps and middens. . . . The large-small dichotomy is interpreted as reflecting the periodic assembling of small groups into several large groups" (Wright 1973:21–22). Shortly after this interpretation was published, Russell Handsman and Charles McNett (1974:26, 31) proposed that the large-small site dichotomy might reflect increasing population size and plant husbandry, necessitating more semipermanent villages. However, no unequivocal evidence of plant tending or plant domesticates has been found. While maize, introduced from the piedmont, may have been added to the subsistence base as early as A.D. 700 (Ford 1974:400), there are no convincingly early dates for, or unambiguous identifications of, any plant domesticate east of the Appalachian Mountains before the beginning of the Late Woodland period. Plant domesticates may have been tended in the Maryland-Virginia tidewater before ca. A.D. 800–900, but they probably contributed very little to the annual diet (Smith 1989:1569).

Patuxent River, Maryland. Of particular importance to an understanding of the Mockley phase is Laurie Steponaitis's (1986) regional survey of the southeastern Patuxent River basin in southern Maryland. The purpose of Steponaitis's research was to investigate the transition from mobile to more sedentary lifeways that occurred between the Late Archaic through Late Woodland periods, ca. 4000 B.C. to A.D. 1600. Toward this end, she conducted a surface reconnaissance of 1.1 percent of the 459-square kilometer (177.2-mi^2) study area. With controlled surface collection techniques, seventy artifact clusters were identified which contained temporally diagnostic artifacts. Analysis of the artifact clusters resulted in the definition of 125 components for the fifty-six hundred years under study. Change in residential mobility through time was measured by examining functional variation in the assemblages, component assemblage diversity, intracomponent artifact density, and component size distribution (Steponaitis 1986:105, 118, 201, 264).

Steponaitis's study indicates that a dramatic change in settlement organization occurred during the Mockley phase. The coastal lowlands were used more intensively than interior areas; there were important differences in the content of artifact assemblages between coastal and interior components; the number of artifacts within each component increased; large, special-purpose sites appeared for the first time; and there was an increase in the relative frequency of large components, especially in the lowlands and along estuaries. Collectively Steponaitis (1986:285–86) has interpreted these patterns as evidence for a decline in residential mobility and an increase in logistical resource procurement. Simply put, small parties were sent out to collect specific resources (goods) and bring them back to the residential base where the majority of the group (consumers) lived. Such a strategy generally involves fewer residential moves (Binford 1980:15).

In examining potential causes for the decline in residential mobility during the late Middle Woodland period, Steponaitis (1986:286) noted that there is no evidence for population growth in the lower Patuxent basin during this time. Nor were resources more abundant than before. However, there is some evidence to suggest that a combination of environmental stress and changes in social relations may have caused a shift in the settlement and subsistence patterns.

Paleoenvironmental studies in the Shenandoah Valley indicate that during the transition from the Sub-Atlantic to the Scandic climatic episode, there was a period of possible environmental stress (A.D. 210–645) when temperatures were lower and dryness increased (Carbone 1976:200). Recently, Grace Brush (1986:150–51) analyzed pollen samples taken from sediment cores collected in the Magothy River, Maryland. Between A.D. 400 and 500, an abundance of dry-weather plants were present, such as holly and chestnut, which seems to support the earlier climatic reconstruction of Victor Carbone (1976).

As is the case for the Chicacoan locality, a high percentage (77%) of late Middle Woodland points and knives in the Patuxent River basin were made from rhyolite and a smaller percentage (4.6%) from argillite (Steponaitis 1986:277–81). The latter stone probably came from sources in southeastern Pennsylvania. Steponaitis (1986:286–87) has suggested that interregional exchange peaked during this time, as the result of a strengthening of alliance networks. The interval of increased dryness between A.D. 400 and 500 may have caused a greater dependence on alliances as a way of reducing risk which, in turn, created a social demand for surplus and storage beyond the domestic mode of production.

In 1988 a series of Mockley phase features were excavated at the Patuxent Point site (18CV272) near Solomons, Maryland, on the east side of the lower Patuxent River. The features include a very large storage pit 3 meters (10 ft) in diameter and 2 meters (6.5 ft) deep, with a four-post structure providing overhead cover, five smaller pits, and an arc of postmolds delineating the remnants of a possible oval house pattern. The largest pit appears to be too big for the storage needs of a single household; it may well have been built for the storage of surplus goods collected by a larger cultural group, of which this household was a part. A diversity of local estuarine and terrestrial resources were harvested, and all seasons but summer are represented in the animal and plant remains excavated from the pits (Gardner et al. 1989).

Rappahannock River, Virginia. An extensive late Mockley phase component, known as Woodbury Farm site no. 1 (44RD48), was discovered on the outer coastal plain near the Rappahannock River's north bank in Richmond County (see fig. 27). The large midden (class 1) covers 3.34 hectares (8.2 a) of the headland on the west side of Farnham Creek, ranking second in size only after the Mockley phase component of the Boathouse Pond site (44NB111) in nearby Northumberland County (fig. 29).

Both sites share a number of additional characteristics. Each one is horizontally extensive but vertically very shallow, with most of the midden confined to the plow zone. The middens of the two sites are composed mainly of gray-black soil. Oyster shell is scattered over both sites, but it is not the major constituent of the midden refuse. The two

29. *Aerial view of the Woodbury Farm site no. 1 (44RD48), looking west. The site appears as dark stains in the cultivated field adjacent to the creek.*

sites are situated on necklands adjacent to coves off tributaries. Both sites yielded a higher percentage of Mockley Net-impressed sherds (86% at Woodbury Farm) than Mockley Cord-marked sherds, and some of the rhyolite points are heavily reworked or are made from old bifaces and flakes (see fig. 12*l*) These data lead to the postulation that the Mockley phase component of Woodbury Farm site no. 1, like the late Middle Woodland component of the Boathouse Pond site, represents a village where a local or regional band gathered as a complete unit for several months during a particular season(s), with a portion of the group, perhaps, resident during most of the year. The occupations probably date between A.D. 550 and 900, and may date closer to A.D. 700–900 (Potter 1982:194–97, 334, 338).

James River, Virginia. Located about 40 kilometers (25 mi) downstream from the falls on the inner coastal plain along the south bank of the James River, the Mockley phase component of the Maycocks Point site (44PG40; see fig. 27) is a shell midden composed of freshwater mussel (Opperman 1980:1). In some areas, the shell is almost 1.5 meters (5 ft) deep. Six distinct stratigraphic zones were observed during the excavation of five 10-by-10-foot (approximately 3-by-3-m) units. The stratigraphy and radiocarbon dates point to at least two occupations, one around A.D. 325 and the second about A.D. 825 (Barber 1981:4–6).

Analysis of the 6,540 animal bones from the Maycocks Point shell midden provided some interesting results. The faunal subsistence patterns of the earlier and later Mockley occupations differ very little. Although a variety of mammals, birds, reptiles, and fish are present in the archaeological samples, the subsistence pattern focused on a limited number of animals, primarily white-tailed deer, turkey, turtles, sturgeon, gar, and freshwater mussels. Two basic habitats were exploited: the freshwater tidal river and the deciduous forest edge. Seasonal data derived from the faunal analysis indicate Maycocks Point was occupied year-round by at least some portion of the cultural group who used the site (Barber 1981:17–21).

East of Maycocks Point, on the outer coastal plain near Newport News, Virginia, archaeological excavation at the Skiffes Creek site (44NN7) uncovered two small Middle Woodland oyster-shell middens (see fig. 27). The most recent of the two shell middens contained Potts points, Yadkin Triangular points, and a ceramic assemblage composed primarily of Mockley ware (Geier 1983:208). This late Middle Woodland shell midden represents a single, short-term stay by a small group of people. Seasonal evidence indicates a probable fall occupation, with the residents focusing on gathering mollusks and hunting white-tailed deer (Barber 1983:181–86).

Not far downriver from Newport News, excavations by the Colonial Williamsburg Foundation's Department of Archaeological Research identified Mockley phase components at two archaeological sites on the Hampton University campus (Edwards et al. 1989:27–55). At site 44HT36 (see fig. 27), a number of prehistoric features were scattered across the site, including at least four storage pits: three were roughly 91 centimeters (3 ft) in diameter and 46 centimeters (1.5 ft) deep, and a fourth pit was 1.4 meters (4.7 ft) in diameter and 1.16 meters (3.8 ft) deep. A radiocarbon date of A.D. 20 ± 70 was derived from charcoal found in the bottom layer of the largest pit. The small number of artifacts recovered and the nature of the features suggest that the Mockley phase component represents "perhaps two noncontemporaneous encampments occupied by small groups of people" who used the site as a place to cache goods (Edwards et al. 1989:30).

At the second site (44HT37), two clusters of prehistoric features were evident. One cluster consisted of two small shell-filled pits, both about 61 centimeters (2.0 ft) in diameter and 37 centimeters (1.2 ft) deep. Charcoal from one of the pits (feature 1003) was radiocarbon-dated to A.D. 40 ± 80. Nearby, excavation of a small secondary burial pit revealed the partial remains of a juvenile and an adult (Edwards et al. 1989:47–49). The second cluster of prehistoric features included at least two storage pits, both about 91 centimeters (3.0 ft) in diameter and depth. A radiocarbon determination of A.D. 300 ± 70 was obtained from charcoal found in one of the pits (feature 1024). Paleobotanical remains from feature 1024 included fragments of a pinecone, hickory nut, and walnut; one seed each of bedstraw and smartweed; and one "possible maize kernel fragment" (Edwards et al. 1989:51).

While it is tempting to interpret such information as evidence "for the possible limited cultivation of maize" (Edwards et al. 1989:3), such an interpretation is at variance with a recent synthesis of the origins of agriculture in eastern North America (Smith 1989). Not only is the identification of the charred corn kernel uncertain, but the radiocarbon date was obtained from associated charcoal, rather than from the "possible maize kernel fragment." Use of accelerator mass spectrometer (AMS) radiocarbon dating to date carbonized kernel fragments directly has dramatically changed the timetable for the initial introduction of corn. "The earliest convincing macrobotanical evidence of the presence of maize in eastern North America is the directly dated carbonized kernel fragments from the Icehouse Bottom site (A.D. 175) [in Tennessee] and the Harness site (A.D. 220) [in Ohio]. . . . Along the Atlantic and Gulf coastal plains . . . , forager economies based almost exclusively on wild species of animals and plants (with some *Cucurbita* [gourd and squash] cultivation) persisted until the A.D. 800 to 1100 shift to maize-centered agriculture" (Smith 1989:1569).

The Rappahannock Complex

DEFINITION

The Rappahannock complex is named for one of the more common types of Late Woodland period ceramics found in the lower Potomac River basin—Rappahannock Fabric-impressed pottery (McNett 1975:235). The term *complex* denotes a recurrent group of cultural remains found at a series of related archaeological components for which comprehensive information is lacking. As William Fitzhugh (1972:112) noted, "Either a large type site is unknown or insufficient samples are available to define the range and variation of the . . . [archaeological culture], and the formal procedure of phase definition awaits further information." Diagnostic artifacts of the Rappahannock complex were described in chapter 2.

Although components of the Rappahannock complex can date as early as A.D. 900 and as late as the middle 1600s, this chapter focuses on components dating from A.D. 900 to 1500. In the Chicacoan locality, it was possible to subdivide that period into two temporal units— Late Woodland I and Late Woodland II. However, most researchers have been unable to subdivide the Late Woodland period into finer temporal units. It must be remembered, therefore, that this discussion of the Rappahannock complex concerns the same period of time, A.D. 900–1500, covered by the Late Woodland I and II periods in the Chicacoan locality.

POTOMAC RIVER BASIN SITES AND LOCALES

Elsewhere on the outer coastal plain of southern Maryland and northern Virginia, changes similar to those observed in the Chicacoan locality occurred in Rappahannock complex settlement patterns. Charles McNett and Ellis McDowell (1974) described a dispersed agricultural settlement situated on the southern shore of Cuckold Creek, in Charles County, Maryland (see fig. 27). A black midden soil mixed with oyster shells marks the location of the former habitations. The people who lived there, probably during the early Late Woodland period, made a shell-tempered pottery similar to Townsend ware. The scattered middens hugging the banks of Cuckold Creek are thought to be the remains of a series of hamlets or farmsteads that were interspersed among the garden plots lining the creek.

As noted for the Chicacoan locality, specialized oyster-gathering camps continued to be an important part of the settlement and subsistence system. At the White Oak Point (44WM119) site, the gathering and preparation of oysters was stepped up during the Late Woodland period, particularly after A.D. 1300. The average number of oysters per volume of midden increased sharply, and mammals and fish contributed a greater proportion of available meat to the diet of those living on-site. It appears, therefore, that large quantities of oyster meat were being dried for storage and trade. Most of the oyster-gathering camps were used between March and May. This shift to intensive gathering and drying of oysters may have come about as a result of scheduling conflicts with spring planting (Waselkov 1982a: table 41, 207–8).

Another item of interest from the White Oak Point site is a large section of channeled whelk (*Busycon canniculatum*), cut into a roughly rectangular shape and ground smooth on its outer surface (fig. 30). This was found in a stratum dated by superposition to ca. A.D. 1400– 1500 (Waselkov 1982a:248, 288). The object was probably intended as a blank for the manufacture of stylized human maskettes, like those discovered in a late high-status burial at Potomac Neck, near the Potomac Creek site (see chap. 5; Potter 1989:162).

Farther upriver in the vicinity of Piscataway Creek, Maryland, a number of archaeological components give a glimpse of Rappahannock complex settlement patterns in the freshwater zone. About 3 kilometers (1.86 mi) from the mouth of Piscataway Creek, situated on a cove along the creek's eastern bank, is the Farmington Landing site (18PR4). This is the largest-known local component of the Rappahannock complex, covering about 1 hectare (2.47 a). The dark midden, features, faunal remains, and artifacts indicate the site was a permanent early Late Woodland village, probably occupied sometime between A.D. 900 and 1300 (Veatch 1974; McNett 1975:236–37). Not only is the Farmington Landing component similar in size to the Late Woodland I village at Boathouse Pond (44NB111), it is also located near areas of Mattapex and Woodstown sandy loam soils (Veatch 1974:4).

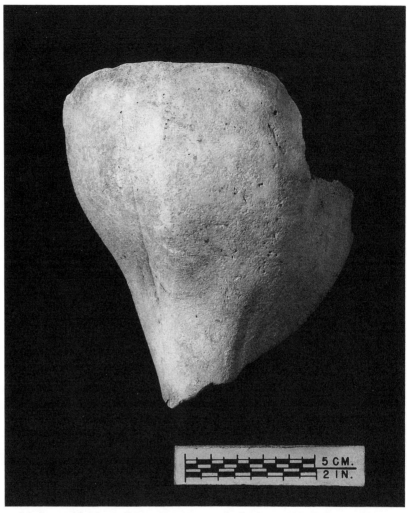

30. Large blank cut from a Busycon canniculatum shell discovered at White Oak Point (44WM119). Shell blanks such as this were probably used to make the stylized human-face maskettes like those from Potomac Neck, Va. (see fig. 46). (Photograph by Victor E. Krantz)

Several smaller components of the Rappahannock complex lie a short distance east and west of Farmington Landing. To the east, near the head of Piscataway Bay, the Piscataway site (18PR7) component "does not suggest a uniform settlement but rather occasional occupation probably by small numbers" of people (Woodward and Phebus 1973). The investigators inferred that it served as a fish camp during anadromous fish runs in late winter and early spring.

Nearby, on the terraces adjacent to an unnamed stream flowing north into Piscataway Creek, an early Late Woodland component (18PR143) was discovered and excavated during archaeological investigations preceding construction of a sewer line. The small component consisted of a diverse assemblage of artifacts—Townsend pottery, flakes with cortex, quartzite cobble cores, bifaces, a knife, drill, and chopper—associated with a scattered hearth. A number of activities are indicated by the range of artifacts, including quarrying, stone tool manufacture, and possibly the gathering of plant foods (Gardner 1976:41–45).

Another small component of the Rappahannock complex is located about 3 kilometers (1.86 mi) west of Farmington Landing at the Accokeek Creek site (18PR8). The Townsend ceramics discovered here originally were thought to be "trade pottery" associated with the Potomac Creek component (Stephenson et al. 1963:109–13, 191). Given the repeated use of the site throughout prehistory and the nearness of other Rappahannock complex components, it is just as likely that the Townsend pottery was deposited during an early Late Woodland occupation of the site.

Judging from an examination of the Piscataway Creek locale, the Rappahannock complex settlement system was centered on an intermediate-size village supported by outlying hamlets and specialized extractive or foray sites. The village was sited near the juncture of Piscataway Creek and the Potomac River to take advantage of the arable sandy loam soils of the floodplain and the variety of resources found in the creek, adjacent marshlands, and surrounding deciduous forest. The special-purpose sites were associated with the harvesting of seasonally abundant animals and plants or the collecting of specific resources found away from the floodplain.

SITES AND LOCALES IN ADJACENT AREAS

Patuxent River, Maryland. To the north in the lower Patuxent basin, the frequency of components larger than 0.6 hectare (1.48 a) increases over time, with the greatest number of components between 0.6 and

3.0 hectares (1.48–7.41 a) occurring in the Late Woodland period. The large Late Woodland components generally are associated with lowland terraces and estuarine settings. In addition to a substantial increase in the areal extent and number of components, there is also an increase in the number of artifacts within components and a decrease in the use of nonlocal raw material for stone tools. Collectively, the evidence implies population growth, an increase in the size of residential groups, greater residential permanence, and the growing importance of farming (Steponaitis 1986:254, 258, 288).

Rappahannock River, Virginia. To the south, along the Rappahannock River, the situation appears to have been the same as described for the tidewater Potomac. Many of the sites known for the river basin, however, were discovered and investigated in the late nineteenth or early twentieth centuries. Information on how the collections were made or the exact sites from which they came is often sketchy or lacking altogether. Even when collections can be associated with a particular site, it is often impossible to estimate the extent of each occupation or component.

Indian Town Farm (44LA80), originally discovered by William Dinwiddie in 1891, is typical of the very large sites found on the Rappahannock River's outer coastal plain (see fig. 27). It is a large shell midden (class 4) located in Lancaster County, Virginia, on the east side of the Corrotoman River, along an unnamed cove (fig. 31). An examination of the original surface collections made by Dinwiddie and surface collections made during a one-day reconnaissance of the site in 1978 points to reoccupation and/or continuous use of the site from at least the beginning of the Late Woodland period up until the seventeenth century. The oyster-shell and dark-earth midden is huge, covering approximately 9.3–10.13 hectares (22.97–25.0 a). In a wooded portion of the site, where there is no indication of previous cultivation, the midden has a uniform depth of 10 to 15 centimeters (3.9–5.85 in). The site is very much like the Woodbury Farm no. 1 (44RD48) and Boathouse Pond (44NB111) sites in terms of its extensive nature, midden composition and depth, and environmental setting. Indeed, all of the major sites along the lower Rappahannock River, like the Indian Town Farm site and Woodbury Farm site no. 1, were occupied in varying degrees from the late Middle Woodland through the early contact period (Bushnell 1937). Similar circumstances have been noted for the major Algonquian sites of northeastern North Carolina (Green 1986:236).

Thus far, the description of Late Woodland cultures has been con-

*31. Aerial view of the Indian Town Farm site (44LA80), looking
northwest. Most of the 9 to 10 hectare (23 to 25 a) site lies in the woods and
fields to the right of the cove.*

fined to components of the Rappahannock complex. Like the previous Mockley phase, these components are concentrated on the coastal plain. However, for the period after about A.D. 1300, components of a different archaeological culture, known as the Potomac Creek complex, are found along the fall line from the Rappahannock River northward to Baltimore, with their greatest concentration below the falls of the Potomac River on the inner coastal plain. The appearance of the Potomac Creek people on the prehistoric landscape coincides with other changes in the area's Late Woodland cultures. In order to understand these and later developments requires an examination of the Potomac Creek complex.

The Potomac Creek Complex

HISTORY AND DEFINITION

Quite often it is necessary to study the history of archaeology before studying the archaeology of prehistory. In the case of the Potomac Creek complex this is certainly true. Without the benefit of a discussion of the people, places, and things involved in its definition, it would be difficult to understand this archaeological culture.

The history of the Potomac Creek complex begins with the excavation of the Potomac Creek site (44ST2), a palisaded village perched on a neck of land near the Potomac River in Stafford County, Virginia (fig. 32). Since the days of Thomas Jefferson, Potomac Neck has been regarded as the site of Patawomeke, a Virginia Algonquian Indian village visited by Captain John Smith in 1608. Between 1935 and 1937 a group of amateur archaeologists headed by Judge William Graham unearthed five prehistoric and historic Indian cemeteries at the Potomac Creek site. The discovery of human skeletal remains prompted Judge Graham to invite Dr. T. Dale Stewart, a physical anthropologist with the Smithsonian Institution, to visit the site. After the judge's death in 1937, Stewart continued the excavations for three consecutive summers beginning in 1938 (Stewart 1988).

In the spring of 1940 an anthropology graduate student from the University of Chicago, Karl Schmitt, came to the Smithsonian Institution to begin analyzing the archaeological collections from the Potomac Creek site. For two months Schmitt familiarized himself with the notes and collections resulting from previous excavations. Then he joined Dr. Stewart for the last field season at Potomac Creek. Upon completion of the excavations, the remaining unstudied archaeological collections were shipped to the University of Chicago where Schmitt continued his analysis (Schmitt 1965:1). The results were presented in Schmitt's 1942 master's thesis, "Patawomeke: An Historic Algonkin Site."

Concurrent with the six years of intermittent excavations at the Potomac Creek site, Mrs. Alice L. L. Ferguson was digging at several prehistoric and historic Indian sites, known collectively as the Accokeek Creek site, on her property across the Potomac River in Prince Georges County, Maryland. One of these six sites (18PR8) was a large village surrounded by numerous palisades (see fig. 32). Ferguson thought this was the site of Moyaone, a village of the Algonquian-speaking Piscataway Indians that also was visited by Captain John Smith in 1608 (Potter n.d.: 10–12).

Since both the Potomac Creek site and the large village of the Accokeek Creek site were considered to be early seventeenth-century Algonquian villages, Schmitt (1965:25) made "a cursory examination of Mrs. Ferguson's material" in order to compare it with the Potomac Creek collection. Schmitt's comparative study resulted in a lengthy list of 102 archaeological traits shared by the two sites (Schmitt 1965:25–

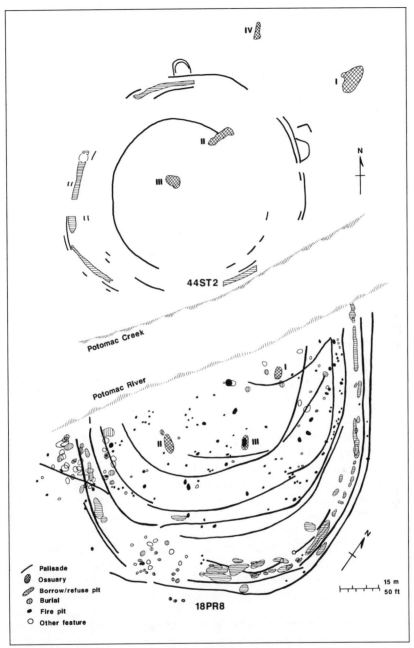

IV

I

II

III

N

44ST2

Potomac Creek

Potomac River

I

II

III

Palisade
Ossuary
Borrow/refuse pit
Burial
Fire pit
Other feature

N

15 m
50 ft

18PR8

32. Plan of partial excavations at the Potomac Creek site (44ST2)
compared to the plan of complete excavations at the Accokeek Creek site
(18PR8). (Illustration after Stewart 1988; Stephenson et al. 1963:fig. 6)

29). Later, Schmitt reduced the list to the following essential characteristics: Potomac Creek pottery; obtuse-angle clay pipes with incised or dentate designs; shell gorgets with drilled-dot designs; shell maskettes with stylized human faces bearing the weeping eye motif; secondary communal reburial of human remains in large, oval pits (ossuaries); and concentric palisaded villages with surrounding defensive ditches. This collection of shared archaeological traits defined what Schmitt (1952:63) called the Potomac Creek focus.

Schmitt's use of the word *focus* reflects the archaeological classification system popular among many Plains and Eastern archaeologists during the 1940s and 1950s. Today, the term *focus* is no longer used by professional archaeologists because of its association with the Midwestern Taxonomic System—an archaeological classification scheme developed in 1939 and based solely upon similarities in the form and content of archaeological assemblages (McKern 1939). This was one of the great weaknesses of that system, which treated culture as an agglomeration of things divorced from the functioning cultural system of which they were a part, hence Schmitt's emphasis upon listing all the archaeological "traits" observed at each site. With the advent of radiocarbon dating, further research at stratified archaeological sites, and the publication in 1958 of Willey and Phillips's *Method and Theory in American Archaeology*, the Midwestern Taxonomic System had become obsolete by the early 1960s.

Like the phrase itself, many of the original defining traits of the Potomac Creek focus have not withstood the test of time. Over forty years of archaeological research since Schmitt's thesis have revealed that ossuaries and obtuse-angle clay pipes with incised or denate designs are found at sites from the Delmarva peninsula south through coastal Maryland, Virginia, and northeastern North Carolina (Custer 1984; Ubelaker 1974; Potter 1982; McCary and Barka 1977; Green 1986; Phelps 1983). Although Schmitt (1965:23) was aware that the ossuaries and clay pipes were not confined to the areal distribution of Potomac Creek pottery, he nevertheless included them as defining traits of the Potomac Creek focus. Schmitt also knew that the shell gorgets with the drilled-dot designs and the shell maskettes with stylized human faces were found only at the Potomac Creek site and the Potomac Neck locale, respectively; to date, they have not been found on any other sites in southern Maryland or northern tidewater Virginia. As for the "defensive ditches," the one at the Accokeek Creek site was not a continuous ditch but a series of discrete borrow pits dug inside a palisade line (Stephenson et al. 1963:38–39, 55–57, 196).

Likewise, it is questionable if the shallow, discontinuous "defensive ditch" at the Potomac Creek site ever functioned as such. Rather, the ditches at both sites were most likely dug for earth that was tossed up against the palisade as an embankment (Stephenson et al. 1963:55). This conforms to several seventeenth-century accounts of Susquehannock Indian forts in Maryland, which were described as "a house or a number of houses surrounded by stakes of wood and a bank of earth" (Marye 1935:203). Thus, only one salient characteristic remains to distinguish components of the Potomac Creek complex—Potomac Creek pottery and a related ware called Moyaone.

William Henry Holmes was the first to describe Potomac Creek ware in his classic study *Aboriginal Pottery of the Eastern United States* (1903:155–56). He based his description on sherds collected from the surface of the type site at Potomac Creek, Virginia. Later descriptions by James Griffin (Manson et al. 1944:406–9), Karl Schmitt (1952:63, 1965:10–11), and Robert Stephenson (et al. 1963:113–20) expanded and refined Holmes's original description.

Briefly, Potomac Creek pottery (fig. 33*a, b, d, e*) consists of small to large coil-constructed vessels with globular bodies, everted or straight rims (some with appliqué strips), and rounded bases. The paste is composed of a compact, hard clay tempered with 20 to 35 percent crushed quartz (or occasionally with other local rocks) and/or medium to fine sand grains. There are two types within the ware group—Potomac Creek Cord-marked vessels and Potomac Creek Plain. Within the former there are two varieties depending upon whether the vessel exterior is cord marked only, or cord marked with twisted cord, cord-wrapped stick, or cord-wrapped paddle-edge impressions below the rim exterior. The cord-impressed technique was used to create three varieties of decorative motifs: vertical, horizontal, and geometric (Falk 1981:53). The Potomac Creek Plain type was first cord marked and then smoothed to a plain surface. It, too, was often decorated with cord-impressed designs below the exterior of the rim (Stephenson et al. 1963:119–20).

A minority pottery associated with the Potomac Creek ceramic tradition is Moyaone ware. Originally described by Schmitt (1965:11–12) as "Potomac Creek Sand-Tempered," the pottery description was revised and expanded by Stephenson (et al. 1963:120–25) as a result of his analysis of the Accokeek Creek site collection. Moyaone vessels are small-to-medium globular jars or simple bowls. The paste consists of a compact clay with fine-grained micaceous sand occasionally mixed with crushed quartz or coarser sand. There are three types: Moyaone

33. Potomac Creek (a, b, d, e), *Moyaone* (c), *and Shepard* (f–k) *pottery. (Courtesy of the Smithsonian Institution)*

Cord-impressed (see fig. 33c), Moyaone Incised, and Moyaone Plain (Egloff and Potter 1982:112). Moyaone pottery from the White Oak Point site in Virginia is radiocarbon-dated to A.D. 1310 ± 50 and 1460 ± 45 (Waselkov 1982a:258).

Potomac Creek ware is generally believed to date from approximately A.D. 1300 through the seventeenth century (Clark 1980:8; Egloff and Potter 1982:112). However, it may date as early as A.D. 1200. At the Robbins Farm site (7K-F-12) in southern Delaware, two or three Potomac Creek Cord-marked vessels and two Keyser Cord-marked vessels were found in a storage/refuse pit radiocarbon-dated to A.D. 1200 ± 55 (Stocum 1977:40–48; Custer 1984:180). This date seems to be supported by two others from features containing Keyser pottery—A.D. 1185 ± 60 from the Biggs Ford site (18FR14) in Maryland and A.D. 1220 ± 80 from site 44LD14 in Virginia—both clustering around A.D. 1200 (Kavanagh 1982:79; Rust 1986:41). However, the radiocarbon date from the Biggs Ford site is suspect, since it comes from a mixed, multicomponent context (Maureen Kavanagh, personal communication 1989). The end date for Potomac Creek ware is securely fixed by both radiocarbon dates and association with seventeenth-century European artifacts (see table 4).

Appliqué rim strips initially were prevalent on Potomac Creek pottery but decreased in popularity as direct rims, some with notches, increased. Likewise, over time Potomac Creek plain ware increased in popularity to become the dominant type by the second quarter of the seventeenth century. Potomac Creek pottery occurs as a major component of the ceramic assemblage on sites around the falls of the Rappahannock River, northward along the fall line to Washington, D.C., and northeast to Baltimore, Maryland. Its greatest concentration is restricted to the inner coastal plain of the Potomac River, where it is directly associated as the dominant ceramic ware with all but one (the Yaocomacos) of the early seventeenth-century Conoy Indian groups of Maryland, as well as with the Tauxenent and Patawomeke Indians of Virginia (Egloff and Potter 1982:112; Cissna 1986:15; Moore 1990a; Potter 1982:133–35).

In 1955 Clifford Evans observed that "the Potomac Creek Series is late pottery in this area [tidewater Potomac], probably coming from the north and definitely without local indigenous development" (1955:126). In fact, some archaeologists believe that the entire archaeological culture, not just the pottery, is intrusive. This supposition leads to a discussion of migrations, native oral traditions, and the origins of the Potomac Creek complex.

ORIGINS

Exactly where did the makers of Potomac Creek pottery come from? Did they migrate to the inner coastal plain of the Potomac River, or did their culture develop locally, through the diffusion of ideas and norms exchanged with other peoples? These questions have given rise to a number of alternative hypotheses.

The Montgomery complex hypothesis. The first person to offer an explanation for the origins of the Potomac Creek complex was Karl Schmitt. During the course of his master's thesis research in the early 1940s, Schmitt noticed the disparity between the archaeological remains from other sites in the Maryland-Virginia tidewater and those from the Potomac Creek and Accokeek Creek sites. There were no obvious tidewater antecedents for the Potomac Creek complex. However, west of the fall line, in the piedmont province of the middle Potomac Valley, there were numerous small Late Woodland villages, like the Shepard site (18MO3) in Montgomery County, Maryland, that exhibited "a material relationship" to the Potomac Creek and Accokeek Creek sites (Schmitt 1965:30). "Perhaps," Schmitt hypothesized (1965: 30), "in very late prehistoric times a number of small groups living on the [piedmont] plateau coalesced and built large fortified villages in the tidewater province. A possible stimulus to such a movement and banding together would be a desire for security from tribes, possibly Iroquoian, to the west and north."

Schmitt's proposed migration, dubbed the Montgomery focus hypothesis (Cissna 1986:29), has been echoed subsequently by several archaeologists (MacCord et al. 1957:28, 1984; Clark 1980; Gardner 1986:88). The basis for the hypothesis is the apparent similarity between the archaeological remains of the Potomac Creek complex and those of the Shepard and related sites, which are now grouped together under the archaeological rubric of the Montgomery complex (Schmitt 1952:62; Slattery and Woodward n.d.:174).

Components of the Montgomery complex are confined mainly to that portion of piedmont Maryland and Virginia drained by the Potomac River and its tributaries. Diagnostic artifacts include Shepard Cord-marked pottery, Levanna Triangular points, and obtuse-angle clay pipes with dentate or incised designs (Kavanagh 1982:70; MacCord et al. 1957:15–16). The people lived in relatively small hamlets and villages, ranging from less than 0.4 to 0.8 hectare (0.9-2.0a) in extent. The dead were generally buried in shallow, individual graves or occasionally in storage pits, usually in flexed positions with few or no grave goods. Village patterns are only partially known, consisting of an oval arrangement of storage pits surrounding a plaza. From this and partial postmold patterns, it is inferred that the houses were circular (Slattery and Woodward n.d.:11, 128, 159; Slattery et al. 1966:49; Kavanagh 1982:70; Clark 1980:13–14; MacCord 1984:9). Two, or possibly three, of the ten known Montgomery complex villages were palisaded (cf. Clark 1980:13, 17; MacCord 1984:9; Slattery and Woodward n.d.: 159, 177–82). The villages were situated near floodplain soils, such as Huntington silt loam, conducive to slash-and-burn techniques. A series of radiocarbon determinations from several villages dates the Montgomery complex to A.D. 900 or 1000 until about A.D. 1300, although three radiocarbon dates from the Rosenstock site (18FR18) in Frederick County, Maryland, indicate that this particular village was occupied at least until A.D. 1450 (Kavanagh 1982:71, 82, 88; Clark 1980:8; MacCord 1984:7; Slattery and Woodward n.d.:161–63).

As is the case with the Potomac Creek complex, pottery is the salient characteristic of the Montgomery complex. The dominant pottery type, named Shepard Cord-marked (see fig. 33f–k), consists of vessels with slightly constricted necks, gobular bodies, semiconical or rounded bases, and cord-marked exteriors. Rim strips were often added to produce what is sometimes referred to as a collared rim. Crushed quartz or granite was used to temper the compact, clayey paste. Vessels were decorated either with cord-wrapped sticks or cord-wrapped paddle-edge impressions encircling the rim in rows or in a series of short vertical or oblique lines or with incised lines, gashes, and punctates (Kavanagh 1982:70; MacCord 1984:9; Slattery and Woodward n.d.:163–69).

The similarity between Shepard Cord-marked and Potomac Creek Cord-marked pottery is obvious. As Carl Manson and Howard Mac-Cord (1985:21) have succinctly stated, the shared ceramic attributes include "overall cord-marking; conoidal [vessel] shapes; simple [direct] rims, as well as those with an added rimstrip; abundant cord and cord-wrapped dowel impressions for ornamentation on neck and rim areas; and the use of crushed stone for tempering." However, the attributes of Shepard Cord-marked and Potomac Creek Cord-marked pottery are also very much like those of a host of Late Woodland pottery from New Jersey to North Carolina. As Maureen Kavanagh (1982:79–82) has clearly summarized:

Ceramic attributes such as vessel sizes and shapes, grit tempering, cord-marked exterior, collared rims, and cord-marked designs on the vessel collars or necks are generalized attributes which show very strong affiliations with the Owasco pottery of New York State of the Oak Hill Phase and with some Shenks Ferry [Blue Rock phase] of Pennsylvania. [The] relationship of the Montgomery Complex to events occurring to the east is still not clear. The Potomac Creek pottery appears to be very similar and its "refinement" of many of the cord decorative techniques found on the Shepard vessels seems to be an outgrowth of the latter. However, this interpretation lacks supporting chronological evidence, and the techniques in common are found in many other pottery types throughout the Eastern United States. The long duration of the Montgomery Complex in the Piedmont (at least to A.D. 1450) also would seem to indicate that the relation between these two ceramic traditions is a complex one.

The difficulty with comparing diagnostic artifacts is that archaeologists end up tracing the diffusion of time-markers—in this case, pottery types—rather than the movement of prehistoric populations (Rouse 1986:171–72). Even when the totality of each archaeological culture is taken into account, trait list comparisons only provide additional evidence of the same kind to "prove" the migration hypothesis. Further comparison of the archaeologically observable characteristics of the Montgomery and Potomac Creek complexes would do little more than confirm that they were two Late Woodland cultures composed of people who made grit-tempered, collared, cord-marked pots decorated in similar motifs; used Levanna Triangular points to tip their arrows; made a variety of bone and antler tools; grew corn; smoked dried plant materials in obtuse-angle clay pipes; kept dogs; and lived in villages with a circular plan, which may or may not have been palisaded depending on the state of local and regional politics (Slattery and Woodward n.d.:159; Barse 1985:146–59; Schmitt 1965:26–29; Stephenson et al. 1963:191–98).

There are two cultural characteristics, however, where the archaeological complexes seem to differ. Houses of the Montgomery complex were probably circular (Slattery and Woodward n.d.:159; Clark 1980:14; MacCord 1984:9). At the Potomac Creek component of the Accokeek Creek site, the "shapes of the houses are not certain but probably were rectangular, though some may have been circular" (Stephenson et al. 1963:197). A site plan of the village contains such a profusion of postmolds that even a master player of connect-the-dots would be hard-pressed to define house patterns (Stephenson et al. 1963:fig. 6). In 1971 reexcavation of a portion of the Accokeek Creek

site by Melburn Thurman (1972:2) resulted in the definition of the
south end and two sides of a structure, 3 by 5 meters (9.8 by 16.4 ft),
with parallel sides and an oval end. At the Potomac Creek site, Schmitt
(1965:8) stated that "no definite house type was discovered," even
though a longhouse is clearly visible on the site plan prepared by T.
Dale Stewart (1988). One end and two sides of the longhouse were
uncovered, measuring 6 meters (20 ft) wide and at least 18 meters (59
ft) long. Thus, there is a probability of circular houses at Montgomery
complex villages, one small longhouselike structure at the Accokeek
Creek site, and one longhouse at the Potomac Creek site.

   Unlike the highly equivocal and limited nature of the house pattern data, the information on burial practices is more reliable and
more abundant. At Montgomery complex villages, the bodies of the
dead were buried in individual graves in a foetal position (primary
flexed burials). Exceptions to this include the bones of two people reburied in bundles (bundle burials) and a burial in which the body was
placed with the spine and legs in a straight line (extended burial), all
discovered at the Shepard site, as well as three disinterred burials from
the Winslow site (18MO9) and one from the Fisher site (44LD4). The
latter are described as graves with only scattered small bones remaining, possibly indicating that the bodies had been removed after burial
(Slattery and Woodward n.d.:158–59).

   Mass secondary reburial in ossuaries was the norm for the common people of the Potomac Creek complex (Ubelaker 1974; Potter
1989; Jirikowic 1990:369). However, a single bundle burial was reported from the Potomac Creek site (Schmitt 1965:20), and "occasional individual burials . . . seem to have taken place during the
entire history of the village" at the Accokeek Creek site (Stephenson
et al. 1963:60). Alice Ferguson, the landowner–turned–amateur archaeologist who excavated the Accokeek Creek village, noted that
"none of the latest types of village pottery, however, were found in
individual burials or in Ossuaries Nos. 1 and 3. While it is believed that
the earliest burials were all individual, the custom of individual burial
apparently persisted to a minor extent after the establishment of the
ossuaries" (Stephenson et al. 1963:64). Reexamining her report on
the excavations and fieldwork, it is clear that at least twenty-three of
the fifty-six individual burials contained only "previllage pottery"—
Ferguson's phrase for pottery earlier than the Potomac Creek ceramics
associated with the village. This means that no more than thirty-three
individual burials could have been associated with the earliest phase
of the Potomac Creek component at the Accokeek Creek village. And

of the fifty-six individual burials, twenty-seven were flexed (Stephenson et al. 1963:66). Unfortunately, there is no way of determining how many of these may have come from the Potomac Creek component.

At first glance, the differences in the burial customs of the Montgomery and Potomac Creek complexes appear to be striking. If, however, the village at Accokeek Creek is earlier than the one at Potomac Creek, as a few researchers have suggested (McNett 1975:245–50; Clark 1976:197), then some of the individual burials at Accokeek Creek may represent a continuation of primary inhumation by the first Montgomery complex immigrants to the inner coastal plain.

About the time of the proposed movement of the Montgomery complex people, ca. A.D. 1300–1400 (Clark 1980:8; MacCord 1984:7), communal ossuary burial had been practiced by the Carolina Algonquians for five to six hundred years (Phelps 1983:36, 40–43). Among the Virginia Algonquians of the James River, ossuary burials date to at least the middle of the thirteenth century A.D. and probably earlier (Outlaw 1990:85–91). All of this is contrary to previous speculation that ossuaries in the Chesapeake region were originally associated with the people of the Potomac Creek complex (McNett 1975:246; Clark 1976:206, 211, 213–16).

To the south and west in the piedmont and ridge and valley provinces of Virginia, secondary interment in accretional burial mounds had been practiced since the beginning of the Late Woodland period, ca. A.D. 800–1000 (Hantman 1990:683–84; MacCord 1986:3–24). Thus, the concept of communal secondary burial, whether in mounds or ossuaries, had been in existence among adjacent cultures of the piedmont and coastal plain for several centuries before the hypothesized movement of the Montgomery complex.

Further credence is given to the Montgomery complex hypothesis when the local chronologies of the Potomac River piedmont and coastal plain are compared. About the time of the proposed migration, ca. A.D. 1300, another archaeological culture, which previously had dominated the upriver end of the Potomac River, moved into the western piedmont. Called the Mason Island complex, its agricultural villages are identified by a limestone-tempered pottery known as Page Cord-marked ware and by Levanna Triangular points (fig. 34a, b). These people had been pushed out of the upper Potomac and northern Shenandoah Valley of Virginia by villagers of the Luray phase, an archaeological culture characterized by shell-tempered Keyser Cord-marked pottery; small, isosceles Madison Triangular points (see fig. 34c, d); and palisaded, agricultural villages. People of the Luray phase

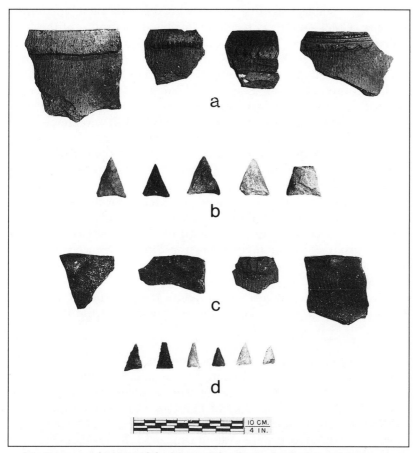

34. Pottery and points of the Mason Island complex (a, b) *and Luray phase* (c, d) *from the Keyser site (44PA1):* a, *Page Cord-marked pottery;* b, *Levanna Triangular points;* c, *Keyser Cord-marked pottery;* d, *Madison Triangular points. (Courtesy of the Smithsonian Institution)*

appear to have spread throughout the remainder of the Potomac piedmont by the fifteenth century, eventually displacing the Mason Island villagers and any remnant groups of the Montgomery complex (Dent and Jirikowic 1990:73–76; Gardner 1986:88–89; Kavanagh 1982:82).

About the same time that the Mason Island complex appeared in the western piedmont, the Potomac Creek complex appeared in the interior coastal plain of the Potomac River. Two large, palisaded villages were established—first, Accokeek Creek and then, apparently, Potomac Creek—in areas formerly inhabited by groups of the Rappahannock complex. This phenomenon is referred to as site unit intrusion; it is the settling of new sites by a particular people in areas previously uninhabited by them. "The shifting of villages from one locality to another is an example [of immigration]. If the villagers crossed a cultural boundary, one may detect their movement by finding sites containing a foreign cultural complex intrusive among sites which have the local complex" (Rouse 1986:174).

The Eastern Shore hypothesis. A second hypothesis postulates migration from the opposite direction, from the Eastern Shore (Cissna 1986:31). According to Nanticoke traditions recorded in the early nineteenth century, the Nanticokes separated from the Delawares at an early date and moved south to settle on Maryland's Eastern Shore. Subsequent population growth caused the Nanticokes to divide into several groups, one of them being the Piscataways who moved to Maryland's western shore between the Susquehanna and Potomac rivers (Feest 1978b:240).

In a speech delivered in 1660 before the governor of Maryland (Arch. of Md.:3:402–3), the brother of the tayac of the Piscataways stated

> that long a goe there came a King from the Easterne Shoare who Commanded over all the Indians now inhabiting within the bounds of this Province (nameing every towne severally) and also over the Patowmecks and Sasquehannoughs, whome for that he Did as it were imbrace and cover them all they called Uttapoingassinem this man dyeing without issue made his brother Quokonassaum King after him, after whome Succeeded his other brothers, after whose death they tooke a Sisters Son, and soe from Brother to Brother, and for want of such to a Sisters Sonne the Government descended for thirteene Generations without Interruption until Kittamaquunds time [A.D. 1636].

Linguistic evidence also confirms a close relationship between the Algonquian-speaking Piscataways, Nanticokes, and Lenape Delawares (Feest 1978b:240; Goddard 1978:73; Cissna 1986:41–46).

This close cultural relationship also is expressed archaeologically, in the form of design similarities on pottery. Design motifs, because they are stylistic attributes, are more sensitive indicators of cultural interaction than functional or technological attributes like vessel form, size, or tempering material (cf. Griffith and Custer 1985:18; Custer 1987:110–11). Daniel Griffith and Jay Custer (1985), in their study of shell-tempered Townsend and grit-tempered Minguannan ceramics of Delaware, point out the increasing frequency of Potomac Creek and Moyaone-like designs on Townsend and Minguannan pottery after A.D. 1300. The latter two ceramic wares share similar design motifs and techniques with the Overpeck and Bowmans Brook ceramics of the lower Delaware Valley. All of these Late Woodland wares are found in areas inhabited historically by coastal Algonquian cultures (Griffith and Custer 1985:17–18). From the lower Delaware Valley through the Delmarva peninsula over to Maryland's western shore, these groups were the Unami-speaking Delawares, Nanticokes and related groups, Patuxents, and Conoys. While similarity in design motifs and techniques should not be interpreted as a one-to-one equation of pots to particular ethnic groups, the resemblance of Potomac Creek stylistic attributes to Townsend and Minguannan design motifs seems to indicate close regional interaction between the Potomac Creek, Rappahannock, Slaughter Creek, and Minguannan archaeological complexes of the tidewater Potomac, Maryland, and Delaware.

The in situ or local development hypothesis. Another alternative hypothesis is that the people of the Potomac Creek complex developed in situ or locally, rather than migrating to the area from someplace else. If this is so, then the similarity of Potomac Creek ceramics and design motifs to Late Woodland ceramics to the west, northeast, and east is nothing more than a reflection of the widespread cultural interaction of the groups living below the falls of the Potomac River. These groups were in the advantageous position of controlling the great natural route running roughly east-west along the Potomac. It is probably no coincidence that the name of the werowance's village of Patawomeke has been translated as "trading center" or "traveling traders or peddlers" (Barbour 1971:296; Tooker 1901:32). As culture brokers in the prehistoric exchange networks, the groups living in the inner coastal plain would have come in frequent contact with villagers of the Montgomery complex to the west, as well as with other groups, including those on the Eastern Shore and in southern Delaware. Thus, the shared ceramic attributes observed archaeologically are evidence of the transmission of ideas and the circulation of goods from one people to another—in a word, diffusion.

A similar argument has been used to account for the presence of the sand / crushed quartz-tempered Gaston simple-stamped pottery on Late Woodland sites in the core area of the Powhatan chiefdom, around the inner coastal plain of the James River (Turner 1988:9–16). Before the protohistoric period, Townsend ceramics were the majority ware of this area. The occurrence of Gaston Simple-stamped pottery in very late prehistoric times is interpreted as evidence that the James River groups were using their strategic location within the regional trade networks to enhance their power within the chiefdom. According to this hypothesis, therefore, it should come as no surprise that Potomac Creek–like ceramics occur as a minority ware as far south along the fall line as Richmond, Virginia (Mouer et al. 1986:138–39).

A consideration of the hypotheses. It has been said many times that hypotheses cannot be proved, they can only be disproved (cf. Meggers 1955:123–24; Rouse 1986:2). Of the three hypotheses, the one with the least support from the existing archaeological data base is the in situ or local development hypothesis. While diffusion is generally considered to be the preferred explanation for the abandonment of old traits and the adoption of new ones, particularly when the source for the innovation is nearby (Adams et al. 1978:487), there should be evidence of a transition marking the decrease in the popularity of the old trait and a corresponding increase in the popularity of the new one. In the case of Potomac Creek pottery, if diffusion was responsible for the development of these ceramics in the inner coastal plain of the Potomac River, there should be archaeological evidence for a transition from the manufacture of Townsend to Potomac Creek pottery. Currently, there seems to be only one example which might support this thesis.

At the Potomac Creek site, a large pit discovered during the excavations contained a diversity of Rappahannock Fabric-impressed, Rappahannock Incised, Potomac Creek Cord-marked, and Potomac Creek Cord-impressed pottery, as well as variants of Potomac Creek / Townsend ware. The pit, designated feature 6, measured 3 meters (10 ft) in diameter and 1.2 meters (4.5 ft) deep, with a U-shaped profile. It was found beneath the western section of the hypothetical defensive ditch (Schmitt 1965:9). Most likely, it was originally dug as a storage pit; the stratigraphy and pottery indicate that it probably dates after the construction of the first series of palisades but before the excavation of the ditch.

A reexamination of the feature contents proved most illuminating (fig. 35). Apparently Schmitt (1965:9) did not analyze all the sherds from the pit, because his tally is less than the total number of sherds from this provenience in the Smithsonian Institution collections. The Rappahannock Incised sherds represent at least nine different vessels

35. *Rappahannock and Potomac Creek/Townsend pottery from feature 6 at the Potomac Creek site (44ST2): a, Rappahannock Fabric-impressed; b, Potomac Creek–like paste of sand and crushed quartz temper with Townsend-like Rappahannock Fabric-impressed exterior surface; c, e–j, Rappahannock Complex Geometric Incised pottery; d, Potomac Creek–like paste of crushed quartz temper and constricted neck / everted rim form with Townsend-like Herringbone Incised motif. (Courtesy of the Smithsonian Institution)*

embellished with both simple and complicated incised motifs (cf. Griffith 1980:30; using Griffith's classification system they are RI2, RI4, RI7, and RI8). A minimum of six Potomac Creek vessels came from the pit, excluding a miniature pot which Schmitt (1965:9) described as "Potomac Creek Sand Tempered." All the vessels have direct rims (usually considered a late attribute) and cord-marked exteriors, albeit only two have cord-impressed designs. The most intriguing sherds are from two vessels which combine Potomac Creek and Townsend ceramic attributes. One is tempered with coarse sand, like Potomac Creek ware, but the simple jar form and fabric-impressed exterior of the vessel are Townsend characteristics (fig. 35b). The second vessel has an everted rim and is tempered with micaceous sand and crushed quartz, both Potomac Creek characteristics, but it is decorated with an incised, complex geometric design similar to those on the Rappahannock Incised vessels from the same feature (fig. 35d). While these vessels are suggestive of a possible transitional period in the manufacture of Townsend and Potomac Creek ware, much more evidence is required to demonstrate it. Then, too, there are other explanations, such as intermarriage, alliance, and conquest, to name just a few, which can account for this apparent crossing-over of ceramic attributes.

The final blow to the local development hypothesis comes in the form of the site unit intrusions represented by the Potomac Creek components at the Accokeek Creek and Potomac Creek sites. Given the current understanding of both the local chronologies and the development of prehistoric cultures in the piedmont and inner coastal plain, the Potomac Creek components at the two sites represent a foreign archaeological complex occupying areas formerly inhabited by people of the Rappahannock complex (McNett 1975:273–76). Although the distinguishing characteristic between the two cultural complexes is pottery, there are differences not merely in trait distributions but in site distributions as well. Like the sudden appearance of blips on a radar screen, the villages at Accokeek Creek and Potomac Creek pop up on the prehistoric landscape sometime during or shortly after A.D. 1300–1400. There are no local antecedents for the Potomac Creek components at either archaeological site. As Adams, Van Gerven, and Levy observe (1978:487–88), "Migration is the obvious explanation for anomalous site distributions . . . [for] there is hardly any other way of accounting for the total abandonment of sites or the foundation of new ones."

If the existing archaeological data do not support the hypothesis that the Potomac Creek complex developed locally, where did the Potomac Creek people come from—the piedmont Potomac or the Eastern Shore? The greatest difficulty with the Eastern Shore hypothesis is that archaeologists have not discovered a trail of sites linking the Potomac Creek complex to the Delmarva peninsula or Delaware Valley. Perhaps this is because it is assumed that such a trail should be marked by Potomac Creek–like ceramics (MacCord et al. 1957:25). Contrary to such an assumption, Irving Rouse (1986:10), in his book on prehistoric migrations, has remarked that "we should not expect to be able to trace population movements in terms of single cultural complexes. . . . [Rather,] population movements have to be inferred from patterns of change in people's complexes."

With that in mind, the most likely ancestors of the Potomac Creek people are the villagers of the Montgomery complex. Existing evidence points to a gradual immigration of some Montgomery complex groups from the Potomac River piedmont downriver to just below the fall line as the Mason Island villagers moved into the western piedmont. The immigration of Montgomery people probably occurred ca. A.D. 1300–1400. Although no villages of Montgomery complex immigrants are found in a 40-kilometer (24.8-mi) stretch from below Seneca Creek, Maryland, to Washington, D.C., this should come as no surprise. The Potomac Valley begins to constrict in that area, as it approaches the Great Falls of the Potomac River, leaving little arable floodplain to support groups of village agriculturalists (McDaniel 1987:228).

It is also clear that not all of the Montgomery complex people had left the Maryland piedmont by A.D. 1400, and some of them may never have left. At least one group of villagers, represented by the Rosenstock site, may have remained in the upper Monocacy River valley until ca. A.D. 1450. Perhaps, as other archaeologists have suggested, some Montgomery complex people later moved to the northeast and joined groups of the Shenks Ferry archaeological culture, along the lower Susquehanna River in Pennsylvania, while others may have been absorbed into the cultural tradition of the Mason Island complex (MacCord et al. 1957:28; Clark 1980:13; Kent 1984:125–26; Gardner 1986:83).

It is likely that the first Montgomery complex immigrants to the inner coastal plain kept to the Maryland and District of Columbia shore of the Potomac River. Later immigrants to the area, or colonists from the vicinity of Piscataway Creek or the Anacostia River, apparently settled on the Virginia side (McNett 1975:245–46). By at least the early fifteenth century, the migration was complete, and the interior coastal plain was populated by groups identified archaeologically as the Potomac Creek complex.

Acceptance of the Montgomery complex hypothesis does not preclude further consideration of the Eastern Shore hypothesis. They are not necessarily mutually exclusive. The Piscataway oral history recorded in 1660, upon which the Eastern Shore hypothesis is based, was a response by the Piscataway tayac's brother to a question from the governor of Maryland, Philip Calvert. What Calvert asked was "how Uttapoingassinem came to be King whether by Succession or Election" (Arch. of Md.: 3:402–3). He did not ask the tayac's brother where the Piscataways came from. If the brother's reply is taken to be a direct answer to a direct question, then he simply related that the position of tayac passed by inheritance through thirteen rulers, the first of whom came from the Eastern Shore. Rather than documenting a migration of the Conoys from the Eastern Shore to southern Maryland (Feest 1978b:240), the passage could be interpreted as documenting the formation of an early intergroup alliance ruled by a paramount chief who came from the Eastern Shore. On the other hand, as Timothy Earle (1987:299) has noted, it is common for the leaders of chiefdoms to "emphasize their foreign origins [real or fictive], an assertion that serves to legitimize rule by a group set off and connected to a universal (rather than a local) order."

Harvesters of the Chesapeake to Village Agriculturalists

Because shell middens are so obvious, are archaeologists putting too great an emphasis on the part shellfish played in Mockley phase settlement and subsistence practices? Leland Gilsen (1979:23), for example, has proposed that late Middle Woodland settlement and subsistence systems were based upon a dual adaptation which emphasized "shellfish as the primary resource, with the fish run as the secondary determinant of the settlement patterns." According to Gilsen (1979:21), shellfish are a low-risk, high-return resource because they are relatively abundant, sedentary, and, therefore, predictable. In terms of exploitation, shellfish are harvested more like plants than animals. Although anadromous fish are highly mobile, the annual fish runs are also predictable and abundant. They occur in the riverine portions of the drainage systems where various techniques of mass capture, such as the impounding weir, can be used.

Gilsen's model of settlement and subsistence strategy predicts that the main seasonal villages or base camps would be located on or near major ecotones in the estuarine portions of the rivers during late summer, fall, and early winter. The emphasis would be upon shellfish collecting supplemented by plants, waterfowl, turtles, fish, and deer. During late winter, spring, and early summer, secondary villages or base camps would be established in the riverine portions of the drainage systems near spawning areas or fish concentrations. Subsistence activities would focus on catching anadromous fish, supplemented by plants, waterfowl, turtles, small mammals, and deer (Gilsen 1979:23–26). Gilsen has proposed that Mockley phase components are the archaeological manifestations of the terminal intensive gathering and hunting subsistence economy (Gilsen 1978:15).

This model is founded upon Gilsen's idea (1978:11) of "estuarine efficiency." It is his position that the relatively high natural productivity of the Chesapeake Bay estuary could support greater population densities at a gathering and hunting level of subsistence. Thus, intensified plant husbandry on the outer coastal plain would be a relatively late phenomenon (Gilsen 1978:11–16).

Based upon a comparison of the Chicacoan data to information from other sites and locales, a slightly different model of Mockley phase settlement and subsistence is suggested. In the Chicacoan locale the early part of the late Middle Woodland period (ca. A.D. 200–550) was characterized by small and intermediate-size coastal shell middens and small interior sites. Family-size groups of collectors probably were responsible for the creation of the small shell middens, while the small interior sites represent temporary, specialized activities to exploit resources in the interior uplands. Periodic assembly of larger, band-size groups is indicated by intermediate-size shell middens like Plum Nelly (44NB128), which may have served as residential bases.

In contrast to Gilsen's suggestion (1979:23), it does not seem likely that shellfish were the primary resource. While a significant percentage of the Mockley phase economic base came from estuarine and riverine resources, especially mollusks, deer provided as much (or more) caloric input to the diet as mollusks. "The notion that molluscan resources have constituted the bulk of any group's subsistence must be rejected," Waselkov (1978b:21) has argued, "if only because of the Vitamin C and thiaminase and iodine poisoning sure to result from such a diet."

At sites that served as residential bases, such as Plum Nelly (44NB128) and Maycocks Point (44PG40), a broad range of animals and plants were taken from the area immediately surrounding the sites. Although a diffuse adaptive strategy was employed in the catchment areas of the more permanent habitations, the subsistence pattern also focused on specific animals to provide the mainstay of the group's protein—mainly white-tailed deer, turkeys, turtles (terrestrial and aquatic), anadromous fish such as sturgeon, and both fresh- and salt-water mollusks. This focused adaptive strategy resulted in the collecting of large quantities of specific resources by task groups who brought the foodstuffs back to the residential bases (Steponaitis 1986:287).

While a dual settlement strategy of primary residential bases in the estuarine zone and secondary residential bases in the riverine zone may have existed, Douglas McLearen and L. Daniel Mouer (1989) have proposed an alternative model for the lower James River. They suggest a gradual change from a fusion-fission cycle to more permanent settlements during the period ca. A.D. 200–800 (McLearen and Mouer 1989:23). Such a change seems to have occurred in the outer coastal plain of the Potomac and Rappahannock rivers, as well. Sometime after A.D. 550, and most likely between A.D. 700 and 900, very large midden sites appeared, such as Boathouse Pond (44NB111) and Woodbury Farm no. 1 (44RD48). These extensive estuarine sites seem to have been major residential bases or villages where local or regional bands came together for extended periods during seasonally optimum times of the year, with some members of the group resident throughout most of the year. As residential mobility decreased, boundary definition between groups would have intensified.

The decrease in residential mobility was, like most cultural phenomenon, probably caused by a number of factors. As a result of Steponaitis's research (1986:264–85), resource abundance and population growth do not appear to have had a significant effect. On the other hand, a dry interval sometime during the early part of the Mockley phase (ca. A.D. 400–500) may have triggered an intensification in preexisting trade and alliance networks. The distribution of rhyolite and other exotic stone materials throughout the coastal plain is evidence that some form of exchange network existed during the Mockley phase. The social and political relationships that developed as part of trade relations provided a margin of economic and social security for times of uncertainty. Increased social demand for more goods received through trade networks required surplus production and storage facilities beyond the immediate needs of the group (as at the Patuxent Point site, 18CV272, Maryland). This, in turn, contributed to reduced mobility and an increased focus on collecting specific resources by sending small task groups out from the major residential bases (Stewart 1989:68; Steponaitis 1986:284; Binford 1980:17).

Between A.D. 700 and 900 additional changes are evident in the archaeological record of the lower Northern Neck. The diversity of species found at oyster-gathering camps drops and the volume of oysters gathered increases, reflecting an intensification in oyster gathering and preparation. A distinctive local pottery, Nomini ware, emerges alongside the characteristic late Middle Woodland Mockley ceramics. Some of the rhyolite points from components at Boathouse Pond (44NB111) and Woodbury Farm site no. 1 (44RD48) are heavily reworked, and others are made from old bifaces and flakes. At the same time, a local variant of the Potts point occurs. Named the Nomini point, it was found in contexts dated A.D. 700–900 at the White Oak Point site (44WM119) and is made primarily from local quartz and quartzite. By the ninth century A.D., the direct procurement of and/or trade in rhyolite blanks from the rhyolite formations of western Maryland ceased.

Collectively, all of the changes occurring between A.D. 700 and 900 seem to be evidence of the further "localization of groups" (Binford 1964:485), when the prehistoric cultures of the Northern Neck were becoming more provincial and somewhat distinct from cultural developments south of the Rappahannock River basin, north of the Patuxent River basin, and west of the fall line. "The basis for localizing these groups into more restricted territories" was not agriculture, as Binford (1964:485) earlier hypothesized (see Smith 1989). Instead, by sending out parties of collectors who focused on the intense hunting and gathering of select species, such as white-tailed deer, turkeys, anadromous fish, and mollusks, while harvesting a wide variety of natural resources in the catchment areas surrounding residential bases, the Mockley phase groups were able to maintain more permanent settlements.

The seemingly abrupt termination around A.D. 900 of the procurement and exchange of rhyolite by Mockley phase groups of the coastal plain coincided with the appearance of agriculturally based village sites in the piedmont, along the middle Potomac River and its tributaries. The pottery found in those villages is very different from the shell-tempered Mockley and Townsend wares of the coastal plain. Called Shepard Cord-marked, it is characterized by crushed granite and quartz temper, cord-marked exterior surfaces, collared rims created by adding a clay strip, and primarily cord and cord-wrapped stick decorative techniques. The similarities between Shepard ceramics and the ceramics of northern groups belonging to the Owasco archaeological culture are striking (Curry and Kavanagh 1991:16). "Given the lack of an indentifiable Middle Woodland resident group in the Piedmont, it appears that there was an expansion of northern agricultural groups into the Monocacy Valley [Maryland] and Piedmont Potomac at least by A.D. 1000 and perhaps as early as A.D. 900" (Curry and Kavanagh 1991:16).

At about the same time, another cultural boundary emerged in Virginia, more or less approximating the fall line from the Rappahannock to the James rivers. This is often referred to as the Algonquian-Siouan boundary because it coincides with the historically documented early seventeenth-century division between the Algonquian-speakers of the tidewater and the Siouan-speaking Manahoacs and Monacans of the piedmont (Egloff 1985:241; Hantman 1990:677–78). Although not all scholars agree that the Manahoacs and Monacans were Siouans (Mouer 1983; McLearen and Mouer 1989:24), they do agree that an archaeologically identifiable cultural boundary came into being about A.D. 900. This development, plus the movement of northern groups into the Potomac Valley piedmont, had profound consequences on the Late Woodland cultures of the tidewater Potomac and, ultimately, on the course of early seventeenth-century Indian-English relationships.

Sometime after the beginning of the Late Woodland period, there appears to have been a dispersal of the population in the Chicacoan locality. Between A.D. 900 and 1300, there were no large village sites, the number of intermediate-size sites increased, and the total number of small sites decreased. Such a pattern can be interpreted as a change from one large village to several smaller villages or hamlets. Although 50 percent of the intermediate-size and large sites of the previous Mockley phase were still occupied during the early Late Woodland period, occupation of the large sites was not as extensive. Use of the Boathouse Pond site (44NB111), for example, shrank from 5.26 to 0.81 hectares (12.9 to 2.0 a). A similar situation occurred at Woodbury Farm site no. 1 (44RD48) in the Rappahannock basin. Other investigators also have noticed the co-occurrence of Mockley phase and Late Woodland sites in similar locales, but with the latter located in areas containing soils particularly suitable for cultivation (Green 1987:141).

The change in settlement patterns observed in Chicacoan and nearby localities resulted from several factors, the two major ones being the introduction of agriculture and an adjustment to a pronounced dry period between A.D. 1000 and 1200. Elsewhere in Maryland and Virginia, shifts in settlement pattern combined with radiocarbon dates (table 9) tend to confirm the interpretation that plant husbandry diffused from adjacent piedmont groups to those in the tidewater portions of the middle Chesapeake, probably around A.D. 900 (see also Smith 1989:1569). It is unnecessary to invoke mass migrations throughout coastal Maryland, Virginia, and North Carolina in order to bring corn, beans, and squash to the tidewater (Green 1987:143). Consideration is due James A. Tuck's suggestion (1978:325) "to look for evidence of some commitment to settled life prior to the introduction of agriculture. This commitment might have served as a sort of 'preadaption' to the type of existence necessary to cultivate vegetable products successfully." The residential bases or villages of the Mockley phase, represented by the year-round occupation of the Maycocks Point site, are testament to the degree of residential permanence achieved during this time. Such sites, inhabited by at least part of the group during the growing season, would have afforded the preadaptive conditions Tuck referred to.

The dry climatic interval of A.D. 1000–1200 may have provided additional impetus for adopting plant husbandry as a supplement to the intensive gathering and hunting economy of the previous late Middle Woodland period. Evidence from Virginia's lower Northern Neck is supportive of Steponaitis's speculation (1986:288–89) that families of the late Mockley phase may have had more children due to greater residential permanence and increased food production stimulated by participation in alliance networks. By the Late Woodland period, population growth and increased demands for food beyond existing means fostered plant husbandry and the further development of village life. The dry climatic interval only added to the resource stress that possibly led to farming. Nevertheless, it was probably not until several hundred years later, ca. A.D. 1300–1400, that farm produce increased to the point where it became a significant part of the total subsistence base (Green 1987:89–106).

About the same time that agricultural production intensified, some groups of the Montgomery complex immigrated to the inner coastal plain of the Potomac River. Exactly what prompted the migration is not known. Schmitt (1965:30) hypothesized that it may have been a defensive reaction to pressure from groups, possibly Iroquoian, to the west and north. While the linguistic identity of these groups is unknown, people of the Mason Island complex apparently came down the Potomac River from the west around A.D. 1300, settling in the Potomac piedmont (Kavanagh 1982:75, 77). Temporal overlap of the

Table 9. Radiocarbon dates from sites containing plant domesticates from the Potomac and James River basins and adjacent areas

Archaeological site	Comments	Uncorrected dates, years A.D.	Reference
Gnagey, Pa. (36SO55)	Corn, beans, and squash	Site dates are 920 ± 80, 1030 ± 80, and 1190 ± 65	George 1983:5
Cresaptown, Md. (18AG119)	Corn and beans. Charred corn kernels from feature 275 were radiocarbon dated to A.D. 855 ± 60	A series of additional dates from the site range from 965 ± 105 to 1635 ± 70	Curry and Kavanagh 1991:6–7
Moore, Md. (18AG43)	One corncob fragment, one corn kernel, and one possible bean seed	Site dates are 1400 ± 70, 1420 ± 50, and 1500 ± 50	Pousson 1983:146–48
Paw Paw, Md. (18AG144)	Five carbonized corn kernels	1010 ± 65	Curry and Kavanagh 1991:7
Rosenstock, Md. (18FR18)	One carbonized corn kernel	Site dates are 1015 ± 60 and four dates between 1335 ± 60 and 1475 ± 60	Curry and Kavanagh 1991:14
Shepard, Md. (18MO3)	Several lumps of charred corn kernels fused together	Site dates range from 320 ± 240 to 1630 ± 280; however, two dates of 1220 ± 60 and 1200 ± 50 probably date the main occupation	Curry and Kavanagh 1991:15; MacCord et al. 1957:22
Winslow, Md. (18MO9)	Several carbonized corncobs	Site dates are 825 ± 150, 1285 ± 100, and 1315 ± 80	Curry and Kavanagh 1991:14
Hughes, Md. (18MO1)	Corncobs (1990 field season) and possible bean seeds (1991 field season)	Site dates are 1290 ± 55, 1370 ± 60, 1440 ± 50, and 1530 ± 60	Dent and Jirikowic 1990:51; Richard J. Dent, personal communication 1991
Posey, Md. (18CH281)	Possible corn fragment	1575 ± 90	Barse 1985:158; Boyce and Frye 1986:10
Stearns, Md. (18CV17S)	Corn	C^{13}/C^{12} date, 1459 ± 125	Wayne E. Clark, personal communication 1989
Reedy Creek, Va. (44HA22)	Corn and beans	1150 ± 65	Coleman 1982:188, 206, 208
Spessard, Va. (44FV134)	Squash seeds and corn cupules	1160 ± 80	Jeffrey L. Hantman, personal communication 1988

Table 9. (continued)

Archaeological site	Comments	Uncorrected dates, years A.D.	Reference
Point of Fork, Va. (44FV19)	Corn	1030 ± 75	L. Daniel Mouer, personal communication 1988
Reynolds-Alvis, Va. (44HE470)	Squash and bean seeds	920 ± 75	Gleach 1987b:221–23
White Oak Point, Va. (44WM119)	One corn kernel, one corn cupule, and one corn embryo	1310 ± 50 and 1460 ± 45	Waselkov 1982:240, 312
44HT37, Va.	Possible corn kernel fragment from feature 1024	300 ± 70	Edwards et al. 1989:51

Mason Island and Montgomery complexes and extensive borrowing between the ceramic traditions of the two archaeological cultures belie any conflict and point to the likelihood of peaceful coexistence and intermarriage. William Gardner (1986:78–79) has proposed that the expansion of Late Woodland cultures, like the Mason Island complex, was prompted by population growth and overexploitation of their territories—conditions that possibly were exacerbated by the pronounced dry period of A.D. 1000–1200.

Regardless of the specific causes behind the spread of the Mason Island villagers, their appearance and that of the Luray phase people in the middle Potomac basin occasioned a movement of some villagers of the Montgomery complex from the eastern piedmont down the Potomac River to the inner coastal plain. This is documented in the archaeological record by the abandonment of small villages in the eastern piedmont and the establishment of new, larger villages in the inner coastal plain between A.D. 1300 and 1400. As others have noted (Adams et al. 1978:488), "migrations based on site distributions are nearly always conceived as internal migrations within the same general area."

By at least the early fifteenth century, the piedmont emigrants had colonized the Potomac coastal plain around and below modern Washington, D.C., where they are identified archaeologically as the Potomac Creek complex. Even though people of the Rappahannock complex inhabited this area earlier in the Late Woodland period, site densities indicate they were probably not as populous as their successors (Johnson 1991:58; Vrabel and Cissna n.d.; McNett 1975:235–37). Most likely, the Potomac Creek villagers settled in a previously underpopulated area.

Earlier it was mentioned that Potomac Creek pottery and, by extension, the Potomac Creek complex can be identified with the majority of the seventeenth-century Conoy Indians of southern Maryland, as well as with the Patawomeke and Tauxenent Indians of Virginia. It is probable that most of those groups spoke subvarieties of an Eastern Algonquian language (Rountree 1989:7–8; Cissna 1986:41–48; Goddard 1978:73–74). If the Potomac Creek complex developed from the Montgomery complex, it follows that some of the Montgomery people probably spoke an earlier form of Algonquian. Some archaeologists might question how this can be, since the founders of the Montgomery complex probably were northern farmers with close affinities to the Owasco archaeological culture. The name Owasco usually evokes images of proto-Iroquoian peoples in the minds of many archaeologists. But, contrary to such opinion, some of the groups who gave rise to the Owasco culture were proto-Iroquoian speakers, while other Owasco groups spoke a proto-Algonquian language. The Munsee Delaware Indians of the upper Delaware Valley spoke an Algonquian dialect yet developed from an Owasco-like early Late Woodland culture, called Pahaquarra to distinguish it from the Owasco culture that Iroquoian speakers came from (Kraft 1975:59–60, 1986:120). Indeed, many of the same ceramic styles and types characterize both Pahaquarra and Owasco. To quote the archaeologist who defined the Owasco culture, William Ritchie (1969:300), "It would thus currently appear that Owasco culture was produced and shared by various groups whose linguistic affiliations included both Algonkians and Iroquoians." Most likely, the riverine-oriented ancestors of the Montgomery and Potomac Creek complexes came from the region of southeastern New York, northeastern Pennsylvania, and/or northwestern New Jersey (see Evans 1955:126–27).

There are a number of similarities between the design motifs and techniques of Potomac Creek, Moyaone, Townsend, Minguannan, Overpeck, and Bowmans Brook ceramics. Also, adoption of the ossuary burial ritual by the Potomac Creek people is probably indicative of an ideology increasingly concerned with maintaining both community solidarity and an external network of social relationships among similar ethnic groups. It also reflects a different view of the individual's place in society than the earlier practice of single burials in households or scattered around the village. Apparently, this curtailing of individual freedom "coincided with a time when territorial, as well as social, boundaries were being made more distinct" (Jirikowic 1990:369), perhaps due to stress brought on by increased warfare (Maureen Kavanagh, personal communication 1990). From a broader perspective, the sharing of ossuary or ossuarylike practices and ceramic design motifs among groups of the Potomac Creek, Rappahannock, and Slaughter Creek complexes is an archaeological reflection of their participation in a panregional cultural tradition that approximates the historic distribution of the coastal Algonquians.

After A.D. 1400 there is increasing evidence for intergroup hostilities, until by A.D. 1500 warfare became endemic throughout most of the Middle Atlantic region (Gardner 1986:88–89). The multiple palisade lines surrounding the Potomac Creek complex villages at Accokeek Creek and Potomac Creek are mute testimony of village expansion and longevity and the constant need for defense. As R. Michael Stewart (1990:97) has summarized, "The appearance of fortified and planned villages circa A.D. 1300 and later implies a nucleation of settlement patterns stimulated by a variety of factors including: population growth, changing political conditions, economic strategies involving more tightly integrated work groups, and changes in fertility and mortality rates as a consequence of agriculture."

Unlike the major palisaded villages of the Potomac Creek complex, most of the major villages of the Rappahannock complex were spread out over large areas. In the Chicacoan locality the areal settlement pattern of the Late Woodland II period is similar to the early seventeenth-century settlement pattern observed by the English colonists. The sixteenth- and seventeenth-century werowance's village of Chicacoan was a large, internally dispersed village located in the necklands along the east bank of the Coan River, with outlying houses and hamlets and favored spots for gathering shellfish within a convenient walk or canoe ride of the main village. Beyond a 2-kilometer (1.24-mi) radius of the village, there were a number of small hunting and gathering sites used by small groups of people for brief periods of time.

Coalescence of most of the Chicacoan population into one village, when examined in light of other archaeological data, might be symptomatic of a larger pattern of change in the social and political structure of Late Woodland tidewater Potomac society. At the White Oak Point site there is evidence for intensified oyster gathering and production after A.D. 1300, with the apparent aim of producing dried oysters for storage and trade. Most of the oyster-gathering camps were occupied sometime between March and May, perhaps to avoid conflicts with spring planting. Also, during the period A.D. 1300–1400 agricultural production intensified, and ceramic motifs and techniques, as well as the practice of ossuary burial, were widely shared among certain Late Woodland groups. Taken together, all of this points to the growing importance of external social and political relations, consolidation of a regional network, and the production of surplus food to provision feast giving, trade, and warfare—in a phrase, the possible emergence of a chiefly elite.

CHAPTER 4

"Ye King of Patomeck":
The
Rise of
Complex Societies

Introduction

AMONG THE NATIVE ALGONQUIAN GROUPS of the Virginia-Maryland tidewater, the time after A.D. 1500 was characterized by increasing social and political centralization and the formation of complex societies. Following Joseph Tainter's definition (1988:37), "Complex societies are problem solving organizations, in which more parts, different kinds of parts, more social differentiation, more inequality, and more kinds of centralization and control emerge as circumstances require." Complex societies also tend to be made up of potentially stable and independent social units. For this reason, they have been characterized by Herbert Simon as "nearly decomposable systems" (quoted in Tainter 1988:23).

It is possible that some incipient form of complex society originated in the inner coastal plain of the Potomac Valley before A.D. 1500. Certainly, such societies existed in the area by the early sixteenth century. Referring to an earlier alliance between the Piscataway Indians of Maryland and the Patawomekes of Virginia, the Piscataway tayac's brother said in 1660 "that long a goe there came a King from the Easterne Shoare who Commanded over all the Indians now inhabiting within the bounds of this Province [Maryland] . . . and also over the Patomecks" (Arch. of Md.:3:402–3). From the first "king" or tayac until 1636, he told the Maryland governor, thirteen generations of tayacs had ruled. Calculating an average of nine years per reign for the tayacs who ruled after 1636, James Merrell (1979:551) has estimated that the chiefdom "was at least 100 years old, and probably even older, since earlier rulers were not as exposed to European disease." Evidence from the ground supports the notion that the Piscataways and Patawomekes may have been allies before John Smith's exploration of the Potomac Valley in 1608. It is not fortuitous that the main area of the Potomac Creek archaeological culture closely approximates the historic territory of the Piscataways and four of their five associated groups, the Nacotchtanks, Pamunkeys, Nangemoys, and Potapocos, as well as the Tauxenents and Patawomekes of Virginia (see fig. 1). Simply put, the Potomac Creek complex is the archaeological expression of these peoples, from late prehistory through early historic times.

It seems likely, therefore, that no later than the early 1500s an interdistrict alliance developed in the inner coastal plain of the Potomac River. The alliance included at least three to five groups in Maryland and two in Virginia. If seventeenth-century Piscataway oral history was accurate, this interdistrict alliance was led by a paramount leader vested with some degree of centralized power and authority. By the late sixteenth century, the larger polity began to break apart when some groups, like the protohistoric Patawomekes who were themselves a small chiefdom, broke away. Other groups, principally those living along the Maryland shore of the Potomac River, continued to acknowledge a paramount leader. That entity was known historically as the Conoy chiefdom.

It does not seem mere coincidence that the largest and most centralized seventeenth-century Algonquian polities of the Potomac River were located in the inner coastal plain—just east of the fall line—in an environmental setting similar to the area where the Powhatan chiefdom began. Yet none of the scholars who have proposed hypotheses for the development of the Powhatan chiefdom have ever used the Conoys and Patawomekes as an independent test for their ideas. Therefore, it is instructive to examine some of the explanations advanced for the formation of the Powhatan chiefdom.

The Powhatan Chiefdom: Hypotheses concerning Its Development

Most of the hypotheses concerning the development of the Powhatans as a chiefdom include two or more of the following elements: environmental diversity, whether between the outer and inner coastal plain and/or between the coastal plain and the piedmont; environmental stress; increased population density; and external cultural stress (Binford 1964:484–95; Feest 1966:78; Mouer 1981:8–18; Smith 1971:234–35, 246–47, 256; Turner 1976:236–54, 264–65; Rountree 1989:148–50). The basic argument is something like this. Powhatan's chiefdom evolved from a number of tribally organized groups whose territories were located in the inner coastal plain. The greater availability of wild plants, animals, and agricultural soils in those territories, coupled with the introduction of domesticated plants, gave the resident groups an economic advantage over others. As agricultural produce assumed greater importance in the economy, populations grew, the number of cultural groups multiplied, and intergroup competition for preferred resources increased, favoring the development of more complex forms of social and political organization.

According to Lewis R. Binford, the preferred resource was anadromous fish. Because that type of fish can be caught only at certain places, "people who lived near 'access windows' of this kind had an effective monopoly over a critical resource which they were able to manipulate for their own political advantage throughout the region" (Binford 1983:215). On the other hand, E. Randolph Turner has argued that the preferred resource was Class I soils, those best suited for modern agricultural use. "By the end of the Late Woodland period (if not earlier) severe population pressure on key agricultural soils was being experienced in at least the core area [the inner coastal plain] from which the [Powhatan] chiefdom evolved" (Turner 1985:210). With only a slightly different twist, Gerald P. Smith (1971:256) has suggested that increasing population pressure depleted scattered resources, such as deer, stream frontage, and agricultural land, more rapidly than concentrated resources, like anadromous fish. As the situation worsened, sociopolitical concern shifted from the problem of coordinating subsistence efforts to the problem of gaining access to depleted resources, resulting in the creation of "stratified multicommunity organizations" (Smith 1971:256).

Although L. Daniel Mouer (1981:17) has agreed "that population/ resource ratios are . . . pivotal in the formation of social complexity," he also emphasized the importance of external pressures. The numerous freshwater swamps and fish spawning grounds of the inner coastal plain attracted piedmont groups eastward, putting pressure on the Algonquians living on the coastal plain near the fall line. This is not radically different from Helen C. Rountree's (1989:149) position that "the paramount chiefdom may have originated near the fall line because of its being a boundary with non-Algonquian peoples." Rountree saw the Algonquians living near the fall line "as more exposed than others to the movements of 'foreign' Indians coming down the larger rivers from the northwest, so that as a means of defense, chiefdoms and eventually a paramount chiefdom would form near the fall line on the rivers" (Rountree 1989:149–50).

A different variation on the fall-line theme has been proposed by Christian F. Feest (1966:78–79). Powhatan political organization developed because of ecological differences between the coast and the piedmont, which served to stimulate trade between groups living in these two areas. This led some members of Algonquian society to specialize in trade, eventually securing monopolies possibly gained through warfare. Once trade monopolies became hereditary, wealth could accumulate in the hands of a few. Stress brought on by warfare or severe droughts may have encouraged an extension of trade restrictions over other groups within existing loosely knit defensive alliances or ethnic confederacies. Stability for such intergroup alliances came about only through the successful adoption of other forms of cultural integration, like the rite of passage into manhood called the *huskenaw*.

Finally, both Feest (1966:78, 1978a:254) and Rountree (1989:150–51) have considered the irregular European contacts of the sixteenth century as a likely source of external stress influencing—if not encouraging—the development of the Powhatan chiefdom. Rountree (1989:141–42), in particular, has suggested "that the chance of the Powhatans escaping epidemics [of alien European diseases] in the late sixteenth century is very slim." If such epidemics occurred, they could have caused great mortality among the Powhatans and disrupted their social organization to the degree that "an ambitious chief who wanted to become paramount chief would have found circumstances aiding him" (Rountree 1990:25).

The Potomac Creek Chiefdom: Possible Factors in Its Development

ENVIRONMENTAL CONSIDERATIONS

When the protohistoric Piscataway-Patawomeke alliance is viewed in light of the factors proposed for the formation of the Powhatan chiefdom, similarities appear. Like the area surrounding the falls of the James and York rivers, the topography and hydrography of the area around and below the Great Falls of the Potomac River affected certain aspects of resource availability and human mobility (see frontispiece). Historically, as now, most of the freshwater marshes and swamps were located in the inner coastal plain. Here, too, is where anadromous and semianadromous fish spawn (Bromberg et al. 1989:7–9; Cronin 1986:188–90; Lippson 1973:10–11, 28–29, 34–35; Carter et al. 1983:54–55). Thus, the inner coastal plain of the Potomac River was an "access window," to use Binford's phrase, to the major fish spawning grounds.

Anadromous fish had been an important resource to the local people since 1500 B.C., and they were even more important to the larger Late Woodland populations who depended upon stored food supplies. The late winter and early spring fish runs provided them an ample and ready source of protein in the leanest months of the year, when agricultural surpluses and nut harvests stored from the year before were nearly depleted. An ethnohistorical testament to the importance of fish in the peoples' diet is preserved in the names of the three upper villages dotting the right bank of the Potomac River on John Smith's 1612 map—Namassingakent, Assaomeck, and Namoraughquend—which are translated "fish—plenty of," "middle fishing place," and "fishing place" (Barbour 1971:286, 293).

Moving down the Potomac River from Great Falls, the river valley suddenly opens up just above Theodore Roosevelt Island (formerly Analostan or Mason's Island), presenting a panoramic view of modern Washington, D.C. (see fig. 8). From this point, expanses of level to gently sloping river terraces occur wherever rivers or large creeks enter the Potomac. In the inner coastal plain such areas can be found at the confluences of the Potomac River and the Anacostia River, Piscataway Creek, Pomonkey Creek, Mattawoman Creek, and Nanjemoy Creek on the left bank and Hunting Creek, Dogue Creek, Occoquan Bay, Aquia Creek, and Potomac Creek on the right bank. It is no coincidence that those are the same places where Indian villages and hamlets are shown on John Smith's 1612 map (see fig. 1) and where, in many instances, late prehistoric or early historic archaeological components are recorded (Bromberg 1987:188–192; Bromberg et al. 1989:14; Cissna 1986:18–29; Vrabel and Cissna n.d.; Michael F. Johnson, personal communication 1992).

The local occurrence of broad, open river terraces in the inner coastal plain contrasts sharply with the nature of the river terraces west of the falls, in the piedmont. Here, the valley walls hug the river more closely, creating a deep, narrow floodplain containing suitable agricultural soils throughout, although the variation in soil productivity is less than in the coastal plain (Vokes and Edwards 1974:56, 149–

50). This situation may have favored agricultural groups in the inner coastal plain. The soil associations found on the broad, open river terraces of the coastal plain contain a variety of silty and sandy loams of moderate to low natural fertility. Those low in natural fertility, as it happens, are often the best soils for growing corn during periods of drought.

Several severe droughts are documented for the Virginia-Maryland area during the late sixteenth to mid-seventeenth centuries, and present-day droughts seriously damage crops one out of every three years. Such agriculturally limiting environmental conditions would favor soils that were more productive during periods of drought, albeit not as fertile.

Of greater scope than the local or regional effects of drought was the major environmental episode known as the Little Ice Age. This was a period from roughly the fourteenth to the eighteenth centuries when annual temperatures in the Northern Hemisphere averaged about 3½° cooler than at present. The result was a reduction in the number of frost-free days, particularly in more northern regions. This would have shortened the growing season for village agriculturalists living at higher elevations farther up the Potomac and its tributaries in the Great Valley and Appalachian Mountains.

Evidence from the northern Shenandoah Valley indicates one way villagers offset the loss of agricultural produce was by hunting more. In doing so, each village would have had to increase its hinterland, the territory necessary to supply its subsistence needs. Expansion of village hinterlands led to competition and ultimately conflict (Gardner 1986:88–89; MacCord 1984:17–18). By the fifteenth century, or perhaps somewhat earlier, villagers of the Luray phase had moved down the Potomac Valley and were living as far east as the Hughes site (18MO1), 35 kilometers (22 mi) above the falls of the Potomac (Stearns 1940; Dent and Jirikowic 1990:73–75).

THE FALL LINE AS A DYNAMIC CULTURAL BOUNDARY

The reshuffling of different archaeological cultures and, possibly, different ethnic groups in the Potomac piedmont during the fourteenth through sixteenth centuries may have affected the Potomac Creek people in much the same way the presence of "foreign" Indians apparently affected the protohistoric Powhatan groups. Warfare or the threat of warfare certainly is implied by the single palisades and, later, double ones surrounding the late prehistoric and protohistoric towns at Accokeek Creek and Potomac Creek (Schmitt 1965:6–8; Stephenson et al. 1963:50–55). Unlike the situation around the falls of the James and York rivers where the "foreign" Indians were probably non-Algonquian speakers, some of the Luray phase villagers may have been non-Algonquian speakers or they may have spoken an Algonquian language like that of the Shawnee (Gardner 1986:92; see also MacCord 1986:31). Currently, there is no evidence to attribute any linguistic affiliation to the Luray phase people.

The fall line had been a dynamic place since at least 2,000 B.C., but it became particularly so during Late Woodland times. It was not a natural defensive perimeter or Mother Nature's version of the Great Wall of China. Unlike the rivers that flow over the fall line, people moved across it in both directions.

That was certainly true in central Virginia where, during late prehistory, piedmont and coastal plain groups passed over the fall line of the James River. Sometime before the settling of Jamestown, something akin to a "cold war" developed between the Monacans of the piedmont and the Powhatans of the coastal plain, turning the formerly dynamic boundary of the fall line into a culturally sanctioned buffer zone, free from complete external control by either of the two contending parties (Mouer 1986:18–23). Creation of a cultural buffer zone had the added benefit of creating a natural haven for deer, at a time when deer populations in the coastal plain may have been declining due to overhunting (Turner 1978:45–46).

Other evidence for the dynamic nature of the fall line comes from the Rappahannock River. Karl Schmitt, who analyzed material from the Potomac Creek site, was the first to recognize that Potomac Creek pottery had been collected by David I. Bushnell from prehistoric sites at and above the falls of the Rappahannock (Schmitt 1965:21; Bushnell 1935; see also Manson et al. 1944:411–12). A reexamination of Bushnell's collections showed that, indeed, four of the sites mentioned by Schmitt definitely contain Potomac Creek pottery: a site (44SP26) opposite Laucks Island in Spotsylvania County, Virginia, and the Forest Hall (44SP34), Richards Ford (44CU14), and Jerrys Flat (44CU15) sites. The pottery is late Potomac Creek, with direct rims, some distinctively notched by transverse paddle-edge impressions; horizontal, diagonal, and geometric cord-impressed designs; interior and exterior smudging; crushed quartz or medium-grained sand temper; compact paste fired harder than most local late prehistoric ceramics; and relatively thin vessel walls (fig. 36).

Mouer (1986:19) has suggested that local variations of Potomac Creek pottery were being made by the Monacans and Manahoacs liv-

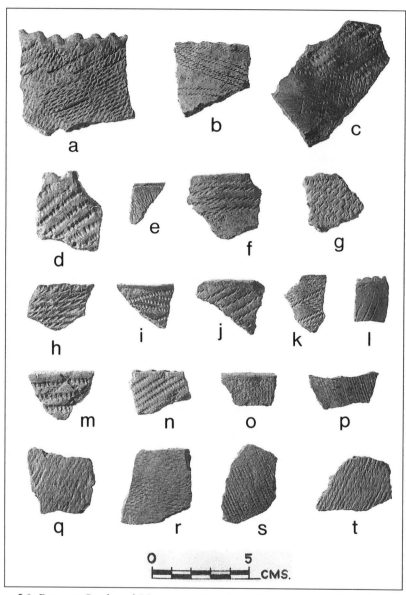

36. Potomac Creek and Moyaone pottery from sites above the falls of the Rappahannock River: a, o–t, Potomac Creek Cord-marked; b–k, m–n, Potomac Creek Cord-impressed; l, Moyaone Incised. Provenience: a, Rappahannock River 12.8 kilometers (8 mi) south of Remington, Va.; b–t, Jerrys Flat (44CU15). (Courtesy of the Smithsonian Institution)

ing in the piedmont portions of the Rappahannock and James river valleys. However, "pottery found in this area [central Virginia] which is typed as Potomac Creek is only rarely decorated with the corded horizontal designs that are common to the north" (Mouer et al. 1986:139). Yet it is precisely the attributes of varied cord-impressed design motifs and distinctive rim treatments that are the hallmark of Potomac Creek pottery and its predecessor, Shepard pottery.

Examination of Late Woodland ceramics from the upper Rappahannock River and the inner piedmont of the James River in the collections of the Smithsonian Institution indicates that the most common Late Woodland pottery type is Albemarle Fabric-impressed, followed by Albemarle Cord-marked (Evans 1955:145). This has been confirmed by the recent work of Jeffrey L. Hantman (personal communication 1990) and others from the University of Virginia (see also Gardner and Carbone n.d.). Albemarle pottery shares the characteristics of crushed quartz or other local rock temper, cord marking, and bag-shaped vessel form with Shepard and Potomac Creek pottery. Unlike the latter two ceramics, Albemarle pottery from central Virginia is rarely decorated, nor are added rim strips or scalloped rims common (fig. 37; Evans 1955:39–44). On the other hand, 70–75 percent of Shepard pottery has added rim strips, and 88 percent is decorated with either cord-impressed or incised designs (Slattery and Woodward n.d.:165–69). Early Potomac Creek pottery is characterized by appliqué rims and cord-impressed geometric designs, while later Potomac Creek vessels have direct rims, some with transverse paddle-edge notches, and cord-impressed decorations (Manson and MacCord 1985:35–39). At the Potomac Creek site, 72 percent of all rimsherds were decorated with some variation of a cord-impressed design motif (Jirikowic 1989:14). Thus, Albemarle pottery is very different when it comes to rim treatment and decorative motifs, the very characteristics that define Potomac Creek and Shepard pottery and, by extension, the archaeological complexes to which they belong.

The appearance of Potomac Creek components at sites up to 19 kilometers (12 mi) west of the falls of the Rappahannock is evidence of interaction between members of the Potomac Creek complex and the late prehistoric Manahoacs, limited westward movements by Potomac Creek groups, or both. The presence of the "late" Potomac Creek Cord-impressed rimsherds indicates that such events probably occurred sometime during the fifteenth or early sixteenth centuries.

Notching the rims with a cord-wrapped paddle edge was a common technique used by Luray phase potters to decorate Keyser Cord-marked vessels (Manson et al. 1944:403–4; Stearns 1940:7; Dent and

37. Rimsherds of Shepard (a), *Potomac Creek* (b), *and Albemarle* (c) *pottery. (Courtesy of the Smithsonian Institution)*

Jirikowic 1990:58–61). The technique was probably acquired by Potomac Creek potters after Luray phase groups expanded into the piedmont Potomac. An extreme example of the blending of various Late Woodland ceramic traditions comes from the Accokeek Creek site where an interesting variation on Keyser Cord-marked ceramics was found. The pottery, represented by sherds from a minimum of seventy to eighty vessels, combines attributes from Keyser, Page, Potomac Creek, and Moyaone ceramics (Stephenson et al. 1963:129–30).

TRADE AND EXCHANGE

Pots and clay smoking pipes, too, were being exchanged between Luray and Potomac Creek peoples (Schmitt 1952:63). A small amount of Keyser Cord-marked pottery was found at the Potomac Creek site (fig. 38), some Potomac Creek pottery was found at the Keyser Farm site (44PA1), and clay smoking pipes with distinctive flaring or expanded

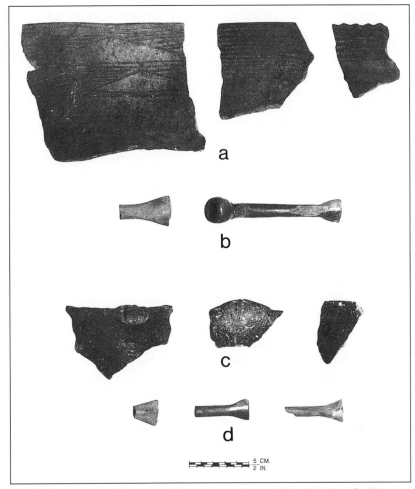

38. Potomac Creek pottery (a) and triangular pipe bits (b) from the Keyser site (44PA1), compared to Keyser pottery (c) and triangular pipe bits (d) from the Potomac Creek site (44ST2). (Courtesy of the Smithsonian Institution)

triangular bits were discovered at both places (Schmitt 1965:11–14; Manson et al. 1944:401–2, 406–9). Even more intriguing, sherds of Potomac Creek and Keyser pottery, from a minimum of two vessels each, were found together in a pit at the Robbins Farm site (7K-F-12) in southern Delaware. No other pottery was found in the feature, which appears to have been used briefly for storage, then for trash disposal (Stocum 1977:41–43). It has been suggested that the Robbins Farm discovery represents "an initial expansion of nonlocal populations using markedly different ceramics" (Custer 1984:171). Because no similar exotic Late Woodland components have come to light since the find was first reported, it is more likely that the Potomac Creek and Keyser pots were brought to Delaware through trade between people of the local Slaughter Creek complex and the Potomac Creek and Luray archaeological cultures. The trade could have been accomplished either by hand-to-hand broad-based exchange or by traders through focused exchange (Stewart 1989:52–56, 63).

Further evidence of limited exchange between coastal plain groups and Luray villagers is the sporadic occurrence of marine-shell beads and pendants at Luray phase sites (Gardner 1986:90–92; Manson et al. 1944:398; Stearns 1940:10–11; MacCord and Rodgers 1966:12). While the quantity of shell and ceramic trade items recovered archaeologically is small, perishable goods also were probably exchanged. More than likely, however, the visible traces of trade material in Luray phase villages indicate that interaction between Luray and Potomac Creek peoples involved both conflict and periodic, focused exchange.

By the early seventeenth century, the names of two werowance's villages of the Potomac Creek complex—Nacotchtank and Patawomeke—attest to their importance in the native exchange network. William Tooker (1894:389–93) translated Nacotchtank to mean "at the trading town." Patawomeke has been translated by Philip Barbour (1971:296) as "trading center." The territory controlled by the werowances of both villages lay to the east of the fall line and straddled the great natural trade route of the Potomac River, connecting Chesapeake Bay and the Appalachian Mountains. Nacotchtank and Patawomeke probably functioned something like " 'gateway communities' situated astride constricted exchange paths," which provided opportunities for the werowances to control long-distance trade (Earle 1987:296).

Near the head of modern-day Aquia Creek, in Patawomeke territory, was "a great Rocky mountaine like Antimony; wherein they [the Patawomekes] digged a great hole with shells and hatchets: and hard by it, runneth a fayre brooke of Christal-like water, where they wash a way the drosse and keepe the remainder, which they put in little bags and sell it all over the country to paint there bodyes, faces or Idols" (Smith 1986c:166). All over the country meant at least as far away as the south bank of the James River, where George Percy observed the Algonquian werowance of Quiyoughcohanock (mistakenly referred to as Rapahanna by Percy) with "his face painted blue, besprinkled with silver ore, as we thought" (Percy 1967:14). Control of antimony ore must have enhanced the status of the werowance of Patawomeke and increased his power to some degree, since the ore was deemed a luxury commodity by Powhatan society (Rountree 1989:55). Yet, trade alone is not a sufficient condition to cause political complexity (Binford 1983:227–31; Earle 1987:296).

EUROPEAN CONTACTS BEFORE 1607

The exact nationality of the first shipload of Europeans to see the Chesapeake Bay probably will never be known, but most likely they were either Spanish or French. In 1527 and 1529 the Chesapeake was portrayed as the Bahía de Santa Maria on the official Spanish *Padrón General* maps. The Jesuit scholars Clifford Lewis and Albert Loomie (1953:7–11) believed that the information concerning the bay was furnished by Pedro de Quexos about 1525. If so, it was knowledge he probably gained during Indian slave-hunting expeditions with Francisco Gordillo along the Atlantic coast in 1521 or from a 1525 reconnaissance mission under his command which traveled from the tip of Florida to just south of Cape Fear (Quinn 1977:144–45).

Also about this time, an Italian, Giovanni de Verrazano, explored the Atlantic coast in 1524 as commander of the French ship *La Dauphine*. Apparently starting as far south as Long Sound, South Carolina, Verrazano sailed northward to Nova Scotia. The following year Estevão Gomes, a Portuguese in the service of Spain, traversed the coast from Cape Charles north to Cape Cod. Neither voyage accurately documented the location of the Chesapeake Bay (Quinn 1977:154–63). However, as the Spanish empire began shipping loot from its New World dominions back home, French pirates preying on the Spanish ships began visiting the shores of the south Atlantic, from Florida to Virginia. One such French vessel was probably in the Chesapeake Bay in 1546, where the local Indians traded "as many as a thousand marten skins [possibly muskrat] in exchange for knives, fish-hooks and shirts" (Lewis and Loomie 1953:13; Quinn 1977:241–42).

In 1561 Pedro Menéndez de Avilés, surveying the coast with two small vessels, entered a great bay at 37° latitude. This was the Chesapeake Bay, which he named the Bahía de Madre de Dios. While in the southwestern Chesapeake, near the mouth of the James River, the Menéndez expedition took an Indian "chief" captive. The Indian, renamed Don Luis, was taken to Spain and later to Havana where he was instructed in Spanish customs and Christian observance (Quinn 1977:238–39).

After nine years in Spanish captivity, Don Luis was sent with five

Jesuits and four catechists to establish a mission in his native country. In September 1570 the ships bearing the Hispanicized Indian and nine missionaries reached the mouth of the James River (Lewis and Loomie 1953:36; Quinn 1977:281–82). Before the ships left Virginia, one of the Jesuits, Father Quirós, wrote a letter to Juan de Hinistrosa in Cuba in which he stated:

> We find the land of Don Luis in quite another condition than ex-pected, not because he was at fault in his description of it, but because Our Lord has chastised it with six years of famine and death, which has brought it about that there is much less popula-tion than usual. Since many have died and many also have moved to other regions to ease their hunger, there remain but few of the tribe, whose leaders say that they wish to die where their fathers have died, although they have no grain and have not found wild fruit, which they are accustomed to eat. Neither roots nor anything else can be had, save for a small amount ob-tained with great labor from the soil, which is very parched [Lewis and Loomie 1953:89]

Lewis and Loomie (1953:36, 42) suggested that the Jesuits and Don Luis disembarked on the north shore of the James River and with the assistance of some of the natives crossed the peninsula to a site on the south bank of the York River, where they set up their cabin. Soon thereafter Don Luis abandoned the Jesuits, and in February 1571 he returned with other Indians and killed all the missionaries except the boy catechist, Alonso de Olmos (Lewis and Loomie 1953:44–48).

In late spring of 1571, a ship was provisioned and sent to the Jesuit mission under the direction of Vicente González. The supply ship failed to find the mission and was attacked by several canoes of Indi-ans. Some of the Indians were taken captive, and from them it was learned that the mission was destroyed and only the boy survived. A year later Menéndez commanded a punitive expedition to the James and York rivers during which Alonso was rescued and a number of Indians were killed in revenge (Quinn 1977:283–85; Lewis and Loomie 1953:55, 274).

English exploration of the Chesapeake Bay occurred near the end of 1585, possibly in October or November. A party of men were sent by Ralph Lane, governor of the first Roanoke colony in North Caro-lina, to explore the area north of the Carolina sounds. Most of their time appears to have been spent in the lower James River area, where they established good relations with the Chesapeake Indians and may have even lived near them for awhile. By February or March the exploring party returned to the settlement at Roanoke (Quinn 1985:106–8).

With the abandonment of the first Roanoke colony in June 1586 and the loss of Sir Richard Grenville's small garrison left there in July or August, another settlement was attempted in 1587. Intending to establish their colony on Chesapeake Bay this time, the English colonists were unexpectedly set ashore at the site of the first Roanoke venture (Quinn 1985:278–80). The disappearance of these settlers, the Lost Colony, has been a matter of conjecture and speculation for years. David Quinn (1985:341–78) recently suggested that the main body of the colonists moved northward to settle with the Chesapeake Indians near modern Norfolk, Virginia. The surviving English, along with their Indian hosts, are supposed to have been destroyed by Powhatan shortly before Jamestown was settled (for a slightly different interpretation, see Rountree 1990:21–23).

In June 1588 Pedro Menéndez Marqués sent a small packet boat under Captain Vicente González to reconnoiter the Chesapeake Bay, searching for any sign of English colonies. González worked his way up the western estuaries of the Chesapeake to the mouth of the Susquehanna River and then down the Eastern Shore (Quinn 1977:301–2). While he found no trace of English settlements in the Chesapeake Bay region, he did take two Indian youths captive, one apparently from northern tidewater Virginia, not far from the Potomac River, and the other from the Eastern Shore (Lewis and Loomie 1953:56). As he returned south González put in at the Carolina Outer Banks and accidently discovered signs of the abandoned Roanoke colony (Quinn 1977:302).

Until recently, there was nothing to indicate the possibility of any other Europeans in the Chesapeake Bay between 1588 and 1603 at the earliest. In 1989 a sherd from a Bellarmine or Bartman jug bearing a medallion with a date of 1593 was recovered by Darrin Lowery, along with a broken neck from a corked wine bottle and a white clay pipestem, during clam-dredging operations. The objects were found off the west shore of Kent Island (Richard Hughes, personal communication 1989), but whether they came from a shipwreck or an eroded terrestrial site is not known. While it is tempting to speculate that these objects may document an unknown European exploration of the bay ca. 1594 to 1603, there are a number of other plausible explanations.

In 1607, while being held captive by the Powhatans, Captain John Smith was told that a European ship had sailed into the York and Rappahannock rivers the year before. Contact with the natives on the York River was apparently cordial, but the European captain killed the chief or werowance of the Rappahannocks and took several of his people captive (Smith 1986a:51; Rountree 1990:24). There is much speculation over when this event actually took place and who the European captain was (Barbour 1986:1:103, n. 120), with David Quinn (1985:355–56, 360, 370) suggesting it may have been the Englishman Samuel Mace.

Exactly what effect those sporadic and relatively short-lived European contacts had on the development of the Algonquian chiefdoms is a question that is still unresolved (Fitzhugh 1985:189). Historians such as James Axtell (1988:180) view sixteenth-century European contacts and trade as a disruptive factor, "pitting native against native for access to the Europeans' technology and its attendant spiritual power." The end result, according to Axtell (1988:181), was the formation of native confederacies, such as Powhatan's in tidewater Virginia. Aside from "confederacy" being both a misnomer and an anachronism when applied to Powhatan's political organization, its use obscures the fact that the groups that served as Powhatan's building blocks were, themselves, chiefdoms—small, autonomous political units comprising a number of villages or communities under the control of a district chief (Carnerio 1981:45). Indeed, by the late sixteenth and early seventeenth centuries, over fifty groups from Chesapeake Bay to the North Carolina sounds were organized as chiefdoms (see Turner 1985:209–11).

The main point that seems to be overlooked is that the development of centralized native polities was the result of a process that combined social, political, economic, and religious customs and ideas, integrating them into a basic cultural pattern shared by most of the sixteenth-century southern Algonquian societies of the Chesapeake Bay and Carolina sounds region. While European contacts between 1560 and 1600 may have accelerated the formation of the large and complex paramount chieftainship of Powhatan (Fausz 1985:235), Powhatan was not the architect and the invading Europeans were not the primary cause of the cultural framework supporting the region's chiefly societies. Powhatan's chiefdom was an elaboration of a long-standing cultural pattern.

Several scholars (Pendergast 1991:47, 69; Axtell 1988:176; Kent 1984:19) have proposed that the main reason the Susquehannocks moved into the lower Susquehanna Valley during the period from 1550 to 1575 was to gain better access to European-made trade goods. Axtell (1988:176), in particular, has remarked that "more than 125 sites belonging to the St. Lawrence Iroquois have yielded hundreds of thousands of artifacts, but only nine small items of European origin, and none resembling the gifts Cartier presented to the natives in his two voyages up the river. This suggests that in the sixteenth century the Chesapeake-Susquehanna route was more important than the more obvious St. Lawrence for spreading European material culture into the native Northeast."

But Axtell's comment concerning the archaeological sites of the St. Lawrence Iroquois applies to the archaeological sites of the Chesapeake Algonquians as well. Even though many thousands of artifacts have been collected from Algonquian sites in Virginia and Maryland, few sites have yielded European-made trade items. At sites where European goods were found, they usually came from contexts dating after A.D. 1600. Where, then, are the "significant quantities of European goods" that James Pendergast (1991:36) claims the Indians of the Chesapeake Bay had acquired before the arrival of the Jamestown colonists?

If Pendergast is correct, the sociopolitical system of the Chesapeake Algonquians may account for the apparent absence of sixteenth-century European trade material. The werowances of the Chesapeake chiefdoms probably controlled the irregular influx of European trade items among their people, reserving most of it for themselves and acting as middlemen in its trade with other Indian groups, which served to enhance the werowances' power and prestige. Upon the death of the werowances and other elites, their wealth, including any European trade goods, was placed with the werowances' remains in the mortuary temple or was buried in other high-status interments, separate from commoners. Such burial sites would be relatively few in number and difficult to find (Custer and Potter 1988). Thus, European trade goods would appear less visible in the archaeological record of the Chesapeake chiefdoms.

Equally elusive in the archaeological record of the Potomac-Chesapeake tidewater is any evidence to support the notion that sporadic sixteenth-century European contacts unleashed epidemics among the previously unexposed natives. In southern Maryland studies of Late Woodland populations indicate rapid growth before the seventeenth century (Ubelaker 1974:68). Recent analysis of a sixteenth- or early seventeenth-century ossuary (18CA88) from the

Choptank River of Maryland's Eastern Shore also indicates a normal, healthy native population (Chase 1990).

Ethnohistorians often refer to two accounts which they interpret as evidence for sixteenth-century epidemics among the Powhatans. The first is the 1570 letter of Luis de Quirós in which the Jesuit mentioned six years of famine and death. However, rather than being a reference to "the lethal forces of virgin soil epidemics" (Fausz 1985:235–36), it is clear from the rest of the letter that a severe drought caused the suffering (Lewis and Loomie 1953:89–91, 93 n. 4). The other account describes a meeting between Captain John Smith and Powhatan in January 1609, during which "Powhatan began to expostulate the difference betwixt peace and war after this manner. Captain Smith you may understand, that I, having seene the death of all my people thrice, and not one living of those 3 generations, but my selfe, I knowe the difference of peace and warre, better then any in my Countrie" (Smith 1986b:247). As Turner has commented (personal communication in Rountree 1989:141), "Powhatan's statement may merely reflect his being an old man who had outlived his contemporaries," rather than being a reference to "serious epidemics of European diseases in eastern Virginia" (Rountree 1990:25).

Some researchers have gone even further afield, suggesting that European diseases were partially responsible for the sixteenth-century destruction of the Shenks Ferry people of the lower Susquehanna Valley (Pendergast 1991:45 n. 8). The transmission and impact of Old World diseases on native populations was a complex process affected by many factors, including the nature and degree of interaction between Europeans and Indians, native population densities, native intergroup relations, and the etiology of the various epidemic diseases such as smallpox, measles, and influenza (Ward and Davis 1989:1, 7). Only when more studies of excavated skeletal populations are combined with historical and ethnographic data will the effect of epidemics on the Indians of the Chesapeake be more than what George R. Milner has called "just-so stories" (quoted in Ward and Davis 1989:2).

SYNTHESIS AND DISCUSSION

Beginning around A.D. 700–900, as group mobility continued to decrease and distinct cultural boundaries developed along the fall line from the Potomac to the James valleys, the territories of individual groups living in tidewater Maryland and Virginia became somewhat restricted. That condition intensified after about A.D. 1300, as popu-

lations grew, agricultural production increased, and, in the Potomac
Valley, the ancestral villagers of the Potomac Creek archaeological culture moved out of the piedmont onto the inner coastal plain (Potter
1982: 347, 368; Custer 1986:154–55). By late prehistory, "the relatively dense occupation of this whole area," observed Christine Jirikowic (1990:367), "combined with the pressures caused by the close
proximity of hostile neighbors must have limited these people's option
to use mobility as a solution for social and economic problems, thus
forcing them to develop new strategies." Jirikowic's statement is a classic description of the phenomenon called social circumscription (Carnerio 1970:737–38, 1981:64).

The effects of social circumscription were more pronounced on
those groups living on the inner coastal plain near the fall line (see
frontispiece). The reasons for this were threefold. The places where
the Potomac and James rivers cross the fall line were points of contact
between coastal Algonquians and potentially hostile groups to the
west; points for controlling access to critical seasonal resources, such
as anadromous fish and the wild animals and plants of the numerous
freshwater marshes and swamps; and points of constriction for controlling regional trade arteries.

By the fifteenth century successive population disruptions in the
Potomac River piedmont culminated in the eastward expansion of Luray phase groups to the area above the falls of the Potomac (Dent and
Jirikowic 1990:73–76). Nearby, late prehistoric Manahoac groups
were concentrated in the Virginia piedmont along the upper Rappahannock River and its tributary, the Rapidan (Hantman 1990:33–34;
Bushnell 1935:4–10). The presence of hostile or potentially hostile
peoples along the fall line put pressure on the Potomac Creek groups
living on the inner coastal plain of the Potomac River, resulting in the
formation of an alliance based on a shared cultural background and
common needs for defense (see Carnerio 1981:64). Similar circumstances occurred among the late prehistoric Powhatan groups living
below the falls of the James River and around the head of the York.

Control by Potomac Creek and late prehistoric Powhatan groups
of seasonal resources, such as anadromous fish, wild resources from
freshwater marshes and swamps, and arteries of trade and communication gave them an economic and, probably, political advantage over
neighboring groups. As the frequency and intensity of shifting sociopolitical alliances and boundaries increased, competition for natural
resources and exchange networks also increased, perhaps exacerbated
by environmental fluctuations such as severe or prolonged droughts.

The complex interplay of all of those factors gave a selective advantage to cultural groups with more centralized forms of political organization, ultimately giving rise to chiefdoms on the inner coastal plain of the Potomac, York, and James rivers. Undoubtedly, the startling and sporadic appearance of European ships, sailors, traders, and missionaries in the Chesapeake region during the sixteenth century added to the stress already affecting native societies.

Thus far, the discussions and interpretations have emphasized the circumstances and forces which probably caused the development of chiefly societies in the Virginia-Maryland tidewater. In an interesting and provocative thesis, John Haynes (1984:64) examined the structural "principles . . . involved in the transformation of social systems" as they related to the formation of the Powhatan chiefdom. Clearly, understanding how social systems change is as important as identifying the factors that cause them to change (Haynes 1984:2). However, knowledge of Powhatan social organization is limited; there is no information on kinship structure, and evidence for reckoning descent is scarce (Rountree 1989:92–93).

Much of Haynes's (1984:62–63, 160–62) interpretation is predicated upon the assumption that Powhatan society developed from conical clans and ramified descent systems (the internal ranking of clans or people based on genealogical nearness to a common ancestor). Ethnographically, neither the conical clan nor ramage is documented anywhere in North America east of the Rocky Mountains (Knight 1990:5). Furthermore, Vernon Knight (1990:1–23) recently has argued that the hierarchical political organization of many groups in the southeastern United States developed from clans that were exogamous social categories based on parent-child ties rather than descent lines. "The local manifestation of the clan in a given district or village sometimes took the form of a small-scale lineage which, in contrast to the broader clan, was both localized and strongly corporate" (Knight 1990:6). This more closely approximates what is surmised about Powhatan kinship structure. Also, Knight's interpretations will require the rethinking of some recent "evolutionary trajectories described for various Middle Atlantic Late Woodland societies" (Custer 1986:166–68), particularly as they relate to chiefdoms.

The Nature and Function of Chiefdoms

What were the advantages to be gained from centralized polities like chiefdoms? Referring back to the definition of complex societies, it should be kept in mind that they are principally problem-solving organizations. In chiefly societies, political, economic, social, and cere-monial life extended beyond the territory of a single community to include a number of communities bound together under a centralized authority. In order to integrate the communities effectively, chiefly au-thority was linked to the supernatural, with the role of chief cast as a ritually sanctioned intermediary between the secular and the sacred, thereby transcending purely local concerns, as well as the identifica-tion of the chief with his or her natal village or territory (Tainter 1988:25, 28; Carnerio 1981:45, 57; Earle 1987:298).

In a similar manner, chiefs handled worldly risks confronting their societies by serving as both a banker to their people and a culture bro-ker to outsiders. The rank of chief gave them the authority to direct labor and gather economic surpluses, resulting in two economies—the political economy of the chiefdom and the subsistence economy of the supporters' households. As culture brokers, chiefs rarely con-cerned themselves with local exchange unless it involved prestige goods or interaction with outsiders, preferring instead to control long-distance trade as a means of securing exotic items to enhance their status, cement potentially beneficial alliances, and spread knowledge about themselves beyond their local communities (Earle 1987:293, 295; Wells 1980:7; Tainter 1988:25; Feinman and Neitzel 1984:44; Schortman 1989:60).

The downward distribution of goods amassed by the chiefs helped to ensure the loyalty of their supporters, although to maintain that loyalty, chiefs had to return only a fraction of what was gathered through tribute (Tainter 1988:25, 37). However, chiefs were restricted in their actions by the obligations of kinship and by the lack of a stand-ing armed force to back up their decisions. As Joseph Tainter (1988:26) has written "Chiefly ambitions . . . are thus structurally con-strained. Too much allocation of resources to the chiefly apparatus, and too little return to the local level, engender resistance. The con-sequence is that chiefdoms tend to undergo cycles of centralization and decentralization."

In a situation where nearby groups are organized as chiefly soci-eties, the option to decentralize may be an invitation to be dominated by them. "To the extent that such domination is to be avoided, invest-ment in organizational complexity must be maintained at a level com-parable to one's competitors" (Tainter 1988:201). The reason for this built-in pressure is that chiefdoms grow primarily by accretion (Car-nerio 1981:66). As the incipient Potomac Creek and protohistoric Powhatan chiefdoms expanded or exerted their influence, adjacent groups who came under their control were recast in the chiefdom's mold. Other groups not yet part of the larger, centralized polity reorganized at a higher level of integration in order to maintain their political autonomy. Thus, by the early seventeenth century all but one of the tidewater Algonquian groups from the Potomac to the James rivers were organized as small chiefdoms (Rountree 1989:8). The lone holdouts were the Chickahominies, who were ruled by a central political body composed of eight great men, or *munguys* (Feest 1978a:261).

Furthermore, according to a study by Gary Feinman and Jill Neitzel (1984:71–72), the evolution of chiefly societies is not as dependent upon the size of the populations involved as it is on the number of organizational units or districts. For example, the Algonquian chiefdoms of the Chesapeake Bay region had smaller units of corporate production than did adjacent tribal societies. The people of the chiefdoms were more sedentary than their more egalitarian neighbors and the settlements were usually smaller, but there were more of them and they were closer together (Binford 1964:464–65, 473).

Corn, Storage, and Politics

In the early days of Anglo-Algonquian contact and trade, Potomac River maize, especially from the Patawomekes themselves, proved to be the lifeblood of Jamestown. Thousands of bushels came from the Patawomekes' villages. Yet not one corn kernel was found at the Potomac Creek site, the protohistoric village of the Patawomekes (Schmitt 1965:9; Stewart 1988:44). One reason for this apparent gap in the archaeological record has to do with the manner in which Potomac Creek and other significant prehistoric sites in the Potomac Valley were excavated. However, there is more to it than that. Whether corn is found or not has as much to do with aboriginal food processing, storage, settlement patterns, and political organization as it does with the quirks of preservation and archaeological recovery techniques.

Excavations at the Potomac Creek site did not favor the recovery of plant domesticates, like corn. Unless a large portion of charred corncob had popped up on the end of a shovel blade, the untrained laborers hired to do most of the digging during T. Dale Stewart's excavations probably would not have noticed or recognized plant remains. Also, no excavated soil was screened, either from the plow zone or from any of the features (T. Dale Stewart, personal communication 1983). The features (see fig. 32) consisted of hundreds of postmolds; some discontinuous, trash-filled borrow pits or what Schmitt (1965:8) called "a defensive ditch"; and one large pit (feature 6) that was so unique to the site it was referred to simply as "the deep pit." Even during Judge William Graham's earlier digs, "only a few pits were found, indicating that pit storage was not a widespread custom" (Stewart 1988:43). At the Accokeek Creek site, there were no trained archaeologists, no soil screening, and no corn (Stephenson et al. 1963:41–45, 197).

Acknowledging that excavation techniques at Accokeek Creek and Potomac Creek were unfavorable to the recovery of corn and that the use of fluid suspension to recover plant remains was unknown at the time, contemporary archaeologists still puzzled over the absence of corn (Turner in press; Green 1987:101). Perhaps the answer lies in the aboriginal storage methods used and the reasons behind those methods. If one looks beyond the tidewater Potomac, at any of the dozens of Late Woodland villages that have been excavated in the piedmont or Great Valley, one of the most common features is the subterranean storage pit for bulk food preservation (see Manson et al. 1944:379–86; MacCord et al. 1957:7; Stearns 1940; Gardner 1986:77–92; Kavanagh 1982:69–79). And yet in the Potomac coastal plain, subterranean storage pits at villages dating after ca. A.D. 1400 are relatively uncommon. This is clearly the case at the Potomac Creek site, where only one bona fide storage pit was found during Stewart's excavations and only a few possible storage pits were noted by Graham.

The situation at Accokeek Creek is anything but clear. Alice Ferguson (Stephenson et al. 1963:57–58), excavator of the site, stated that "there were many small pits, larger and deeper than the first [fire] pits, and without any traces of fire. Most of them were about 2.5 feet deep [76.2 cm] from the bottom of the plowzone and many of them had irregular discolorations of the sand suggesting the decay of vegetable matter. These may have been storage pits." But there is no way to confirm how many of those "storage pits" were associated with the Potomac Creek occupation, how many were really dug for storage, or the exact number that "many" represents.

When the ground plan for the Accokeek Creek site excavations is examined (see fig. 32), there are sixty pit features shown within the palisaded village that do not fall into any of the following categories: refuse pit (trash-filled borrow pit), fire pit, burial pit, or ossuary (Stephenson et al. 1963:38–39). Presumably those sixty features include some that Ferguson thought were storage pits. As Warren DeBoer has noted (1988:5), theoretically "storage pits are likely to assume shapes that maximize volume while minimizing surface and access area (deep cylinders and bell shapes approximate these requirements)." Even though cross-sectional profiles exist for only a few pits from Accokeek Creek and there are no data on pit volume, by examining the size and shape of the plan views of the sixty pit features, pits can be eliminated that have too small a surface area and, therefore, would inhibit access to the bulk storage of food or, conversely, have too large a surface area to preserve bulk foodstuffs effectively. After eliminating pits at either extreme, thirty-nine features remain. The long, intermittent occupation of the site makes it likely that a certain number of those pits were used before the Potomac Creek people built their village. Other pits may not have been dug for storage at all. Thus, the total number of potential storage pits at the Accokeek Creek site is relatively small compared to the maximum size of the village and its long history (Stephenson et al. 1963:46, 198).

If subterranean storage was not the principal means for the bulk storage of corn, what was? There are two possible answers to this question—one from archaeology and one from ethnohistory. Site plans of Accokeek Creek and Potomac Creek show villages peppered with postmolds, the result of building and rebuilding houses, shelters or shade structures, drying racks, cooking racks, hanging poles, and probably aboveground granaries or corncribs. On the other hand, colonist Henry Spelman (1910:cxii) wrote that the Patawomekes took the dried ears of corn and piled them "up in ther howses, dayly as occation serveth wringinge the eares in peises betwene ther hands, and so rubbinge out ther corne do put it to a great Baskett which taketh upp the best parte of sum of ther howses." Most likely, the houses in which the corn was stored were similar to Spelman's (1910:cv) description of Powhatan's "treasurie" (see also Smith 1986b:173–74): "At Oropikes [Orapaks] in a house . . . are sett all the Kings goods and presents that are sent him, as ye Corne."

The village at Potomac Creek was the principal year-round town for its group, the place where the werowance lived. As such, the village served as a collection point for tribute paid to the werowance by his or her people. Much of the tribute was paid in corn, which was stored above ground, either in granaries or in huge baskets probably kept in the werowance's "treasurie." The reason for this arrangement may have to do with the dual economy of chiefdoms—the political economy of the group and the private household economy of the common people. In such a system, "above-ground (visible) storage was associated with the political economy in contrast to the hidden household stores of the subsistence economy" (Earle 1987:295).

The Virginia Algonquians' use of below-ground storage pits to hide their household stores was described by William Strachey (1953:115): "Their Corne and (indeed) their Copper, hatchets,

Howes, beades, perle and most things with them of value according to theire owne estymation, they hide one from the knowledge of another in the ground within the woods, and so keepe them all yeare, or untill they have fitt use for them." Among the chiefdoms of the Virginia-Maryland tidewater, subterranean storage was probably practiced to a certain degree as concealment against tribute demands and by people living in outlying hamlets that were periodically abandoned or that may have been somewhat distant from the principal town and more exposed to possible attack (DeBoer 1988:9–13). Although the preservation efficiency of storage pits "is no doubt less than cribs, especially for corn storage," observed H. Trawick Ward (1985:99), "they do offer security not found in above ground facilities."

Archaeologically, one should expect fewer storage pits in the larger villages that may have served as the residence of the werowance. Conversely, in hamlets, particularly those farther from the werowance's village, there should be greater evidence of underground storage. Where there are more underground storage pits, there is a greater chance of finding vegetable remains, because many storage pits were turned into handy trash receptacles once their original contents were removed (DeBoer 1988:4).

Similar circumstances occur nearby in North Carolina where the tribally organized piedmont Siouan villages are characterized by many underground storage pits, like the majority of the Late Woodland villages in the Potomac River piedmont and Great Valley of Virginia and Maryland. In contrast, few underground storage pits are found in the villages of the late prehistoric Cherokees, who, like most of the Virginia and Maryland Algonquians, were organized as chiefdoms (Ward 1985:100). Among the Cherokees, agricultural surpluses were stored in aboveground corncribs akin to the "great Baskett[s]" and aboveground granaries of the Algonquian chiefdoms of the Virginia-Maryland tidewater.

A comparison of Montgomery complex villages to those lived in by their descendants, the Potomac Creek people, suggests that the change from belowground to aboveground storage, like the change from primary individual burials to ossuaries, is a reflection of increasing complexity in the sociopolitical organization of Potomac Creek culture. When these and other changes in the archaeological record are considered, it is possible that as early as the fifteenth century complex societies, such as chiefdoms, developed on the inner coastal plain of the Potomac River.

CHAPTER 5

The
Clash
of Cultures

Introduction

THE OPENING YEARS OF THE SEVENTEENTH CENTURY were turbulent times for the native peoples of the Potomac Valley, a prelude to even darker times to come. The Potomac River, once a means of unifying the Algonquian groups along its banks, was becoming a political frontier between rival factions on opposing banks and between the Conoy chiefdom of southern Maryland and the rapidly growing Powhatan chiefdom of tidewater Virginia. This aboriginal frontier was exploited by the invading Englishmen at Jamestown, as they sought to enlist the Patawomekes as allies in their fight against Powhatan. In doing so, they alienated groups of the Conoy chiefdom, who later sided with Englishmen at St. Mary's City in their struggle against the alliance between the Jamestown English and the powerful Iroquoian-speaking Susquehannocks. Ironically, what began as an aboriginal frontier between developing Algonquian chiefdoms became the border between developing English colonies.

Prelude to Invasion

During late prehistory and early historic times, apparently only the more important Algonquian villages or those along cultural boundaries were protected. As the local or regional importance of a village changed or as sociopolitical or ethnic boundaries shifted, so did the need for defense. Examination of the excavation base maps for the Accokeek Creek (18PR8) and Potomac Creek (44ST2) sites indicates at least five to seven major episodes of palisade construction at the former and at least three to five at the latter, depending on whether double palisades were built (see fig. 32; Stephenson et al. 1963:38–39; Stewart 1988). When the Accokeek Creek site was excavated in the 1930s, only half the village remained, covering a little more than 0.81 hectare (2 a; Stephenson et al. 1963:46). The rest was lost to shoreline erosion as the Potomac River widened its channel. At its maximum during the last half of the 1500s, the village covered approximately 1.62 hectares (4 a). The protohistoric village of Potomac Creek encompassed slightly more than 0.81 hectare (2 a) at its zenith, about A.D. 1600 (Schmitt 1965:7). By the end of their histories, both the Accokeek Creek and Potomac Creek villages were probably surrounded by double palisades (Stephenson et al. 1963:38–39; Manson and MacCord 1985:29). The unstable and predatory nature of chiefdoms makes it likely that some of the palisades at the Accokeek Creek and Potomac Creek sites were erected as much to protect against neighboring Algonquian groups as against hostile Siouan and Iroquoian peoples on their borders.

The Potomac Creek site and its nearby successor, the historic Indian Point site (44ST1), represent the protohistoric and historic werowance's villages of the Patawomekes (MacCord 1991:120, 135–39). As such, these sites were probably akin to the capital towns or villages of the North Carolina Algonquians, housing the werowance or *weroansqua*, his or her family, their kinfolk, and the priests (David S. Phelps, personal communication 1991). In 1608 the majority of the 650 to 850 Patawomekes lived in nine outlying hamlets. Two hamlets were located along Potomac Creek, and seven others lined Aquia Creek to its headwaters in the outer piedmont. Near the head of Aquia Creek was the Patawomekes' antimony mine, which lured Captain John Smith to explore the creek personally and so chart the villages along its course. Although the distribution of fair to good agricultural soils in this area is very patchy, two other factors may have contributed to the scattering of hamlets along the creek. The dispersed hamlets could have served as a means of restricting access to the antimony mine and as an early warning system against incursions by the Manahoacs from the southwest (Parker 1985:30, 38).

By the late sixteenth century, if not before, the people of the Luray phase had abandoned their villages above the falls of the Potomac River all the way to the confluence of the Shenandoah River. The apparent cause for this abandonment was the movement of the Iroquoian-speaking Susquehannocks to the lower Susquehanna River valley of Lancaster County, Pennsylvania, sometime between 1550 and

1575. Soon thereafter, they extended their influence southward into the upper Potomac Valley. Archaeological evidence from the Pancake Farm (46HM73) and Herriot Farm (46HM1) sites near Romney, West Virginia, confirms the intrusion of Susquehannock groups into the area (James W. Bradley, personal communication 1992; Brashler 1987; MacCord 1952; Witthoft 1952). The Susquehannocks apparently maintained an outpost in the vicinity of Romney until the early 1600s, when their main village (36LA8; see fig. 27) was at Washington Boro, Pennsylvania (Kent 1984:317).

Not content with controlling the upper Potomac Valley, the Susquehannocks and their enemies, the Massawomecks, were harassing the tidewater Algonquians. This conflict is reflected on Captain John Smith's map by the conspicuous absence of any Algonquian settlements along the western shore of Chesapeake Bay north of the Patuxent River (Cissna 1986:110; Steponaitis 1986:26; Pendergast 1991:33–34). As for the brave souls living along the Patuxent River in 1608, Smith (1986c:105) noted that "they inhabit togither, and not so dispersed as the rest." Such a defensive posture is reflected at the Cumberland site (18CV171), a late sixteenth- or early seventeenth-century palisaded village located along the east bank of the Patuxent River in Calvert County, Maryland (Clark and Hughes 1983).

The dreaded Massawomecks "were a great nation and very populous. For the heads of all those rivers, especially the Pattawomekes, the Pautuxuntes, the Sasquesahanocks, the Tochwoughes are continually tormented by them" (Smith 1986c:119). As Amorlock, a Siouan-speaking Manahoac Indian, vividly expressed it, the Massawomecks had "so many men that they made warre with all the world" (Smith 1986c:176). Exactly who the Massawomecks were is a matter of continuing debate, although it is generally agreed that they were Iroquoian-speakers (Pendergast 1991; Rountree 1989:142; Barbour 1986:1:230; Kent 1984:26). James Pendergast (1991:68) has postulated that the Massawomecks were the same Iroquoians known to the French as the Antouhonorons, who lived in the region east of the Niagara River during the first quarter of the seventeenth century. Antouhonorons (or Entouhonorons) was the early French name for the four western tribes of the Five Nation Iroquois, with only the easternmost tribe, the Mohawk, being identified by the French as Iroquois (Trigger 1976:311, plate 28). This observation fits nicely with the English trader Henry Fleet's (1956:483–86) statement that the Massawomecks consisted of four nations in 1632. Later, after the French had gained a better understanding of the Five Nation Iroquois, they began referring to all five tribes of the league as Iroquois (William R. Fitzgerald, personal communication 1992). Similarly, after 1634, once the English of the Chesapeake region learned more about the Five Nation Iroquois, no contemporary accounts refer to the Massawomecks (Pendergast 1991:72).

By the early 1600s the Algonquians of the Potomac and Rappahannock rivers were keeping a watchful eye open not only for the Massawomecks, Susquehannocks, and Manahoacs but for the Powhatans as well. The rapid expansion of the Powhatan chiefdom in the tidewater region south of the Rappahannock River during the last quarter of the sixteenth century must have caused growing concern among the smaller chiefdoms living in the lower Rappahannock Valley. Not wishing to suffer the same fate as the original inhabitants of Kecoughtan or Chesapeake, whom Powhatan destroyed, some villagers moved from the south to the north bank of the Rappahannock, putting the river between them and the unpredictable paramount chieftain (Strachey 1953:43–44, 67, 104; Potter 1976:21–22, 1982: 65–67).

With more people now living on the north side of the Rappahannock River, the lower Northern Neck became the most densely settled part of tidewater Virginia (Turner 1982:56–57). The profusion of circles and longhouses on John Smith's map, representing hamlets and villages, resembles a strand of beads strung along the Rappahannock's left bank (see fig. 1). Such a linear dispersion of hamlets and villages is probably a reflection of the Virginia Algonquians' custom of considering uncultivated land common ground (Rountree 1989:40). Due to the increased population density along the north shore of the Rappahannock, the people of the various chiefdoms spread themselves over the landscape as a means of asserting their control over the narrow band of prime agricultural land lining that side of the river (see Smith 1972:415).

Preliminary archaeological fieldwork at three estuarine sites near the Rappahannock's left bank supports the notion that the number of smaller habitations increased late in prehistory. Although more fieldwork needs to be done at all three sites, the surface collection data indicate that protohistoric and possibly early historic use of the Indian Town Farm (44LA80) and Woodbury Farm (44RD48 and 44RD49) sites was not as intensive or extensive as earlier occupations (see fig. 27; Potter 1982:190–202).

Historical documents tend to uphold such an interpretation. In a court transaction concerning the division of the Corrotoman estate, a map surveyed December 31, 1817, shows the unnamed cove on which the Indian Town Farm site is located as "Indian Town Creek." The land to the south of the cove is labeled "Indian Town Quarter." These early nineteenth-century place-names and a triangular piece of sheet copper found at the Indian Town Farm site are indications that some portion of the site probably was used during protohistoric and early historic times by a group from the lower Cuttatawomen chiefdom (Potter 1982:192, 362). Indeed, it is possible that this is the hamlet of Chesakawon, which Barbour (1971:287) placed in this locale. Chesakawon was one of four hamlets associated with the werowance's village of lower Cuttatawomen shown on John Smith's map.

The Woodbury Farm sites may have been occupied during the protohistoric and early historic period by a group from the Moratico chiefdom. Again, Barbour (1971:295) proposed that the hamlet of Oquomack was located in the vicinity. Oquomack was one of at least two, maybe four, hamlets affiliated with the werowance's village of Moraughtacund (anglicized to Moratico), as depicted on Smith's map. Further support for limited historic Moratico occupation comes from land patents dating to A.D. 1660 and 1664 that refer to an "Indian field" near the head of Farnham Creek and, in 1667, to Pipemaker's Creek, which flows into Farnham Creek just north of the Woodbury tract (Nugent 1934:408, 441, 501; Ryland 1976:57).

While many of the chiefdoms along the tidal Rappahannock were placing the river between themselves and Powhatan's imperial ambition, other groups like the upper Cuttatawomens were contending with life along the fall-line frontier. Their principal village, where the werowance lived, was located near the confluence of modern Lamb Creek and the Rappahannock. Known to archaeologists as the De Shazo site (44KG3), it was first described by David I. Bushnell in 1937 (see fig. 27). On a portion of the site Bushnell (1937:61–62) observed an embankment and ditch. The best-preserved section of embankment was "approximately 18 inches (45.7 cm) in height and the ditch about the same in depth. Nothing is known of the origin of the embankment and ditch. They are very old and may have been constructed during the days of Indian occupancy, when the embankment would undoubtedly have been surmounted by a palisade." Even though no traces of the embankment and ditch were visible in the 1960s when members of the Archeological Society of Virginia conducted excavations nearby (Howard A. MacCord, Sr., personal communication 1990), similar defenses existed at the Potomac Creek and Accokeek Creek sites and should be expected at a late sixteenth- and early seventeenth-century werowance's village near the fall line of the Rappahannock River—to protect not only against the Manahoacs and Massawomecks but possibly against other Algonquian groups.

Anglo-Algonquian Contact and Conflict, 1607–50s

In 1607, the year the English built James Fort in Virginia, relationships between Indian groups in the Chesapeake Bay region consisted of a complex web of trade and military alliances, raids and warfare. When viewed from the tidal Potomac River (see frontispiece), the situation looked something like this: to the north were the Susquehannocks who lived along the lower Susquehanna River in Lancaster County, Pennsylvania, but claimed as their territory the entire Susquehanna Valley and vast areas on either side of Chesapeake Bay (Jennings 1978:363). Susquehannock raiding parties were striking Algonquian villages along the Patuxent and Potomac rivers. Somewhere northwest of the Susquehannocks were their "mortall enimies," the Massawomecks, who were busy trading with some Eastern Shore groups in the Tangier Sound region while attacking the Susquehannocks, the Tockwoghs and other Indian groups near the head of Chesapeake Bay, the Algonquians of the Patuxent and Potomac rivers, and the Manahoacs of north-central piedmont Virginia (Smith 1986b:230–32, 1986c:176; Pendergast 1991:35; Jefferson 1972:96). The Manahoacs and their piedmont confederates, the Monacans, warred with and sometimes traded with the Algonquians living near the fall line from north of the Rappahannock River to the James River (Hantman 1990:677–80, 685–86). South of the tidal Rappahannock was the heartland of Powhatan's paramount chiefdom, concentrated along the tidal York and James rivers. Most of the tidewater Algonquians living along the Rappahannock River and the south shore of the Potomac River were part of Powhatan's "ethnic fringe" (Rountree 1989:14; Fausz 1985:235–37). But two of the groups with territories on the Potomac's south shore, the Patawomekes and Tauxenents, probably were not within the Powhatan fold.

The Patawomekes, recently divorced from their alliance with the Piscataways and other groups living mainly on the north side of the Potomac River, were caught between them and the expanding Powhatan chiefdom to the south (Smith 1986c:316). At odds with his former allies and hard-pressed by Susquehannock, Massawomeck, and Manahoac raids, the werowance of Patawomeke could ill afford to add Powhatan to his list of enemies. By the same token, given Powhatan's tenuous hold on the Algonquians of Virginia's Northern Neck, he could not afford to alienate the most populous and one of the most powerful groups in the lower Potomac Valley, particularly one that served as a buffer on his volatile northern frontier. For those reasons, the Patawomekes remained autonomous, only acceding to Powhatan's wishes when it was in their best interest to do so. Otherwise, the werowance of Patawomeke was "unwilling to own Subjection to the other Emperors, whom he always affected to treat, rather as Brethren than Superiors" (Stith 1747:240).

Most likely, the Tauxenents were still loosely allied with the Nacotchtanks and Piscataways (Cissna 1986:111–12). In the summer of 1608, Captain John Smith's party of explorers was initially greeted with hostile receptions at Matchotic (Onawmament), Chicacoan (Cecocawone), and Patawomeke (Patawomeck), "but at Moyaones, Nacothtant [Nacotchtank] and Taux [Tauxenent], the people did their best to content" them (Smith 1986b:227). The inhabitants of the unfriendly villages either were part of Powhatan's ethnic fringe or maintained cordial diplomatic relations with Powhatan, "but the latter," observed David I. Bushnell (1940:127), "where the people were well-disposed, are believed to have been allied with the tribes of Maryland, enemies of Powhatan, and who by their actions endeavored to gain the good will of the colonists" (see also Rountree 1990:45). Later seventeenth-century accounts document continuing cultural ties between the Tauxenents and the Indians of southern Maryland, particularly the Piscataways (Marye 1935:197; Washburn 1972:20–21; Harrison 1987:83).

The Englishmen who founded Jamestown quickly became entangled in the web of native intergroup relations. On May 26, 1607, twelve days after landing on Jamestown Island, the colonists were attacked by a combined force of two to four hundred warriors from five different groups belonging to Powhatan's chiefdom. Only the ships' cannons and constant musket fire repulsed the Algonquian attackers (Fausz 1977:224–25). Failing to destroy or dislodge the English invaders, a month later Powhatan changed his strategy. If he could not drive the aliens away with arrows, he would win them over with maize.

In exchange for Powhatan maize, the English traded "Copper, white beades for their women, Hatchetts, . . . Howes to pare their Corne ground, knyves and such like" (Strachey 1953:75). Of all those items, initially it was copper that Powhatan coveted most. Among the southern Algonquians, copper was a symbol of power and authority, reserved for the werowances and other individuals of high status. It was used to reward people and purchase assistance in warfare and was buried with the werowances in the mortuary temples (Potter 1989:153–54). European copper was particularly prized because it was redder and harder than native varieties (Strachey 1953:145).

Before the arrival of the Jamestown colonists, Powhatan acquired copper from several sources: the Great Lakes region, possibly the Virgilina ridge in North Carolina, and the Blue Ridge Mountains in Virginia (Quinn 1985:114, 177–78; Rountree 1989:55). At least one Blue Ridge copper mine was in the territory of Powhatan's nemeses, the Monacans. As Jeffrey L. Hantman (1990:685) has noted, "Whether the Monacan were a direct source of copper, or whether they were a conduit of copper obtained from more western sources, they may well have played a key role in the pre-1607 native copper exchange sphere."

With the advent of the strangers, or *tassantasses* (Strachey 1953:58), at Jamestown, suddenly Powhatan had a potential new source of high-grade copper. There were also the terrifying weapons of the Englishmen, which might be directed against Powhatan's enemies if the strangers were made his "subservient allies" (Fausz 1990:17; Hantman 1990:685–86). Perhaps it is for those reasons that Powhatan allowed Jamestown to survive.

Over the next eighteen months, Algonquians and Englishmen took stock of one another as they traded corn and copper. In the summer of 1608, Captain John Smith's explorations of the Chesapeake Bay were as much missions to gather intelligence on the strengths and weaknesses of Powhatan's chiefdom as they were voyages of discovery (Fausz 1990:19). Smith's treks around the Chesapeake gave Powhatan something to worry about. Not only had Smith made brief and ultimately friendly contact with parties of Susquehannocks, Massawomecks, and Manahoacs (Smith 1986c:170–77), but, as Helen Rountree (1990:46) has commented, "it looked to John Smith—and perhaps also to Powhatan—as if the English had become allies of all the Potomac and Rappahannock river groups."

Things were also beginning to turn sour with the maize trade. Overanxious to maintain good relations with the Powhatans, the Virginia Company of London intervened in Indian affairs. As the Virginia Company's local agent, Captain Christopher Newport sought to appease Powhatan no matter what the cost, over the strenuous objections of Captain John Smith. As the price of Powhatan maize rose, so did Smith's temper. Rather than trade for foodstuff, the irate English captain began taking it by force (Fausz 1990:19).

The rise in Powhatan's valuation of maize corresponded with a de-valuation of copper due to its "abundance and [the colonists'] neglect of prisinge it" (Kingsbury 1933:3:19). "Valuing a basket of corne more pretious than a basket of copper, saying he could eate his corne, but not his copper, " Powhatan asked for English "gunnes and swords" in exchange for Indian maize (Smith 1986b:246). Previously, Newport had acquiesced to Powhatan's terms by giving him twenty swords for twenty turkeys, but Smith refused to follow such "an ill example" (Smith 1986b:220). Even the Virginia Company of London changed its earlier policy of appeasement, and by May 1609 council members advised the Jamestown leaders to "make friendship with . . . those [na-tions] that are fartherest from you and enemies unto those amonge whom you dwell, for you shall have least occasion to have differences with them and by that meanes a suerer league of amity, and you shalbe suer of their trade partley for covetousnes and to serve their owne ends, where the copper is yett in his primary estimacion which Pow-hatan hath hitherto engrossed" (Kingsbury 1933:3:19).

The council's advice was soon put into practice when the First Anglo-Powhatan War erupted in August 1609, beginning "five yeeres intestine warre with the . . . Indians" of the lower York and James river basins (Hamor 1957:2). Three months after hostilities with Powhatan commenced, Captain Francis West and thirty-six colonists sailed north to trade with the Patawomekes. After loading their pinnace with maize, West and his men inexplicably cut the heads off two Indians. Having thus alienated a friendly trading partner and potential ally, West then left his countrymen at Jamestown to starve, preferring in-stead to set sail for England (Percy 1922:266).

A year later, the breach between Patawomeke and Jamestown was patched, probably due to the diplomacy of Captain Samuel Argall, who "partly by gentle usage and partly by the composition and mix-ture of threats hath ever kept faire and friendly quarter with our neighbours bordering on other rivers" (Hamor 1957:3). Trading "with the great king of Patawomeck," Argall "obteyned well neere 400. bush-ells of wheat [corn], pease and beanes (besyde many kind of furrs)" in exchange for copper, beads, hatchets, knives, bells, and scissors worth about "40s. English" (Strachey 1953:46). In the bargain, an English boy by the name of Henry Spelman, who had lived with the Patawo-mekes for a year, was placed in Argall's custody. Regarding Argall's trip, the governor of Virginia, Baron De La Warre, wrote, "The last discovery, during my continuall sicknesse, was by Captaine Argall, who hath found a trade with Patomack (a King as great as Powhatan, who still remains our enemie, though not able to doe us hurt)" (Tyler 1907:213).

De La Warre's parenthetical dismissal of Powhatan was premature. While De La Warre was sailing back to England in March 1611, Powhatan's warriors were attacking the blockhouse at Jamestown. Under the successive leadership of Deputy Governor Sir Thomas Dale and Lieutenant Governor Sir Thomas Gates, much of the James River was secured by defeating the Nansemonds at the mouth of the river and invading the territories of the Arrohatecks and Appamatucks below the falls (Fausz 1990:6, 36–42). With their backs against the fall line, the Powhatans made peace with their ancient piedmont enemies, the Monacans. As William Strachey (1953:105–6) observed, "Powhatan had manie enemies, especially in the westerly Countryes, before we made our Forts and habitations so neere the Falls, but now the generall Cause hath united them."

A lull occurred in the fighting during 1612 and much of 1613, as the English consolidated their gains and the Powhatans regrouped (Fausz 1990:42–43). Hoping to capitalize on his earlier trading success with the Patawomekes, Captain Argall returned in December 1612. In addition to eleven hundred bushels of maize, Argall got something of even greater importance: a defensive military alliance with the Patawomekes against Powhatan (Fausz 1977:282). The following April, Argall outdid himself by kidnapping Powhatan's daughter Pocahontas while she was "among her friends at Pataomecke" (Hamor 1957:4). It was a couple of those "friends" who betrayed Pocahontas into the hands of Argall for the princely sum of "a small Copper kettle and som other les valuable toies" (fig. 39; Hamor 1957:4). A year later, the First Anglo-Powhatan War ended, not with a decisive military victory but with the marriage of Pocahontas to an Englishman named John Rolfe (Rountree 1990:59–60).

Now that the war between the Powhatans and the English was over, the independent Chickahominies, realizing the precariousness of their position, quickly concluded a separate peace with the colonists (Hamor 1957:11–16). The cessation of hostilities also brought about a reduction in the English maize trade with distant Indian groups, like the Patawomekes. No longer did the Virginia planters feel "constrayned yerely to seeke after the Indians, and intreate them to sell us Corne" (Rolfe 1971:6). Their sense of self-sufficiency was only an illusion, however. Reality quickly returned whenever the fragile supply lines to the mother country failed or when greed for the riches of tobacco overcame the colonists' prudence in planting corn. Two years

39. In an engraving from Matthew Merien's Historiae Americanae, . . .
Decima Tertia Pars *(Frankfurt am Main, 1634), Japazaws, holding the
copper kettle, assists Samuel Argall in kidnapping Pocahontas by enticing her
to board the English ship* Treasurer. *(Reproduced by permission of the
Virginia Historical Society)*

after the treaty with the Chickahominies, Deputy Governor George
Yeardley forcibly took corn from them, killing a dozen or more Indians in the process (Smith 1986c:256–57). Yeardley's reckless action accomplished something that neither Powhatan nor his ambitious
brother, Opechancanough, had been able to achieve: it coerced
the Chickahominies into joining the Powhatan chiefdom (Rountree
1990:62).

The period from 1614 to 1622 was one of considerable change.
Drought and disease in 1617 and 1619 took their toll of Englishmen
and Indians alike, "but chiefly amongst the Indians" (Kingsbury
1906:1:310; Fausz 1977:314–15). Powhatan died in April 1618, to be
replaced in name only by his next younger brother, Opitchapam. The

real power behind the paramount chieftaincy was Opechancanough, the next brother in the line of succession. By 1622, his charisma and aggressive leadership had made Opechancanough effectively the paramount chief even though Opitchapam retained the position till his death sometime after August 1629 (Rountree 1990:62, 66, 80). And as the number of Virginia immigrants increased during this time, so did the planting of land-hungry tobacco which, along with the Virginia Company's attempts to convert Algonquians into Anglicans, helped sow the seeds of a second war (Rountree 1990:66–70; Fausz 1977:338–42).

On March 22, 1622, Algonquian warriors from groups living mainly in the James and York river basins, led by Opechancanough, launched a concerted attack against the hated tassantasses, striking their settlements "like violent lightening" (Kingsbury 1935:4:73). When the devastated survivors tallied their losses, they discovered that over one-quarter of the colony's inhabitants were dead. Fortunately for those who lived, Opechancanough failed to follow up his initial success with additional attacks. Once they recovered from Opechancanough's onslaught, the enraged colonists began a series of harsh campaigns against the Powhatans that were designed to keep them on the defensive, take away great quantities of their corn, but never completely destroy them, taking "paynes to burne a few of their houses, everie yeare like a Surgion that wanteth meanes, to keepe one in hand 3 yeares, that maybee Cured in 3 quarters, or 3 monthes" (Kingsbury 1935:4:37; Fausz 1977:357–403).

As the Second Anglo-Powhatan War heated up in the lower James and York river valleys, its effects boiled over into the Potomac River. Captain Henry Spelman, accompanied by Captain Raleigh Crashaw, was commanding a trading voyage to the Potomac River when Opechancanough attacked the English settlements. Spelman was an interpreter for the Virginia colony, exercising a proficiency he gained during the year he lived with the Patawomekes. While Spelman's vessel lay at anchor off the Chicacoan village, "a Salvage stole aboord them, and told them of the Massacre, and that Opechancanough had plotted with his King and Country to betray them also, which they refused, but them of Wighcocomoco at the mouth of the river had undertaken it" (Smith 1986c:304–5). Weighing anchor, Spelman and his men set sail for Wicocomoco where they displayed such a show of force, the Indians "suspected themselves discovered, and to colour their guilt . . . so contented his desire in trade, his Pinnace was neere fraught" (Smith 1986c:305).

At this point Crashaw and Spelman split up, with Crashaw heading upriver "to Patawomeck, where he intended to stay and trade for himselfe, by reason of the long acquaintance he had with this King that so earnestly entreated him now to be his friend, his countenancer, his Captaine and director against the Pazaticans [Piscataways], the Nacotchtanks, and Moyaons his mortall enemies. Of this opportunity Croshaw was glad . . . to keepe the King as an opposite to Opechancanough, and adhere him unto us, or at least make him an instrument against our enemies" (Smith 1986c:305). Learning that Crashaw was at Patawomeke, Opechancanough tried to bribe the werowance into killing him, but the latter refused (Smith 1986c:308).

Shortly thereafter, Captain Ralph Hamor, commanding a ship and a pinnace, arrived at Patawomeke to trade for corn. Explaining that he had no surplus maize, the werowance of Patawomeke offered "40. or 50 choise Bow-men to conduct and assist" the English in an attack to seize maize from his enemies, "the Nacotchtanks and their confederats" (Smith 1986c:309). The joint Anglo-Patawomeke raid was a success, with the victors "taking what they liked, and spoiling the rest" (Smith 1986c:309).

Returning to Jamestown with the much-needed corn, Hamor left Crashaw and five men at Patawomeke. Crashaw, realizing that the English had stirred up a hornet's nest by taking part in the attack on the Nacotchtanks and knowing that Opechancanough had placed a price on his head, "retired into such a convenient place, that with the helpe of the Salvages [the Patawomekes], hee . . . quickly fortified himselfe against all those wilde enemies" (Smith 1986c:309).

Following a plan devised by Crashaw, the governor sent Captain Isaac Madison and thirty-six men to Patawomeke near summer's end. Crashaw's idea was this: base an English force at Patawomeke to help guard the maize fields. Then, through trade with their friends and by force from their enemies, they would gather a sufficient amount of maize at harvest time to supply the colony. Unfortunately, before Crashaw could personally execute his plan he had to leave Patawomeke (Smith 1986c:309).

With Crashaw gone, relations between Madison and his men and their Patawomeke hosts began to deteriorate. "Madyson not liking so well to live amongst the Salvages as Croshaw did, built him a strong house within the fort, so that they were not so sociable as before" (Smith 1986c:312). Things went from bad to worse when English paranoia was mixed with native politics. A defeated werowance, "beat out of his Country by the Necosts [Nacotchtanks]," sought assistance from the werowance of Patawomeke. When the Great King of Patawomeke "would not helpe him revenge his injuries," the defeated werowance fed false information to an English interpreter named Poole who was with Madison's party (Smith 1986c:312–13). The troublesome and untrustworthy Poole believed his informant and told Madison that the Patawomekes were plotting with Opechancanough to kill them. Acting on Poole's misinformation, Madison indiscriminately slaughtered thirty or forty Patawomeke men, women, and children, took the werowance and his son captive, and sailed to Jamestown. After being held for awhile, "the poore kinge of Patomecke" and his son were returned to their people for a ransom of corn (Kingsbury 1935:4:89).

In March 1623 Captain Spelman and nineteen colonists were killed while on a trading voyage to the Potomac River, somewhere within approximately 51 kilometers (30 mi) of present-day Washington, D.C. Although there has been considerable debate over who committed the deed—the Nacotchtanks or the Patawomekes—the one man who lived to write about it blamed the Nacotchtanks. The sole survivor was Henry Fleet, one of twenty men who went ashore with Spelman. All those who left the ship were presumed dead by the five men remaining on board, who survived to tell the tale back at Jamestown. Fleet, however, was "taken prisoner and detained five years" by the Nacotchtanks (Fleet 1956:482; Smith 1986c:320–21; Kingsbury 1935:4:89).

The following November the governor of Virginia, Sir Francis Wyatt, led a punitive military expedition to the Potomac River "to revenge the trecherie of ye Pascoticons [Piscataways] and theire assocyates" (Kingsbury 1935:4:450). Wyatt's purpose was not only to avenge the death of Spelman, "the best linguist of the Indian Tongue of this Countrys," but also to renew the English alliance with the Patawomekes by attacking their enemies, the Piscataways and Nacotchtanks (Kingsbury 1935:4:89). The English force, composed of Wyatt, three captains, and ninety men, "putt many to the swoorde" and burnt the Piscataway and Nacotchtank houses and corn (Kingsbury 1935:4:450; Fausz 1977:504–5).

To help ensure the preservation of the Anglo-Patawomeke alliance and prevent future misunderstandings on the part of his captains, Governor Wyatt "thought fitt, for this present yeare [1624] to restreine all perticuler trade for Corne, within the Bay, and to appropriate that trade, only for the publique benefit of the Colony" (Kingsbury 1935:4:447). Wyatt put Captain Hamor in charge "of the good Shipp the William and John," granting him "full power and authorite, to trade, in any River, or Rivers within the Bay" but forbidding him "to compell by any waies or meanes any Indians whatsoever to trade more than they shalbe willing to trade for; or to offer any violence to any except in his owne defence" (Kingsbury 1935:4:447).

Meanwhile, across the Atlantic in May 1624, the Court of King's Bench dissolved the charter of the Virginia Company of London, paving the way for Virginia to become a royal colony later in the year (Dabney 1971:39). Back in Virginia, about harvesttime, Governor Wyatt and sixty militiamen defeated some eight hundred Pamunkey and other warriors and cut down enough Indian maize "to have Sustayned fower Thousand men for a Twellv mounthe" (Kingsbury 1935:4:507). With the demise of the Virginia Company's idealistic policy of Christianizing the Powhatans and a de-escalation of combat after 1624, the Virginia English began planting more tobacco than ever before. In 1626 Virginia harvested 132,000 pounds of tobacco; by 1629, over one million pounds were produced (Fausz 1977:509–13, 557).

During the late 1620s, as the Second Anglo-Powhatan War was slowly coming to a close in the lower James and York river valleys, the Chesapeake beaver trade began in the Potomac Valley. Chief among those who sought their fortune in furs was the former maize trader and interpreter Captain Henry Fleet (Fausz 1988:60). Held captive by the Nacotchtanks for five years, Fleet "by that meanes spake the Countrey language very well" and was ideally suited to trade among the Potomac River Algonquians (Hall 1925:72). Fleet's former captors, the Nacotchtanks, were now under the protection of the Massawomecks, probably the Five Nation Iroquois, acting as their middlemen in the fur trade. This strange partnership began sometime in the late 1620s, after the Conoys suffered severe losses from Massawomeck attacks (Feest 1978a:243).

While Fleet and others were busy in the Potomac, William Claiborne made three exploratory voyages to the northern Chesapeake. Although he was one of Virginia's top ten planters in 1630, Claiborne's explorations convinced him of the profit to be made from pelts. When the tobacco boom of the 1620s went bust in 1630, Claiborne received backing from London merchants and, in 1631, obtained a royal trading patent for the Chesapeake Bay (Fausz 1984:7, 1988:59–61).

Aware of the inferior quality and quantity of beaver pelts from the Potomac, Claiborne chose to go farther north. Soon after his patent was granted, Claiborne established a trading post on Kent Island in the middle Chesapeake. From that settlement, Claiborne began a trading partnership with the Susquehannocks, skilled warriors, fur trappers, and traders. The following year, 1632, the decade-long war between the Powhatans and the Virginia English finally ended, due perhaps to a great drought that year that severely reduced the corn supply, causing the colonists to initiate trade with the Indians (Kent 1984:34; McCartney 1985:57).

Unfortunately, peace had a short life span on the seventeenth-century Chesapeake frontier. The spark that ignited the new conflict was the founding of the colony of Maryland at St. Marys City in 1634. Ironically, Sir George Calvert, the first Baron Baltimore, heard of Claiborne's fur-trading venture while visiting in Virginia. Wanting a piece of the action and a southern proprietary, Sir George applied for a royal charter upon returning to England. By the time it was granted, he was dead, and his son, Cecil Calvert, the second Baron Baltimore, became the recipient of a royal charter granting him the northern two-thirds of the Chesapeake Bay. Apparently the people who doled out royal charters and patents did not realize that Baron Baltimore's charter contradicted William Claiborne's trading patent. That oversight kept the Chesapeake in turmoil for the next quarter century (Menard and Carr 1982:175; Fausz 1985:225, 1988:65–67).

With the assistance of Fleet, Governor Leonard Calvert, the second Baron Baltimore's brother, selected a site for St. Marys City along a river the English called St. Georges (now St. Marys), on the north side of the Potomac River, about eight miles from Chesapeake Bay. At first, Calvert sought to settle farther up the Potomac. When Wannas, tayac of the Piscataway and paramount leader of the Conoy chiefdom, told Calvert that "he would not bid him goe, neither would hee bid him stay, but that he might use his own discretion," the governor wisely chose not to "seate himselfe as yet so high in the River" (Hall 1925:72). That decision, important to both Marylanders and Piscataways, meant that English settlements would not encroach on the Conoy heartland for several decades (Merrell 1979:555).

St. Marys City was located in the territory of the Yaocomacos, a small group belonging to the Conoy chiefdom (see frontispiece). The werowance of the Yaocomacos apparently was pleased that the Maryland English chose to settle within and adjacent to his village, since he and his people were being hounded to death by the Susquehannocks. Indeed, the harassment was so great, the Yaocomacos "had the yeere before our arrivall there, made a resolution, for their safety, to remove themselves higher into the Countrey where it was more populous, and many of them were gone thither before the English arrived" (Hall 1925:74).

Claiborne, upset with the Calverts for trying to take over his trade and Virginia's territory, rallied Susquehannock trappers and Virginia allies to his side. Governor Calvert, acutely aware of his colony's vulnerability, sought a commercial and military alliance with the Conoys. With no love lost on either the Susquehannocks or the Virginia English, the Conoys realized the potential danger of their own situation and readily agreed to a pact with the Marylanders (Fausz 1984:9–10).

The Maryland-Conoy alliance was further strengthened by the death of the tayac, Wannas, at the hands of his brother, Kittamaquund, in 1636. Upon assuming the paramount chieftaincy, Kittamaquund initiated a period of greater interaction between his people and the Maryland English. Kittamaquund's policies were stimulated, in part, by his own need for English protection from those Piscataways who never forgave him for murdering his brother. By befriending the Jesuits, promoting their missions, and personally accepting Catholicism, Kittamaquund set an example that was followed by the baptism of some 130 Indians. In the process, the Jesuits were gathering not only the natives' souls but their lands, which they received as gifts from Indian converts. Of even greater importance, shortly before his death Kittamaquund gave Maryland authorities the right to choose his successors (Merrell 1979:556–57; Fausz 1988:75).

Most of Kittamaquund's efforts to speed his people's acceptance of European ways were short-lived, however. Four years after his death in 1641, the Jesuits left Maryland for a time. When priests returned in the 1650s, they were not as successful among the Indians as they had been while Kittamaquund was tayac. And, rather than appointing the tayacs, the provincial governors usually ended up merely approving candidates already chosen by members of the chiefdom (Merrell 1979:561–62).

At least two of Kittamaquund's actions did have long-term consequences for the Conoys. By assuming the position of tayac through fratricide and with no brother or nephew to succeed him, Kittamaquund disrupted the matrilineal succession to the chieftainship, an effect felt by the Conoys till at least 1666. Also, by giving provincial authorities the right to chose his successors, Kittamaquund in effect made the chiefdom tributary to the English colony, obliging them "to help fight Maryland's enemies, protect Maryland's frontiers, and build Maryland's forts" (Merrell 1979:559).

In 1637 the Susquehannocks' growing concern over a possible Maryland attack against Kent Island prompted them to give Palmer's Island, near the mouth of the Susquehanna River, to Claiborne. A second trading post, staffed by some of Claiborne's Kent Island veterans, was soon up and running, thanks to the assistance of Susquehannock warriors-turned-lumberjacks. All was for naught, though, and by the end of 1638 both Kent and Palmer's islands were under the Calverts' control (Fausz 1988:72–73). Counting on the profits to be gained from the Susquehannocks' prime beaver pelts, the Calverts did not anticipate the Susquehannocks' fierce loyalty to their old ally, Claiborne. Rather than trade with those who had fought against their friend, the Susquehannocks took their pelts, and the Calverts' hoped-for profits, overland to the Swedes at newly constructed Fort Christina on the site of present-day Wilmington, Delaware (see frontispiece; Fausz 1988:73). In addition, other European goods continued to flow to the Susquehannocks from Dutch factors operating in the lower Delaware Valley (Kraft 1986:198–99; Kent 1984:34–35).

In 1642, supplied by both the Swedes and Dutch, the Susquehannocks began ten years of warfare against the Maryland English and their Conoy allies (Fausz 1988:76). Also, in that year, John Mottrom, a merchant-planter formerly of St. Marys City, Maryland, but more recently from York County, Virginia, established the first permanent English settlement on the south side of the Potomac. Not far from the Coan River's L-shaped bend, Mottrom built Coan Hall on land he bartered from Machywap, werowance of the Chicacoans. The personal relationship between those two men served as the basis for generally peaceful interaction between Englishmen and Algonquians during the early years of English settlement in Chicacoan (Potter and Waselkov in press).

Farther south in Virginia, things were not so peaceful. Continued colonial expansion in the York and James river basins heightened intercultural tensions, triggering the third and final Anglo-Powhatan War. Repeating his earlier stratagem, Opechancanough and warriors from the remaining Algonquian groups of the James and York valleys launched a surprise attack against the Virginia English on the morning of April 18, 1644. This time there were too few Powhatans and too many English. Two years later the war was over, Opechancanough was dead, the centralized political power of the Powhatan chiefdom was destroyed, and all Virginia Algonquian groups were made tributary to the colonial government (Turner 1985:215–16; Rountree 1990: 84–88).

Meanwhile, back in Chicacoan, which the English eventually named Northumberland, a county government was functioning by at least 1645 (Hiden 1957:11–12; Hening 1823:294, 299). As the cost of the Third Anglo-Powhatan War rose, the Virginia Assembly suddenly realized there were colonists living in Northumberland who were not paying their share of the war levies. However, the English inhabitants of Northumberland were not about to pay taxes for an Indian war in which they were not involved. Their position was supported by William Claiborne's argument, made before the governor and council of Virginia, that the war should not be prosecuted against the Indians living in the Northern Neck, since they apparently did not participate in Opechancanough's attack (Potter 1976:40–41; McCartney 1985: 58; Rountree 1990:86–87).

Claiborne had returned to Virginia in 1643 from a five-year self-imposed exile in England. More determined than ever to regain the trade and territory lost to the Calverts, Claiborne found his task easier when he was restored to his seat on the Virginia council and, with the outbreak of the Third Anglo-Powhatan War, was appointed Virginia's first major general of militia (Fausz 1988:73–78). From such powerful positions, Claiborne fought Powhatans in Virginia and fostered the overthrow of fellow Englishmen in Maryland. As J. Frederick Fausz (1984:12) has observed, "while the Susquehannocks ravaged the colony, and the Civil War in England forced Calvert's allies from power, Claiborne used his trans-Atlantic Puritan contacts between 1642–52 to disrupt, discredit, infiltrate, and finally to replace the government of the Lord Proprietor in Maryland."

During depredations against Calvert's colonists and their Conoy allies, the Susquehannocks availed themselves of the opportunity to trounce other traditional Algonquian enemies. In 1648 they marched "into the Kings owne Colony of Virginia, have caried thence the King of Patowmeck prisoner, and expelled his and eight other Indian Nations in Maryland, civilized and subject to the English Crown" (Plowden 1648:19). The following year, the Susquehannocks' distant allies, the Hurons of the Great Lakes, were destroyed by the Senecas, one of the Five Nation Iroquois and enemies to the Susquehannocks. Two years later, the Mohawks, another member of the Five Nations, attacked the Susquehannocks but were unsuccessful. Fortunately for the Susquehannocks, the 1652 treaty with Claiborne's Puritan allies meant they could concentrate on fighting their linguistic relatives, the Iroquois. Unfortunately for the Marylanders and Conoys, being friends with the Susquehannocks meant they were enemies to the Iroquois, a fact that became more evident as the decade passed (Kent 1984:38; Jennings 1982:220–21).

The end of the Susquehannock Indian War in Maryland and the Third Anglo-Powhatan War in Virginia brought some stability to the two colonies, fostering further settlement. During the late 1640s and early 1650s, the English population along the lower Potomac and Rappahannock rivers grew, as evidenced by the proliferation of parishes and counties in Virginia and of administrative units, or "hundreds," in Maryland. Virginia's lower Northern Neck was quickly carved into four counties: added to Northumberland, ca. 1645, were Lancaster, 1651; Westmoreland, 1653; and old Rappahannock, 1656 (modern Richmond and Essex counties, see fig. 8; Hiden 1957:11–12, 14–15). On Maryland's side of the Potomac River, the number of hundreds and people living on them expanded sufficiently beyond the original county of St. Marys (1642) to warrant the formation of Charles County in 1658 (Kellock 1962:14; Carr et al. 1984:19).

Greater stability and increased settlement among the English caused further instability and displacement among the Algonquians. Although the Potomac River beaver trade continued on a small scale till the 1650s, the majority of the new colonists to the area came to raise tobacco, not to trade for pelts (Fausz 1988:70, 87). No longer were the Potomac River Algonquians a discreet distance from English plantations, as they were four decades earlier. Now the invaders were in their midst, and they were in the way.

The first group to feel the direct effect of English settlement in the Potomac Valley was the Yaocomacos. Unrelenting raids by the Susquehannocks and entreaties by Henry Fleet on Governor Calvert's behalf persuaded the werowance of Yaocomaco to welcome the first Maryland colonists into his village. Although the records suggest that the Yaocomacos were planning on moving upriver soon after the colonists came, some of the group seem to have stayed in the vicinity of St. Marys City until at least 1643 (Hall 1925:73–75). In that year, "on the two and twentieth day of this instant month of ffebruary, at an Indian quarter in the woods neare St. Georges creek in St. George's hundred," one John Elkin, planter, shot "a certaine Indian commonly called the king of Yowocomoco" in the throat (Arch. of Md.:4:176–77).

Within eight months, the Yaocomacos moved to the south side of the Potomac River (fig. 40), between the territories of the Chicacoans and the Matchotics (formerly the Onawmanients). The river they settled on bore their name (spelled variously as Yeokomico or Yokomoco) when adjacent lands were patented by Englishmen in October 1643 (Nugent 1934:149–50). They were still residing in that area in August 1652, when the governor and captain general of Maryland, William Stone, complained that the "Yoacomoco Indians and the Matchoatick and divers other Indians on the South Side of Potomake

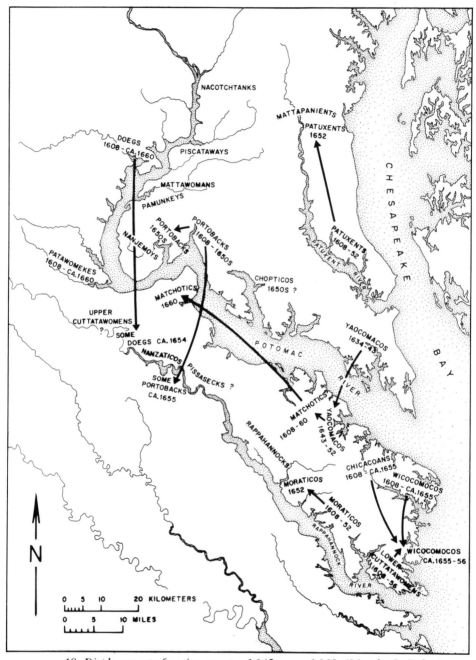

NACOTCHTANKS

MATTAPANIENTS

PATUXENTS
1652

DOEGS
1608 - CA.1660
PISCATAWAYS

CHESAPEAKE

MATTAWOMANS

PAMUNKEYS

PATUXENTS
1608 - 52

PORTOBACKS
1650S
PORTOBACKS
1608 - 1650S

NANJEMOYS

PATAWOMEKES
1608 - CA.1660

CHOPTICOS
1650S ?

POTOMAC

YAOCOMACOS
1634-43

MATCHOTICS
1660

UPPER
CUTTATAWOMENS
? SOME
DOEGS CA.1654

NANZATICOS
PISSASECKS ?

SOME
PORTOBACKS
CA.1655

RIVER

RAPPAHANNOCKS

MATCHOTICS
1608 - 60

YAOCOMACOS
1643 - 52

BAY

CHICACOANS
1608 - CA.1655
WICOCOMOCOS
1608 - CA.1655

MORATICOS
1652

MORATICOS
1608 - 52

RAPPAHANNOCK

LOWER
CUTTATAWOMENS
1608 - 56

WICOCOMOCOS
CA.1655 - 56

RIVER

N

0   5   10   20 KILOMETERS

0   5   10 MILES

40. *Displacement of native groups, 1643 to ca. 1660. (Map by G. Robert Lewis)*

River" were crossing over to hunt in Maryland (Arch. of Md.:3:281). Probably by 1652, the remnants of the Yaocomacos had taken refuge with the Matchotics. The year before, the werowance of the Matchotics sold a neck of land called Rhotancke to six Englishmen. The land purchased by the colonists was located between Yeocomico River and an unnamed creek to the west that bordered Matchotic Indian town (Potter 1976:44).

Although the early court documents contain numerous references to Indian werowances "selling" lands to Englishmen, it is doubtful if the Algonquians really understood the English system of land tenure. The concept of permanent land purchase was foreign to them. Unless the "purchased" lands were fenced in or were being farmed, the Indians assumed that the "unused" lands reverted back to their group's ownership, just as it did among themselves (Rountree 1990:128). As the years passed, the land base on which the Algonquians could fish, farm, hunt, and gather became ever smaller.

By the time the Virginia Grand Assembly met in November 1652, the situation was so critical that the burgesses passed the following act (Billings 1975:72):

> Whereas many Complaints have been brought to this Assemblye touchinge wrong done to the Indians in takeinge away theire lands, or fforceinge them into such narrow Streights, and places That they Cannot Subsist, Either by plantinge, or huntinge, And for that it may be feared, that thereby they may bee Justlye Driven to dispaire, and to Attempt some Desperate Course for themselves . . . [therefore, be it] Enacted that all the Indians of this collonye Shall, and may hold and keepe those seates of Land that they now have, And that noe person, or persons whatsoever be suffered to Intrench, or plant uppon Such places as the Indians Claime, or desire, untill full Leave from the governor, and Councell, or Commissioners of that place.

Earlier in the same year, the Grand Assembly passed an act requiring that 50 acres (20 ha) be set aside for every bowman among the tributary Indians and the sum total of land be surveyed for each Indian group (Billings 1975:68). Exercising their newly granted authority as a frontier county to treat directly with local Indians, the Northumberland County commissioners did more than simply oversee the surveying of the Indians' lands. They moved the Chicacoans and Wicocomocos southward, out of their former territories along the

Coan, Potomac, and Wicomico rivers—prime agricultural and waterfront land that was settled or coveted by the English. In the process the commissioners combined the two chiefdoms into one group. That done, they made Machywap, werowance of the Chicacoans and "so ancient and known a friend to our English Nation," leader of the combined group (Potter 1976:72). The more numerous Wicocomocos objected and threatened to kill Machywap. The county commissioners, in turn, threatened to treat those Wicocomocos who did not acknowledge Machywap's authority as "Enemies to our English Nation" (Potter 1976:46–47, 72). Ultimately, the Wicocomocos prevailed, and by 1659 Machywap was deposed. Thereafter, the combined group was known as the Wicocomocos.

According to John Gibbon, a visitor to the area in 1669–71, Machywap's successor was a Wicocomoco named Pekwem (also spelled Pewem), whom he called "the king of Wickicomoco" (Hiden and Dargan 1966:11). However, the Northumberland County commissioners evidently refused to recognize Pekwem as the werowance, since he is referred to in all the court records as simply one of "ye great men of the Wicocomoco Nation of Indians" (Potter 1976:75–77).

The tract of land surveyed for the eighty-eight Chicacoan and Wicocomoco bowmen and their families consisted of 4,400 acres (1,782 ha) lying on the south bank of Dividing Creek, between the Corrotoman River and Chesapeake Bay (see fig. 40). Although the act of 1652 guaranteed tributary Indians the rights to their lands, particularly those set aside for them, the legislation was ignored more often than it was enforced. No sooner were the Wicocomocos settled on their new reservation than they were in court complaining that two Englishmen had "intruded upon their Land—whereby they [the Wicocomocos] are made incapable of providing food for their livelihood" (Potter 1976:46, 50, 71, 75–76).

Ultimately, all the Algonquians living in the Potomac and Rappahannock valleys faced similar or worse experiences. It was just a matter of time, and the timing depended mainly upon the pace of English expansion along the waterfront, although intertribal and intercultural warfare affected it, too. As the English presence increased, so did the likelihood of Anglo-Algonquian conflict. Most often, disputes arose over property ownership, hunting and gathering rights, the theft or killing of livestock, and the despoiling of Indian cornfields and gardens by free-roaming English livestock (Cissna 1986:149; Merrell 1979:559–60; Waselkov 1983:20–27; Rountree 1990:92–94, 117–24).

Soon after patents were taken out along the north shore of the Rappahannock River, the lower Cuttatawomens moved from their homeland along the Corrotoman River to near Fleet's Bay, sometime between 1653 and 1656. Several years later they apparently moved again, this time to the north where they merged with the Wicocomocos (see fig. 40). By 1652 the Moraticos abandoned their early seventeenth-century territory for land around Totuskey Creek, farther up the Rappahannock River (Nugent 1934:186, 189, 289, 343; Rountree 1990:117, 122–23). Their next-door neighbors, the Rappahannocks, were constantly embroiled in disputes with land-hungry Englishmen through the 1650s. The most serious conflict occurred in 1654, when militia from Northumberland, Westmoreland, and Lancaster counties jointly converged on the Rappahannocks' town to "demand and receive such satisfaction . . . for the severall injuries done unto the said inhabitants [the English]" (Hening 1823:1:389–90). Even though the mandate from the Virginia Assembly stated that the militia was to resort to force only if attacked, the meeting between the militia and the Rappahannocks turned into a brawl, and Taweeren, the werowance of the Rappahannocks, was killed (Rountree 1990:118). The people of the Pissaseck, Nantaughtacund (anglicized to Nanzatico), and upper Cuttatawomen chiefdoms of 1608 probably were still living along the upper reaches of the tidal Rappahannock in the 1650s, when they appear to have consolidated into five newly named towns (Rountree 1990:119–20).

A combination of English encroachment on their lands and the murder of an Englishman by two of their men finally prompted the Matchotics to move farther up the south shore of the Potomac River in 1660. Although the Patawomekes were being harassed by English land speculators and settlers beginning in 1646 and had taken a beating from the Susquehannocks in 1648, they continued to live in their homeland during the 1650s. Their upriver neighbors, the Doegs (formerly the Tauxenents), were still living on what is now Mason Neck in Fairfax County, Virginia. By 1654, some of the Doegs may have moved to lands along the Rappahannock River (Potter 1976:47–50; Waselkov 1983:23–29; Rountree 1990:121–22; Nugent 1934:296; Moore 1991:79–80).

Across the Potomac River in Maryland, the first chiefdom to be supplanted was that of the Yaocomacos. As the number of English hundreds multiplied, some Indians sought protection among the Marylanders while most sought to distance themselves from the invaders. In 1651 the Chopticos, along with other displaced groups, asked for a land grant at the head of the Wicomico River (see fig. 40). Seven years later, the number of English settlers living west of the Wicomico increased to the point that Charles County was formed. Its seat was established at Port Tobacco, the site of the former Indian village located on the river of the same name. Pressured by English settlement in their eastern territory, some of the Potapacos or Portobacks apparently relocated to the Rappahannock River in the mid-1650s, while others moved onto their western lands adjacent to the Nanjemoys, where they were living in 1663 when the queen of Portoback complained about further English encroachment upon her people (Rountree 1990:119–20; Cissna 1986:147–49, 153–54, 157; Marye 1935:185; Feest 1978b:fig. 2). Most of the other groups of the Conoy chiefdom were still living in their original territories in the 1650s, even though some village locations had changed, with corresponding changes in village and, occasionally, group names.

Beyond recording trade relations, intercultural and intertribal disputes and warfare, English settlement, and Algonquian displacement, the historical documents pertaining to the Potomac Valley contain little information concerning the effects of these actions on other aspects of Algonquian culture. It was mainly during the earliest phases of English colonization in Virginia and Maryland that some of the invaders bothered to write about bits and pieces of Algonquian culture, often as a means of educating their supporters in the mother country, extolling their own exploits, or enticing other Englishmen to cross the Atlantic. When the Algonquians ceased to be economically or militarily useful to the English, and the salvation of their souls was no longer a priority, fewer accounts about specific Indian groups and their way of life were written. Additional insights can be gained, however, when the archaeology and ethnohistory are examined.

The Archaeology and Ethnohistory, 1608–50s

CONTACT PERIOD SITES AND ASSEMBLAGES

As a consequence of the sixteenth- and seventeenth-century European accounts describing trade with Indians in Chesapeake Bay, some archaeologists have assumed that Native American sites containing European trade goods would be relatively common. Yet nothing could be further from the truth. Why is this so?

While a certain number of contact period sites undoubtedly have been lost to natural and cultural forces, Herbert Kraft (1989:22–23) came closer to addressing the issue when he suggested that larger, more centralized native polities may have enjoyed a competitive edge in the fur trade over smaller, more egalitarian ones, or that intertribal warfare intimidated or eliminated some native groups from competing in the fur trade. In order to identify contact-period Indian sites it is necessary to identify the factors which influenced the cultural context of trade. The motivations and interrelationships of the competing European nation-states, the nature, purpose, magnitude, and frequency of trade, native belief systems, aboriginal social and political structures, native intergroup relations, and accessibility—access to sources of furs, to European trade outlets, and to sources of European trade goods within native societies themselves—affected the cultural context of trade and, ultimately, the archaeological context and visibility (Custer and Potter 1988).

Equally important are the archaeological and historical criteria for recognizing contact-period sites. Archaeologists in the Chesapeake Bay region often attempt to correlate Native American sites with the historical locations of specific Indian villages mentioned in documents or oral traditions. "If an archaeological site and an historical location are to be proven to be one and the same," Bruce Trigger (1969:306) has cautioned, "they must conform with each other in as great detail as possible in date, geographical location and layout." Many times, though, the archaeological data and historical documentation are inadequate to meet all those criteria. On the other hand, there were many archaeological sites created by Native Americans during the contact period for which no specific references exist in historical records or oral traditions.

Regardless of whether documentation exists or not, archaeologists usually require that an undisputed contextual association must exist between native- and European-made artifacts in order for an archaeological site to be assigned to the contact period (Kraft 1989:20–23; MacCord 1989:123; Custer 1984:178; Trigger 1969:314). As Larry Moore (1990b:1–2) has pointed out, however, European-derived cultural traits are also evidence of European contact (as are European pathogens and plant remains). For example, if several gunflints flaked from native stone using an aboriginal technique were found with other native-made objects in a suspected seventeenth-century context, it would be reasonable to infer that this is a contact-period component even though no European trade goods were associated with them. Clearly, any products that were native-made of native materials but were inspired by or made for use with European-made items are equally indicative of European contact.

In all probability, archaeological myopia, not a lack of sites, has hindered contact-period research. "Given the processes of European fur trade that would have affected native American populations in Delaware" Jay Custer (1984:178) commented, "perhaps the criteria for recognizing European Contact sites should be reevaluated." Thomas Davidson and others (1985:48) have noted that the "persistence of indigenous material culture traditions on Maryland's Eastern Shore probably explains why so few Contact period sites have been identified there. In many cases Contact period sites probably have been classed as late prehistoric because they did not show any obvious evidence of European influence." That statement is also applicable to the situation in the lower Potomac Valley.

Components of the Rappahannock complex. Since 1978 several small contact-period components representing hunting or gathering camps have been excavated in the tidal Potomac. The first of these sites is Blue Fish Beach (44NB147). This shell midden, located along the Potomac River in Northumberland County, Virginia, is a place where a small group of Chicacoans gathered and ate oysters, soft-shell clams, and other shellfish during the first half of the seventeenth century. Two radiocarbon dates of A.D. 1605 ± 70 and A.D. 1645 ± 70 and the presence of European objects confirm the period of occupancy. The European artifacts and materials include a fragment of an iron knife blade, two white clay pipestems, and a wasted core and flake of English flint. Most of the aboriginal artifacts are sherds of Yeocomico Plain pottery from a minimum of seven vessels, consisting of small to medium-size bowls or, in one case, a cup (Potter 1982:204–44).

Another contact-period shellfish-gathering campsite was excavated at the White Oak Point site (44WM119) on Nomini Bay, Westmoreland County, Virginia, in the former territory of the Nomini or Matchotic Indians (Waselkov 1982a:200–208, 252–54, 288–89). Four radiocarbon dates from this component yielded a mean date of A.D. 1590 ± 80. The only European trade item found in the component was a small white glass bead (Kidd variety IIa12; see Kidd and Kidd 1970) associated with a partial burial. Among the aboriginal artifacts recovered (fig. 41) were sherds from eight Yeocomico Plain and two Townsend Corded pottery vessels; a complete obtuse-angle clay smoking pipe; stem and bowl fragments from three other clay pipes, including one stem with a triangular cross section and one bowl with a rocker-stamped dentate decoration; one shell disk bead; two bird-bone beads; several antler-tine projectile points, bone pins, and awls; and one quartz triangular point with serrated edges. Analysis of the vertebrate and invertebrate faunal remains revealed a drop in the spe-

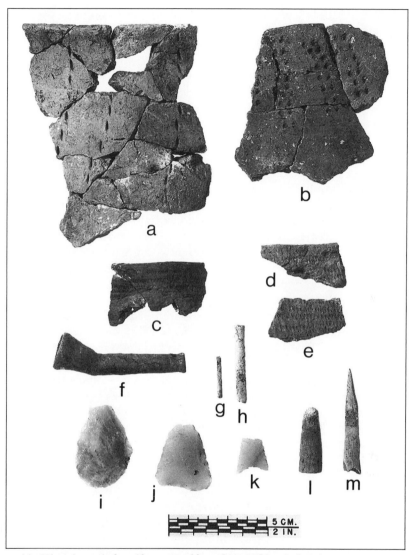

41. Historic-period artifact assemblage from White Oak Point (44WM119): a, b, *Yeocomico Plain rimsherds with punctate decorations;* c–e, *Townsend Corded pottery;* f, *complete clay smoking pipe;* g, h, *bird-bone beads;* i, *ovoid quartz biface;* j, *triangular quartz blank;* k, *serrated quartz triangular point;* l, *socketed antler-tine projectile point;* m, *bone awl. (Photograph by Victor E. Krantz)*

cies diversity index and an increase in the number of oysters per unit of midden, confirming that this was a specialized oyster-collecting camp probably occupied during April and May.

In marked contrast to the seasonal shellfish-gathering camps is Boathouse Pond (44NB111), on the Coan River in Northumberland County, Virginia (see fig. 14). Historical records and archaeological survey data indicate that this is the probable location of the seventeenth-century werowance's village of Chicacoan, shown on John Smith's map as "Cekakawwon." The protohistoric/historic village midden is quite extensive, covering 4.45 hectares (11 a), suggesting that the houses were spread over a wide area. Indeed, some of the Chicacoans may have lived at other sites surrounding the cove called Boathouse Pond, such as site 44NB97, where a surface survey resulted in the collection of a blue glass bead (Kidd variety IIa40) and late prehistoric through early historic aboriginal artifacts. Native-made objects from the Boathouse Pond site that occur with greater frequency after A.D. 1500 include Yeocomico Plain pottery (the dominant type), Rappahannock Incised pottery with reed punctations, Potomac Creek Plain pottery, and clay smoking pipes with dentate geometric designs. Other aboriginal items probably associated with this component are simple geometric-incised Rappahannock Fabric-impressed pottery, Levanna Small Triangular points, and pecked and ground stone celts. Five items of European origin were found during surface-collecting on the densest area of the site—two white clay pipestems with large bore diameters, a rimsherd of Rhenish brown stoneware, the handle to a brown-glazed earthenware vessel, and a spall of English flint. Even though these artifacts came from the plow zone, they might have been used during the historic Indian occupancy of the site (Potter 1982:245–70). Similar European objects were found in association with aboriginal artifacts at other contact-period sites mentioned in this section.

Across the Potomac River from the Boathouse Pond site, at historic St. Marys City, Maryland, intensive test excavations in 1981 uncovered evidence of a late prehistoric and early historic Indian hamlet associated with the seventeenth-century werowance's village of Yaocomaco. The artifacts found during the archaeological investigations consist of both Levanna Large and Small Triangular points and a variety of ceramics. Like the Boathouse Pond site, Yeocomico Plain and Rappahannock Fabric-impressed pottery dominate the ceramic assemblage, with smaller amounts of Rappahannock Incised, Townsend Herringbone, Potomac Creek Plain, and Potomac Creek Cord-impressed pottery. The ceramics were found in three discrete clusters spaced approximately 24 meters (80 ft) apart, suggesting "that these clusters represent the locations of aboriginal houses, or at least, the cooking fires associated with buildings, around which the pottery would have been used" (Miller 1983:32). It is also possible that one of the proposed house sites may have been occupied by the English during the first months of Governor Leonard Calvert's settlement. "In the same area as the most westerly sherd concentration," observed Henry Miller (1983:35), "the excavation squares also yielded a blue glass bead, Indian-made terra cotta pipe fragments, a few wrought nails, and several sherds of early 17th-century European pottery. . . . It is known from the surviving historical records that the colonists used these buildings, and the first Roman Catholic chapel in Maryland was established in one of these Indian houses."

For comparative purposes, it is worthwhile to examine another Rappahannock complex village site of the contact period; this one is located near the confluence of Lamb's Creek and the Rappahannock River in King George County, Virginia. Named the De Shazo site (44KG3), it was probably the seventeenth-century werowance's village of upper Cuttatawomen, also shown on Smith's map of 1612 (see figs. 1 and 27). Excavations there in 1964 and 1973 by members of the Archeological Society of Virginia confirmed the contact-period attribution. Charcoal from a shallow refuse pit yielded a radiocarbon determination of A.D. 1590 ± 120. In the pit fill was an English gunflint, a wrought-iron nail, a white clay pipe fragment, and a rolled copper strip, along with seventeen sherds of Rappahannock Fabric-impressed pottery, one sherd of Potomac Creek Plain pottery, lithic debris, and vertebrate and invertebrate faunal remains. Another pit contained an English gunflint, fifteen wrought-iron nails, four white clay pipe bowls, a sherd of container glass, forty-nine Rappahannock Fabric-impressed sherds, several sherds of plain, sand-tempered ware, and faunal and plant food remains (MacCord 1965:98–104). The two gunflints from this site are made from the same type of English flint as the wasted core and flake from the contact-period component at Bluefish Beach. Of additional interest are two other features discovered during the 1973 excavations. One was an infant shroud burial with four shroud pins around the skull and two shroud pins in the area where the infant's feet would have been. The other feature was a rectangular house pattern approximately 2.7 meters (9 ft) wide and 7.3 meters (24 ft) long. Fill from the wall trench of the house contained sherds of Rappahannock Incised and one sherd of Potomac Creek Cord-marked pottery (VDHR Archaeological Inventory Archives, Richmond).

Components of the Potomac Creek complex. In the freshes of the tidal Potomac, in the area inhabited historically by the Tauxenent or Doeg Indians, a contact-period component was discovered at the Little Marsh Creek site (44FX1471; see fig. 27) on Mason Neck, Fairfax County, Virginia (Moore 1990a). Three native-made gunflints, including one from European flint, were found (fig. 42). Two are chip flints, and the other is a bifacial gunflint. Other artifacts probably associated with this component are one quartz Levanna Small Triangular point,

42. *Native-made gunflints and triangular projectile points from Little Marsh Creek (44FX1471):* a, *bifacial gunflint of local chert;* b, *chip flint of local chert;* c, *chip flint of European flint;* d–f, *crudely made triangular points;* g, *Levanna Small Triangular point. (Photograph by Victor E. Krantz)*

three crudely made triangular points, and Potomac Creek Plain sherds from a minimum of four vessels. The gunflints suggest an occupation dating to the second quarter of the seventeenth century, even though charcoal from a feature yielded a radiocarbon determination of A.D. 1520 ± 90 (Moore 1990a:26–30, 35, 1990b:8). It was not possible to determine conclusively whether the contact-period component resulted from a short-term occupancy or whether it was part of a larger site that has eroded into Occoquan Bay.

Across the Potomac River in Charles County, Maryland, near Mattawoman Creek, test excavations were conducted in 1985 at the Posey site (18CH281; see fig. 27), a small contact-period village or hamlet (Barse 1985:146–59). Because the site is located in an area that was occupied by several different groups of the Conoy chiefdom during the seventeenth century, identification of the precise group is not possible. A small quantity of European trade materials were recovered during the investigation. Included among these objects are wrought nails, bottle glass and ceramic sherds, stem and bowl fragments from white clay smoking pipes, two small brass buttons, and several fragments of unidentifiable iron artifacts. Five metal arrowpoints and one point tip were found (fig. 43); two triangular and one conical point are made from brass, and one triangular and one conical point are made from iron. A single quartz Levanna Small Triangular point was found, along with a small scraper made from European flint. Other artifacts in the collection are flakes from European flint and local stones, a bone tool, one columella and three shell disk beads, and fragments or sherds of native-made pipes and pottery vessels. The fifty pipe fragments include a stem with a triangular cross section similar to the one from the contact component at the White Oak Point site; a pipe bowl bearing a floral motif; two other bowl fragments with white-infilled circular reed punctations; and another pipe bowl decorated with dentate geometric designs. Potomac Creek Plain is the dominant ware in the ceramic assemblage, followed by Yeocomico Plain, Camden Plain, and Potomac Creek Cord-marked pottery. Faunal and floral remains (including a possible carbonized maize fragment), a small refuse pit, and sixteen postmolds were also discovered during the test excavations. The artifact assemblage and a radiocarbon date of 1575 ± 90 (Boyce and Frye 1986:10) indicate that the hamlet probably was occupied sometime during the period A.D. 1600 to 1660.

The Potomac Creek (44ST2) and Indian Point (44ST1) sites in Stafford County, Virginia (see fig. 27), represent the consecutive sites of the protohistoric and historic period werowances' villages of the Pa-

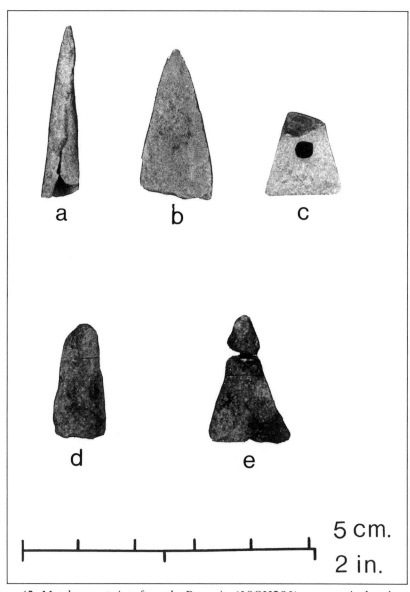

43. Metal arrowpoints from the Posey site (18CH281): a–c, *conical and triangular points of brass;* d, e, *conical and triangular points of iron. (Courtesy of the Maryland Historical Trust, a program of the Maryland Department of Housing and Community Development)*

tawomeke Indians. Reaching its maximum extent about A.D. 1600, the Potomac Creek site housed the Patawomeke elite within the 0.81 hectare (2 a) encircled by its double-palisaded walls. No in situ European trade goods are recorded from any aboriginal features within the palisade lines. The European-made artifacts that were found came from the multiple burial near the northeast palisade lines and an ossuary located 21 meters (70 ft) outside the palisades. Probably by 1608, the former inhabitants of the Potomac Creek site were living in a new village constructed a short distance away at Indian Point (Stewart 1988:3, 136–38; MacCord 1991:135–39).

The large, palisaded village at the Accokeek Creek site (18PR8; see fig. 27) in Prince Georges County, Maryland, is similar to the Potomac Creek site in several respects. It, too, is protohistoric. In all of Alice Ferguson's extensive excavations at the village she thought was seventeenth-century Moyaone, not a single European-made artifact was recorded from any of the aboriginal features (Stephenson et al. 1963:199). And, like Potomac Creek, the last palisades constructed around the 1.62-hectare (4-a) village, sometime in the latter part of the sixteenth century, were double ones. Most likely, too, the majority of the people living within the village walls were the protohistoric Piscataway tayacs, their families and kinfolk, elite supporters, and the priests.

On the other side of Accokeek Creek from the large palisaded village, archaeological test excavations during 1983–84 revealed a site (18PR248; see fig. 27) with a contact-period component. The majority pottery type is Potomac Creek Plain, followed by lesser amounts of Potomac Creek Cord-impressed, Camden Plain (classified by the original investigators as Colono ware), and one sherd of Moyaone ware. Other artifacts probably associated with the contact component include two bowl fragments from Indian-made clay smoking pipes; one large and three small Levanna points; a copper fragment; twenty-three medium-sized drawn round glass beads (nineteen black, Kidd variety IIa6; three red with black cores, Kidd variety IVa1; and one untyped red bead with three green stripes); nineteen white clay tobacco pipe fragments; and two gunflints. Two postmolds were also uncovered. Most likely, the contact-period component represents the debris deposited by the occupants of one or several seventeenth-century Piscataway houses (Vrabel and Cissna n.d.).

Discussion and summary. Although the sample of contact-period camps and villages is small and the temporal contexts are not very tight, nonetheless some observations are worth noting. For example, some of the principal villages persisted in the same locales for long periods of time. Long-lived palisaded villages like Potomac Creek and Accokeek Creek probably did not house the entire population of their respective groups. It was mainly the werowance or tayac, their families and relatives, and other elite supporters who lived within the palisade walls. The majority of the common people lived in outlying hamlets that provided the tribute—including corn—necessary to support the werowance and other elite. Since the werowance's village served as the collection point for paying tribute, a palisaded town where the werowance and elite supporters resided would not have to be totally dependent upon its own agricultural fields. For that reason, werowances' palisaded villages probably did not move often, particularly where agricultural land was limited, as on Potomac Creek. They were enabled to stay where they were because of tribute from the hamlets, which probably did move frequently.

At other towns that most likely served as the werowance's residence, such as the Chicacoan village at Boathouse Pond, village movement, if it can be called that, was a slow process because the houses were not clustered but were internally dispersed within the large area encompassed by the village. By dispersing the houses, factors that might cause one or several households to move (e.g., pests, depleted wood supplies, weeds in the gardens, or soil exhaustion) would not require the movement of the entire village. Indeed, evidence from around the Coan River suggests that some Algonquian villages "moved" about within the same favored locale for over a century. On Maryland's Eastern Shore, Chicone, the principal seat of the Nanticoke emperor, was located on the same tract of land from its earliest documentation in 1608 till at least 1758 (Davidson et al. 1985:44).

As for material culture, certain classes of native-made objects persisted even though European analogues existed. European ceramic containers are not conspicuous on Algonquian villages occupied during the first half of the seventeenth century because there was no reason to use them in lieu of native-made pottery vessels; aboriginal ceramic containers met the Algonquians' cultural needs. As Gregory Waselkov and Eli Paul (1981:312) have observed, "Native groups responded in terms of their own cultural backgrounds, substituting new for old within the framework of their own social, economic, and subsistence systems."After about 1650, however, as some native peoples of the Potomac and Rappahannock valleys began adopting European ways and a nonnative market developed for the barter of their wares, Algonquian potters began to change their pottery to accommodate European ceramic forms and functions.

Copper or brass kettles are not likely to be highly visible in the archaeological record of the tidewater Potomac, at least not in their original form, since the natives probably cut up most of them. The status value that southern Algonquians placed on copper during the early years of contact made copper and brass kettles far more valuable to them as sources of raw material to be converted into gorgets and other social badges of rank and prestige than as cooking utensils. Later, as copper and brass items became more plentiful, devaluing them as a source of status and prestige, the brass kettles continued to serve as sources of raw material for the manufacture of arrowpoints similar to those found at the Posey site, until the bow and arrow gave way to the acquisition and use of European firearms.

The first account of European firearms coming into the hands of Potomac River Algonquians dates to 1622, when the Nacotchtanks captured many "peeses, Armour, [and] sworde, all things fitt for Warre," after wiping out most of Henry Spelman's trading party (Kingsbury 1935:4:61). Most likely, the majority of the "peeses" captured by the Nacotchtanks were self-striking flintlocks. In 1624–25 an inventory of all the firearms among the 1,029 settlers of the Virginia colony revealed six carbines, fifty-five pistols, 981 "peeces fixit" (which included flintlocks with combined battery and pan cover, as well as snaphances), and only forty-seven matchlocks (Brown 1980:84).

Even though English authorities and colonial governments attempted to restrict the sale of guns to the Indians, the lure of profits caused some traders to ignore the restrictions (Waselkov 1983:20; Fausz 1979:45). European firearms, illegal or not, contributed to the loss of native flint-knapping skills. This is graphically illustrated by artifacts from the seventeenth-century Doeg Indian component at the Little Marsh Creek site, where three crudely made triangular points and three native-made gunflints were found (see fig. 42).

The archaeological visibility of European objects and traits at hunting and gathering camps and other short-term, specialized sites occupied by small groups of people will be low. Most of these sites may not contain anything of European origin, even if they were occupied during the contact period. At the White Oak Point site, only the sheer luck of finding a single small, white glass bead in an oyster-shell midden confirmed the contact-period attribution strongly suggested by the four radiocarbon dates and Yeocomico pottery. When present, European artifacts and traits usually will be limited to easily portable, utilitarian items, such as knives and hunting implements, or raw material, like European flint, picked up through the opportunistic collecting of discarded ship's ballast. There will be few personal effects.

In the middens and refuse pits of hamlets and villages, the quantity and variety of European-made objects or traits will be greater than at special purpose, short-term sites, but their occurrence in the archaeological record will be limited to a small percentage of the total site assemblage. Utilitarian items continue to dominate the assemblage of European goods, although there will be more personal effects than at campsites. Recalling William Strachey's (1953:115) observation concerning the Virginia Algonquians' use of storage pits, personally valued items like iron axes and hoes were probably cached away from their houses until needed. Not only were "most things with them of value . . . [hidden] in the ground within the woods," they were also carried to the grave (Strachey 1953:115). And, indeed, it is in Algonquian burial sites that most of the European trade goods from the Potomac Valley were found.

TRADE, STATUS, AND BURIALS

With the beginnings of European contact and trade in the Chesapeake Bay, the Algonquian elite sought to control the flow of European trade material into their society, much as they controlled the flow of prestige goods gathered through tribute from their own people. Nowhere in the archaeological record of the tidewater Potomac is this more evident than in contact-period Algonquian burial sites, particularly ossuaries—the saucer-shaped pits containing the reburied remains of ten to over six hundred people (Jirikowic 1990:358–59). Even though many of the burial sites were excavated in the nineteenth through mid-twentieth centuries by antiquarians or avocational archaeologists who did not systematically excavate and record their findings, the information they did gather gives greater insight into certain aspects of seventeenth-century Algonquian life than historical documents alone.

Not surprisingly, there is no known seventeenth-century description of ossuary burial. Only a few "ethnographic gleanings" provide indirect evidence "that the practice of bone cleaning and ossuary burial did occur" (Ubelaker 1974:10–11). This should be expected, since Europeans probably were not allowed to observe the ossuary burial ceremony or any of the ritual associated with it.

Historical accounts do describe other forms of burial for commoners. John Smith (1986b:169) wrote that "for their ordinary burials they digge a deep hole in the earth with sharpe stakes and the corpes being lapped in skins and mats with their jewels, they lay them upon sticks in the ground, and so cover them with earth." Because corpses are mentioned, Smith's description probably is of primary interments. Henry Spelman (1910:cx), drawing on his experience living with the

Patawomekes, described a form of secondary burial for commoners. The body of the deceased was placed on a scaffold and when "nothing is left but bonns [bones] they take thos bonns from ye scaffould and puttinge them into a new matt, hangs them in ther howses" until the houses were abandoned "and then they are buried in the ruinges of ye house." Perhaps what Smith and Strachey described were the early stages in a mortuary process that culminated in ossuary burial.

Werowances, too, may have gone through a process of primary and secondary burial. A 1622 letter from the council in Virginia to the Virginia Company of London (Kingsbury 1935:4:10), refers to "the takinge upp of Powhatans bones at which Ceremony great numbers of the Salvages were to be assembled." This event took place in 1621, three years after Powhatan's death, and may indicate the customary passage of time between the primary and secondary burial of the elite. However, since Powhatan was the paramount chief, or mamanatowick, this ceremony may have been peculiar to individuals of his rank and may not pertain to mortuary practices associated with district or lesser chiefs.

The reference to the "takinge upp of Powhatans bones" notwithstanding, the remains of all werowances were eventually interred in a mortuary temple (fig. 44). Strachey (1953:94) gave a detailed account of the treatment of deceased werowances:

Within the Chauncell of the Temple by the Okeus [image of a god] are the Centaphies or the monuments of their kings, whose bodyes so soone as they be dead, they embowell, and scraping the flesh from the bones, they dry the same upon hurdells into asshes, which they put into little potts (like the ancyent urnes) the Annotamye of the bones they bynd togither, or case up in Leather, hanging braceletts or Chaynes of Copper, beades, pearle, and such like, as they used to weare about most of their Joynts and neck, and so repose the body upon a little Scaffold (as upon a tomb) laying by the dead bodyes feet all his ritches in severall basketts. . . . Their Inwards they stuff with perle, Copper, beades, and such Trash sowed in a skynne, which they overlappe very Carefully in white skynnes one or twoe, and the bodyes thus dressed, lastly they rowle in mattes, as for the wynding sheetes and so lay them orderly one by one, as they dye in their turnes.

Other contemporary accounts by John Smith (1986b:169) and George Percy (1922:263) corroborate Strachey's description.

The physical separation of the deceased remains of the werow-

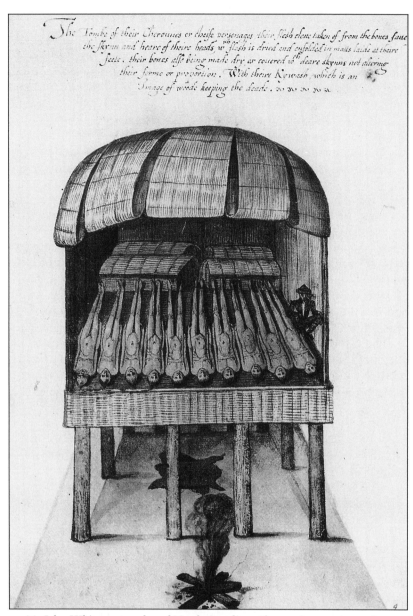

44. John White watercolor of North Carolina Algonquian mortuary for werowances, 1585. Similar structures were built by the Potomac River Algonquians to house the preserved remains of deceased werowances. (Photograph by Victor E. Krantz; reproduced by permission of the University of North Carolina Press and the British Museum)

ances from those of the commoners was reinforced by the Algonquian beliefs about an afterlife (Rountree 1989:138–39). John Smith (1986b:172) wrote that "they thinke that their Werowances and Priestes which they also esteeme Quiyoughcosughes [gods] when they are dead, doe goe beyound the mountaines towardes the setting of the sun, and ever remaine there in forme of their Oke [a god], with their heads painted with oile and Pocones, finely trimmed with feathers, and shal have beades, hatchets, copper, and tobacco, doing nothing but dance and sing, with all their Predecessors. But the common people they suppose shall not live after death." Regardless of whether this was an upper-class ideology (Feest 1978a:262) or one shared by all the people (Rountree 1989:138–39), it is unlikely that werowances were interred with commoners. Constance Crosby (1988:192), paraphrasing Emile Durkheim's famous dictum, has noted, "People invent their Gods and their cosmology in society's own image." A cosmology that admitted only werowances and priests into an Algonquian paradise would not have permitted them to be placed in communal burial pits with commoners.

The stark social differences between elite and commoners did, indeed, follow them to the grave. In 1869 four antiquarians discovered a contact-period, high-status Algonquian burial—the only one recorded from the Potomac Valley (Potter 1989:162–64). Although the information pertaining to the site is sketchy, enough data exist for an adequate interpretation. The multiple burial, located on Potomac Neck, Virginia, near a historic Patawomeke village site (44ST1) at Indian Point, contained the primary, extended inhumations of twelve adults. Native-made shell beads were found around eleven of the skeletons. About the twelfth skeleton (fig. 45), however, was an amazing array of artifacts: five shell mask gorgets with stylized human faces in bas-relief (figs. 46 and 47); five circular shell gorgets; six circular and six quadrangular copper gorgets (fig. 48); four small whelk shells; a native-made earthenware bowl; about four quarts of beads made of rolled sheet copper, shell, bone, and clay; fifteen drawn round beads of blue glass; two flushloop brass bells; and "a cross of white metal of rude construction . . . found in an erect position, sustained by the earth, between the thumb and forefinger of the skeleton" (Reynolds 1881:93). The glass beads and brass bells are typical of the early seventeenth century; along with the *Busycon* mask gorgets, they indicate the interment probably occurred sometime between 1608 and 1630 (Potter 1989:162; Smith and Smith 1989:9).

It has been suggested that the cross found with the twelfth skeleton

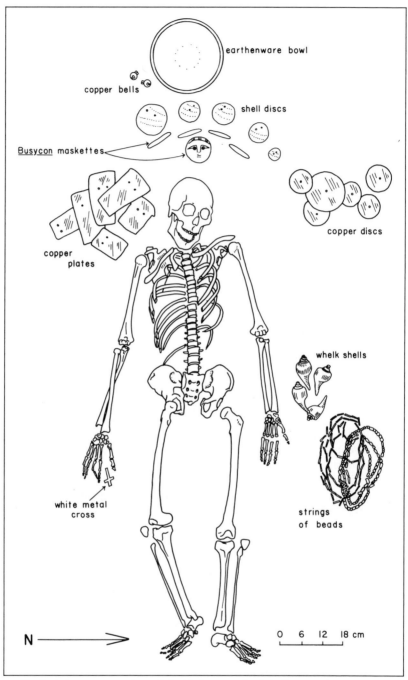

45. Artist's reconstruction of the high-status burial discovered at Potomac Neck, Stafford County, Va. (Illustration by Ellen M. Paige; reproduced by permission of the University of Nebraska Press)

46. Shell maskette with stylized human face from high-status burial,
Potomac Neck, Stafford County, Va. Dimensions: 12.7 × 14.0 cm
(5.0 × 5.5 in). (Courtesy of the Smithsonian Institution)

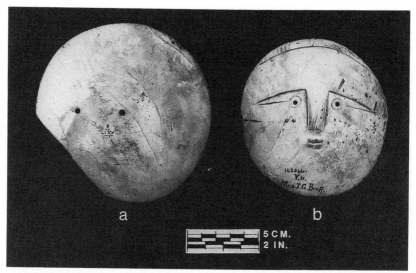

47. Plain, circular shell gorget (a) and circular shell maskette with stylized human face (b) from high-status burial, Potomac Neck, Stafford County, Va. (Courtesy of the Smithsonian Institution)

was distributed by Father Andrew White, a Jesuit priest who visited Patawomeke in 1642 (MacCord 1991:127–28). However, Father White would have given the Patawomekes crucifixes, not crosses, in his attempt to convert them to Catholicism. In 1609, several decades before Father White's visit, the Virginia Company of London instructed the Anglican settlers of Jamestown to "endeavour the conversion of the natives to the true god and their redeemer Christ Jesus, as the most pious and noble end of the plantacion" (Kingsbury 1933:3:14). Even before this pronouncement, Jamestown colonists were erecting wooden crosses, carving crosses in trees, and leaving brass crosses behind as they traveled throughout tidewater Virginia and Chesapeake Bay (Percy 1967:10, 20; Smith 1986c:175). In particular, several of the men who accompanied John Smith during the explorations of the Chesapeake noted that "in all those places and the furthest we came up the rivers [including the Potomac], we cut in trees so many crosses as we would, and in many places made holes in trees, wherein we writ notes and in some places crosses of brasse, to signife to any, Englishmen had beene there" (Smith 1986c:172).

Ethnohistorical accounts confirm that large copper plates or gorgets like those found in this burial were reserved for the Algonquian

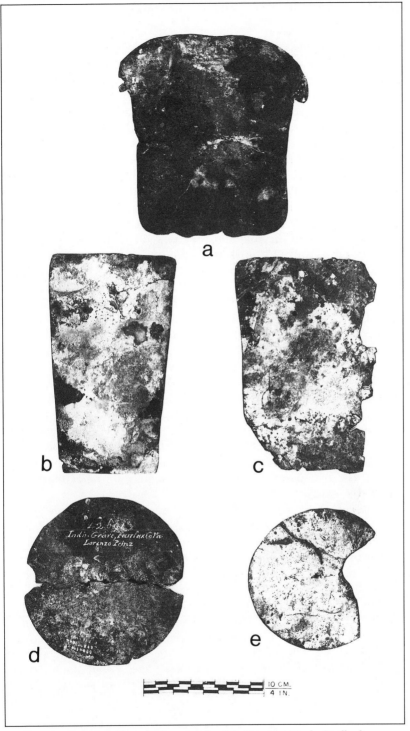

48. Copper gorgets from high-status burial, Potomac Neck, Stafford County, Va. (Courtesy of the Smithsonian Institution)

elite. The copper gorgets and other prestige items accompanying the twelfth individual served as signs or badges of rank in life and continued to do so in death, so that the person could arrive in the afterlife materially and socially prepared (see Brenner 1988:152). A recent study of engraved shell masks suggests that the iconography recalls specific "widespread southeastern Indian myths of the Thunderbird or other similar being, while the masks functioned to gain the supernatural power of this creature for prowess in hunting and warfare" (Smith and Smith 1989:16). Another possibility is that the engraved shell masks from Potomac Neck were tokens of social relationships between high-status individuals engaged in long-distance exchange (see Binford 1983:228). Both interpretations are consistent with ethnohistorical accounts of the role and function of werowances within early seventeenth-century Virginia Algonquian society.

Not far from Indian Point, avocational archaeologists excavating at the Potomac Creek site (44ST2) in 1936 unearthed an ossuary (Ossuary I) about 21 meters (70 ft) beyond the outermost palisade line (see fig. 32). The large oval pit, measuring 11.4 meters (37.5 ft) long, 4.6 meters (15 ft) wide, and 1.5 meters (5 ft) deep, contained the secondary remains of at least 181 individuals of all ages and both sexes. Native-made objects from the ossuary included shell gorgets, clay smoking pipes, and thousands of shell beads, often associated with children's remains. Copper, usually in the form of small, tubular beads, was found with twenty-eight individuals. Less than eighty drawn round beads, mostly of varying hues of blue glass, were recovered from six burials. Other European objects included a pair of scissors and a couple of small flushloop brass bells. Like the high-status burial, the ossuary probably dates between 1608 and 1630 (Potter 1989:164–65).

The two early seventeenth-century burial sites from Potomac Neck not only reflect the social distinctions that separated the elite from the common people in death, as in life; they also reflect the power and authority of the werowances, their kinfolk, and other elite supporters. Possession of status markers and other prestige goods by the elite is exemplified by the type and quantity of objects associated with the twelfth skeleton in the multiple burial, such as the twelve large copper gorgets. In contrast, few status or European items were found in the ossuary burial of 181 commoners. Similar conditions existed at a smaller ossuary (18CH95, Ossuary IV; see fig. 27), probably contemporaneous with the one at Potomac Neck, discovered along the Port Tobacco River in Maryland (Graham 1935:28–33). During this time the authority of the elite was still implicit in the relatively restricted flow of European trade material and prestige goods to society at large, before the beginning of the Chesapeake beaver trade around 1630.

With an increase in trade brought about by the change from maize to furs, European trade material poured into the Potomac-Chesapeake tidewater. The effects of this influx, both subtle and obvious, can be seen at several burial sites dating around 1630 to 1660, especially at one on Potomac Neck. In the fall and winter of 1935, the same avocational archaeologists who dug the ossuary near the Potomac Creek site excavated another aboriginal burial feature in the vicinity. This one was a much smaller pit, 76.2 centimeters (2.5 ft) deep and about 1.8–2.4 meters (6–8 ft) in diameter, containing the individual primary burials of at least ten children and adults. It is possible that some of the deceased were buried at different times, but the excavation records are not detailed enough to verify this (Stewart 1988:6). Some of the artifacts found in the group burial are a small whelk shell, large quantities of native-made disk and columella shell beads, one-half of a shell gorget with a drilled-dot star pattern, a stone pipe, two bone awls, part of a European-made double-tooth bone comb, six or seven metal buttons, a section of copper chain, forty flushloop brass bells, a seventeenth-century brass spur rowel of probable Spanish origin, a Dutch abacus counter made ca. 1588–1612 and worn as a pendant, a small, silver English dram cup dating around 1640, and glass beads. The beads consisted of an unknown number of drawn monochrome blue, red, and green round beads and about two hundred small drawn tubular beads. All of the tubular beads were found with a child burial, and most were red or blue (Potter 1989:165–66; Stewart 1988:86–97, 100–109).

Red tubular beads and some blue ones occur most often on Susquehannock Indian sites dating 1630 to 1680 (Kent 1984:213). In the middle and lower Chesapeake, tubular beads are uncommon on aboriginal or colonial sites; when they do occur, they are found mainly in contexts dating to the mid-to-late seventeenth century (Miller et al., 1983:140–43). Given the presence of the tubular beads, the approximate date of 1640 for the manufacture of the English dram cup, and the Patawomekes' abandonment of their homeland no later than the 1660s (Rountree 1990:121), the group burial probably dates between 1640 and the 1660s.

At Potomac Neck the shift in burial practices for common people from ossuaries to group burials and the presence of greater quantities of European items per number of individuals interred probably reflected the changes in aboriginal social and political organization indicative of the weakening power of the werowances. Increased Anglo-Algonquian contact, first through trade and sporadic fighting and later through English settlement, diminished the werowance's authority through a variety of factors: depopulation through disease and warfare (both intertribal and intercultural), defeats in war, displacement or loss of land, discrediting of the priesthood because of their ineffectiveness against European weapons and diseases, and, perhaps, disruption of clear succession to the chieftainship. As the centralized power of some werowances weakened, so did their control over native tribute and exchange systems.

Ossuaries at two other sites probably dating to the same period, 1630 to 1660—Piscataway Creek (18PR40) in Prince Georges County, Maryland, and Mount Airy (44RD3) in Richmond County, Virginia (see fig. 27)—also exhibit an increase in European objects and native wealth among commoners (Ferguson and Stewart 1940; McCary 1950). Like the group burial from Potomac Neck, the evidence from Piscataway Creek and Mount Airy suggests that the economically restrictive practices formerly enforced by the tayacs or werowances and their advisers had diminished. This change, in turn, increased opportunities for enterprising Algonquians to engage in trade and acquire European goods. Previously, a person's position within the social and political hierarchy led to the possession of status markers. Perhaps by the mid-seventeenth century social positions within Algonquian society could be obtained by individuals who already possessed status markers and wealth gained through trade (see Brenner 1988).

INDIAN TOWNS AND ENGLISH PLANTATIONS

As profits from the fur trade dwindled, more colonists sought their fortunes in tobacco rather than furs. The great European land grab was on. The fact that Algonquians were still living on the land did not deter the English from laying claim to it or settling on it, usually near former or extant Indian farmlands and villages (Potter and Waselkov in press).

The location of seventeenth-century English tobacco plantations, consisting of a post-in-the-ground house and associated outbuildings, usually was chosen with three factors in mind: near the waterfront for ease of transportation, near freshwater springs for drinking water, and near good-quality silty and sandy loam soils suitable for hoe cultivation (Smolek 1984). Those three factors are identical to three of the five possible factors involved in selecting the site of an Algonquian village. A striking example of the convergence of English and Algon-quian settlement patterns is illustrated by the distribution of archaeo-logical sites in the Chicacoan locality (fig. 49). Statistical comparison of the locations of seventeenth-century English plantations with proto-historic-historic Chicacoan sites indicates a high degree of association (Potter and Waselkov in press). There are several reasons for this.

Intensive cultivation of tobacco limited a manageable crop to about 1.2 hectares (3.0 a) per year per individual. Cultivating tobacco using traditional English farming methods, such as short-fallow, plow agri-culture, was impractical because of a shortage of laborers and draft animals. However, by adopting the Algonquian method of planting Native American crops, like tobacco and corn, among the stumps, fallen logs, and ashes of a swidden plot tended by hoe cultivation, a small English population was able to adapt successfully to the seven-teenth-century Chesapeake frontier. Archaeological evidence from the Chicacoan locality also suggests that by the 1640s and 1650s, the colonists recognized the temporarily low fertility of recently aban-doned Indian swidden plots and were selecting those sites as the most vegetation-free locations for their houses, while reserving the nearby nutrient-enriched Indian village sites for their field locations (Potter and Waselkov in press).

The successful settlement of the English in Algonquian territories like Chicacoan reduced the amount of land available to the Indians to sustain themselves. As English colonization continued and the need for additional tobacco lands increased, Indians living in the area of English settlement left voluntarily, were forced out, or were placed on lands set aside for them by the colonial government. The first Potomac Valley Algonquians pressured into the last course of action were the Chicacoans and Wicocomocos. Sometime in the mid-1650s they were combined as one group and moved to a tract of land south of their former territories (Potter 1982:366). Soon thereafter remnants of the lower Cuttatawomen chiefdom merged with them on their reservation near Dividing Creek. With the colonial establishment of this Indian reservation in Northumberland County, the Anglo-Algonquian fron-tier—that zone of mixture and interaction between native and intru-sive societies (Waselkov and Paul 1981:323)—ended in the eastern Northern Neck of Virginia.

The Cuttatawomens and Chicacoans quickly lost their identities as distinct ethnic groups and became, in essence, Wicocomocos (Roun-tree 1990:122–23). In 1705, when Robert Beverley's book *The History and Present State of Virginia* was published, Beverley (1968:233) de-

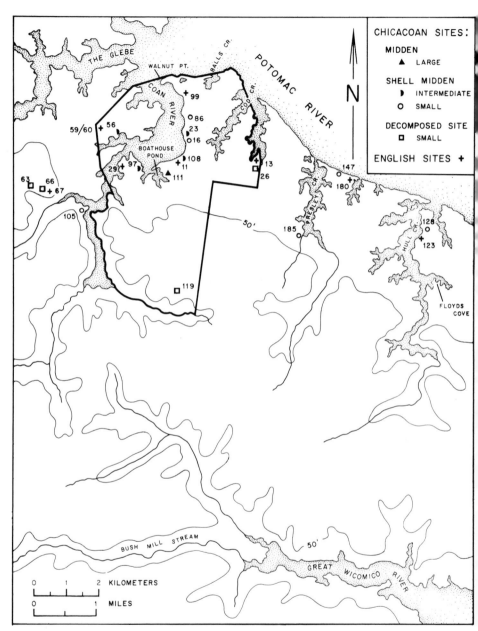

49. Distribution of protohistoric-historic Chicacoan components and seventeenth-century English components in the Chicacoan study area. (Map by G. Robert Lewis; redrawn by permission of the Smithsonian Institution Press)

scribed the Wicocomocos as having "but three men living [only warriors were counted], which yet keep up their Kingdom, and retain their Fashion; they live by themselves, separate from all other Indians, and from the English." By the early eighteenth century, the remaining Algonquians of the Virginia-Maryland tidewater were living on a colonial landscape, or as Beverley (1968:233) phrased it, a landscape "now improv'd (I should rather say alter'd) by the English."

Epilogue

O N JULY 14, 1719, THREE ENGLISHMEN arrived at the house of Elizabeth Tapp, probably located in the vicinity of Dividing Creek, to inventory and appraise the estate of her late husband, William. Son of Taptico, a Wicocomoco werowance, William Taptico or Tapp was the last werowance of the Wicocomoco Indians, but his estate inventory reveals quite an untraditional life-style (Northumberland County, 1718–26, Record Book, fol. 79–80). In contrast to Robert Beverley's (1968:233) remarks about the Wicocomocos a decade and a half earlier, William and Elizabeth Tapp were not living in the customary Algonquian manner.

Materially, the Tapps were living more like their middling-class English neighbors, with goods and livestock valued at over £100 (Horn 1988:82–85). When occasion warranted, William could select from several changes of English garb and bedeck himself from head to toe in hat, coat, vest, breeches, garters, shoes, and "a handkercheif." Their house was furnished with four chests, one large table, another table and six chairs, and four feather beds. Two of the feather beds, in particular, were very well-appointed by early eighteenth-century standards; they were "a Feather bed and bolster, 2 Pillows, 1 Sheet, 1 Blanket, 1 Rugg, 1 Sett Curtains and Vallens [valances], 2 Pillow cases and bedstead," valued at £4 10s., and "1 Great Feather bedd, 1 rugg, 1 Bolster, 1 pair blankets, 2 pillows, 2 Sheets, and one bedstead," also appraised at £4 10s. Englishmen living in St. Marys County, Maryland, during the period 1658 to 1700 owned beds, bedding, and bedsteads with an average value of about £2 10s. James Horn (1988:83) has noted that "planters in the £100-£249 category, however, commonly owned beds of twice this value." A variety of hearth furniture, cooking utensils, bottles, jugs, a dozen spoons, thirty-one pewter plates, and table linen meant the Tapps also could prepare and serve meals in a manner similar to most middling Chesapeake planters.

William Tapp also owned "a parcell of Olde Books" and "some pa-per," possibly indicating that he and/or his wife knew how to read and write English, something that very few of their Algonquian contem-poraries could do. In keeping with his position as werowance, it ap-pears from the inventory that Tapp was an entrepreneur; large quantities of yard goods and nails, as well as the money owed him by both Indians and Englishmen, suggest that Tapp served as a middle-man in trade between natives and colonists (Helen Rountree, personal communication 1991).

The presence of fish hooks, gigs, and line; a canoe, boat rigging, and oars; a large gun and two small ones; and axes and iron wedges indicate William Tapp continued to pursue the traditional male Al-gonquian activities of fishing, hunting, and land clearance (Rountree 1989:88). To supplement their traditional livelihood, the Tapps raised farm animals—six lambs and ten sheep; one bull, eleven cows, six yearlings, and six calves; thirty or forty hogs; and "fowls which the appraisers would not concern themselves with"—to provide them milk, butter, eggs, meat, feathers, hides, and wool. William also had a "young horse" that, judging by the harness and saddlery listed in the estate inventory, he used for both work and riding. Three pairs of wool cards, a spinning wheel, knitting needles, butter pots, "4 English milk-panns and 3 Indian," as well as one broad and two narrow hoes and the cooking utensils, suggest that Elizabeth Tapp had added carding, spinning, knitting, and dairying to the traditional Algonquian tasks associated with her gender—gardening, food preparation, pottery making, and child rearing, among others (Rountree 1989:80–89).

The listing of "4 English milkpanns and 3 Indian" is the only spe-cific reference to Indian-made artifacts on William Tapp's inventory. By calling them Indian milkpans, the English appraisers apparently meant that three of the artifacts were manufactured by Indians but were functionally patterned after a European form. Thus, this is a written reference to what archaeologists originally termed Colono-Indian ware (Noël Hume 1962; Mouer et al. in press). Other archae-ologists now prefer the broader name Colono ware to designate all low-fired, handbuilt pottery found on colonial-period sites, since both Indians and Africans "were capable of making pottery and evidence suggests that both did" (Ferguson 1992:22).

Recently, some archaeologists have claimed that seventeenth-century Colono pots and pipes found in Virginia and Maryland were made primarily, if not solely, by African slaves (Deetz 1988:365–66; Emerson 1988). In addition to this reference in the Tapp inventory,

which indicates that the Northern Neck Algonquians made Colono
vessels for their own use until about 1719, there is conclusive documentary evidence that the Algonquian Indians of the lower Rappahannock River were making both pots and pipes for sale and
exchange to non-Indians as late as December 1686, and the Pamunkeys continued to do so until at least the late 1700s (Bushnell
1937:40–41; Mouer et al. in press). This fact is confirmed archaeologically by discoveries at acculturated Patawomeke and Matchotic Indian
sites in Caroline County and at the Pamunkey Indian Reservation in
King William County, Virginia (MacCord 1969:9–18; Norrisey
1980:25–26; Speck 1928:402–9, figs. 101 and 102).

Seventeenth-century Colono pots made by Indians of the lower
Potomac and Rappahannock river basins were constructed using native pastes and techniques but were stylistically and/or functionally
patterned after European designs. The coil-constructed pottery was
either untempered or tempered with shell or sand, and its plain exteriors were either unburnished or burnished. A variety of vessel forms
were made, such as flat-bottomed jars with inverted rims, globular jars
with constricted necks and everted rims, flat-bottomed bottles with
long necks (fig. 50), and shallow bowls with slightly flattened bases
and straight rims (Dalton 1974:167; MacCord 1969:10, 12–13, 18;
Buchanan 1976:197). These ceramics developed from the late prehistoric, protohistoric, and early historic native ceramic traditions represented by the shell-tempered Yeocomico Plain pottery and from the
quartz and/or sand-tempered Potomac Creek Plain and Moyaone
Plain pottery types.

Seventeenth-century Indian-made obtuse-angle clay smoking
pipes were hand modeled from untempered pastes similar to some of
the Indian-made Colono pottery. Geometric, running deer, and star
motifs were applied to the pipe bowls using solid-point and hollow-
reed punctuations, impressed cords, or the serrated edges of shells or
fossil shark's teeth (fig. 51). Similar pipe forms and decorative techniques had been used in Virginia since at least the thirteenth century
A.D. (Gardner 1986:86; Mouer et al. in press).

As William Tapp's estate inventory and the Colono pots and pipes
illustrate, the creole subcultures spawned by the mixing of Native
American, European, and African cultural traditions on the seventeenth-century Chesapeake frontier make ethnic attribution based
solely on artifacts risky business. Since culture change involves the in-
corporation of objects into a functioning cultural system, the patterning of artifacts and structural features is as important, if not more so,

50. *Indian-made, shell-tempered Colono ware vessel from Lancaster County, Va. (Photograph by Victor E. Krantz)*

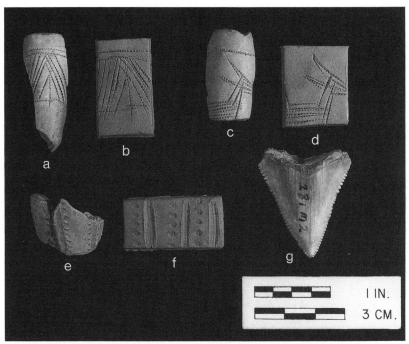

51. Decorated seventeenth-century Indian-made pipe bowls (a, c, e) compared to design motifs (b, d, f) replicated with archaeologically recovered shark's tooth (g). Provenience: a, c, e, Camden site (44CE3); g, De Shazo site (44KG3).

as the origin of the artifacts in correctly identifying the ethnicity of the inhabitants of a particular archaeological site. In the case of William and Elizabeth Tapp, their house was probably built more like an English frame structure than a traditional Algonquian bark-covered, pole-supported *yi-hakan*. The likelihood of this interpretation is indicated by the hearth furnishings and the amount, type, and size of the household furniture owned by the Tapps.

Archaeological identification of acculturated Indian house sites, like the Tapps', is made all the more difficult by their dispersal over the landscape. As the number of Indians living on reservations waned, they were unable to maintain all of their lands. Sections of Indian lands no longer occupied by them were taken over by encroaching Englishmen owning adjacent plantations. By 1705, not only were the Wicocomocos reduced to a few families, they were no longer living on a true reservation. In 1696 William Tapp's father, Taptico, sold the remaining Wicocomoco lands to an Englishman (Rountree 1990:158–59). With no lands of their own, the Wicocomocos became tenants living on an English plantation, a common custom during the late seventeenth and early eighteenth centuries when the majority of non-reservation Indians lived "scatter'd upon the English Seats" (Beverley 1968:233).

The loss of people, land, tribute, and native sovereignty eroded the traditional power base of many of the remaining Algonquian rulers, like William Tapp. Whereas Tapp's predecessors of the early 1600s ruled a chiefdom encompassing 260 square kilometers (100 mi^2) with a population of about 550, Tapp ruled a "Kingdom" composed of a few landless subjects (Beverley 1968:233).

References Cited
Index

References Cited

Adams, William Y., Dennis P. Van Gerven, and Richard S. Levy
  1978   The Retreat from Migrationism. In *Annual Reviews of Anthropology* 7:483–532.

Allen, Durward L.
  1962   *Our Wildlife Legacy*. New York: Funk and Wagnalls.

Anthony, David L.
  1990   Migration in Archeology: The Baby and the Bathwater. *American Anthropologist* 92(4):895–914.

Arber, Edward (editor)
  1884   *Captain John Smith, Works, 1608–1631*. The English Scholar's Library 16. Birmingham: Unwin.
  1910   *Travels and Works of Captain John Smith*. 2 vols. Edinburgh: John Grant.

Archer, Gabriel
  1910 [1607]   A Relatyon of the Discovery of Our River, from James Fort into the Maine. In *Travel and Works of Captain John Smith*, 3 vols., ed. Edward Arber, 1:xl–lv. Edinburgh: John Grant.
  1969 [1607]   A Brief Description of the People. In *Jamestown Voyages under the First Charter, 1606–1609,* Works Issued by the Hakluyt Society, 2d ser., vol. 136, ed. Philip L. Barbour, pp. 102–4. London: Cambridge University Press.

Archives of Maryland
  1883—   *Proceedings of the Council of Maryland*. Baltimore: Maryland Historical Society.

Axtell, James
  1981   Ethnohistory: An Historian's Viewpoint. In *The European and the Indian: Essays in the Ethnohistory of Colonial North America*, ed. James Axtell, pp. 3–15. Oxford: Oxford University Press.

1988   At the Water's Edge: Trading in the Sixteenth Century. In *After Columbus: Essays in the Ethnohistory of Colonial North America*, ed. James Axtell, pp. 144–81. Oxford: Oxford University Press.

Bailey, M. H.
1974   Climate. In *Soil Survey of Stafford and King George Counties, Virginia*, by D. Isgrig and A. Strobel, Jr., pp. 121–23. U.S. Department of Agriculture, Soil Conservation Service. Washington, D.C.: GPO.

Barber, Michael B.
1981   The Vertebrate Faunal Utilization Pattern of the Middle Woodland Mockley Ceramic Users: The Maycock's Point Shell Midden Site, Prince George County, Virginia. Ms on file, Virginia Department of Historic Resources, Richmond.
1983   Vertebrate Faunal Analysis: The Macrodata. In *The Skiffes Creek Site (44NN7): A Multicomponent Middle Woodland Base Camp in Newport News, Virginia* by Clarence R. Geier. Occasional Papers in Anthropology no. 17. Harrisonburg, Va.: James Madison University.

Barbour, Philip L.
1971   The Earliest Reconnaissance of Chesapeake Bay Area: Captain John Smith's Map and Indian Vocabulary. *Virginia Magazine of History and Biography* 79(3):280–302.
1972   The Earliest Reconnaissance of the Chesapeake Bay Area: Captain John Smith's Map and Indian Vocabulary, Part II. *Virginia Magazine of History and Biography* 80(1):21–51.

—— (editor)
1986   *The Complete Works of Captain John Smith.* 3 vols. Chapel Hill: University of North Carolina Press.

Barse, William P.
1985   A Preliminary Archeological Reconnaissance Survey of the Naval Ordnance Station, Indian Head, Maryland. Ms on file, Maryland Historical Trust, Crownsville.

Bastian, Tyler
1974   Some Observations on Points/Knives Associated with the Selby Bay Phase in Maryland. Paper presented at the 5th Middle Atlantic Archaeological Conference, Baltimore.

Bergsland, K., and H. Vogt
1962   On the Validity of Glottochronology. *Current Anthropology* 3(2): 115–53.

Beverley, Robert
1968 [1705]   *The History and Present State of Virginia*, ed. Louis B. Wright. 1947. Rept. Charlottesville: University Press of Virginia.

Billings, Warren M. (editor)
1975   Some Acts Not in Hening's *Statutes:* The Acts of Assembly, April 1652, November 1652, and July 1653. *Virginia Magazine of History and Biography* 83(1):22–76.

Binford, Lewis R.
1964   Archaeological and Ethnohistorical Investigations of Cultural Diversity and Progressive Development among Aboriginal Cultures of Coastal Virginia and North Carolina. Ph.D. diss., University of Michigan. University Microfilms, Ann Arbor.
1980   Willow Smoke and Dogs' Tails: Hunter-Gatherer Settlement Systems and Archaeological Site Formation. *American Antiquity* 45(1):4–20.
1983   *In Pursuit of the Past: Decoding the Archaeological Record.* New York: Thames and Hudson.

Bohannan, Paul
1963   *Social Anthropology.* New York: Holt, Rinehart and Winston.

Boyce, Hettie, and Lori Frye
1986   *Radiocarbon Dating of Archeological Samples from Maryland.* Maryland Geological Survey Archeological Studies no. 4. Baltimore.

Bozman, John L.
1837   *A History of Maryland, from Its First Settlement, in 1633, to the Restoration in 1660.* 2 vols. Baltimore: James Lucas and E. K. Deaver.

Brashler, Janet G.
1987   A Middle 16th Century Susquehannock Village in Hampshire County, West Virginia. *West Virginia Archeologist* 39(2):1–30.

Brenner, Elise M.
1988   Sociopolitical Implications of Mortuary Ritual Remains in 17th-Century Southern New England. In *The Recovery of Meaning: Historical Archaeology in the Eastern United States,* ed. Mark P. Leone and Parker B. Potter, Jr., pp. 147–81. Washington, D.C.: Smithsonian Institution Press.

Bromberg, Francine Weiss
1987   Site Distribution in the Coastal Plain and Fall Zone of the Potomac Valley from ca. 6500 B.C. to A.D. 1400. M.A. thesis, Department of Anthropology, The Catholic University of America, Washington, D.C.

——, Ray Wood, Catherine Toulmin, Elizabeth Crowell, Janice Artemel, Madeleine Pappas, Cynthia Pfanstiehl, and Teresa Kacprowicz
1989   Anacostia Park from a Historical and Archaeological Perspective. Engineering-Science, Inc. Report submitted to Fleming Corporation, Washington, D.C.

Brown, M. L.
1980   *Firearms in Colonial America: The Impact on History and Technology, 1492–1729.* Washington, D.C.: Smithsonian Institution Press.

Brush, Grace S.
1986   Geology and Paleoecology of Chesapeake Bay: A Long-Term Monitoring Tool for Management. *Journal of the Washington Academy of Sciences* 76(3):146–60.

Buchanan, William T., Jr.
1976   The Hallowes Site. Archeological Society of Virginia *Quarterly Bulletin* 30(4):195–99.

Bushnell, David I., Jr.
1935   The Manahoac Tribes in Virginia, 1608. *Smithsonian Miscellaneous Collections* 94(4):1–56.
1937   Indian Sites below the Falls of the Rappahannock, Virginia. *Smithsonian Miscellaneous Collections* 96(4):1–65.
1940   Virginia before Jamestown. *Smithsonian Miscellaneous Collections* 100(whole vol.):125–58.

Carbone, Victor A.
1976   Environment and Prehistory in the Shenandoah Valley. Ph.D. diss., Department of Anthropology, The Catholic University of America, Washington, D.C.

Carneiro, Robert L.
1960   Slash-and-Burn Agriculture: A Closer Look at Its Implications for Settlement Patterns. In *Men and Cultures: Selected Papers of the Fifth International Congress of Anthropological and Ethnological Sciences,* ed. Anthony F. C. Wallace, pp. 229–34. Philadelphia: University of Pennsylvania Press.
1970   A Theory on the Origin of the State. *Science* 169:733–38.
1981   The Chiefdom: Precursor of the State. In *The Transition to Statehood in the New World,* ed. G. Jones and R. Kautz, pp. 37–79. Cambridge: Cambridge University Press.

Carr, Lois Green, Russell R. Menard, and Louis Peddicord
1984   *Maryland . . . at the Beginning.* Annapolis: Hall of Records, Department of General Services.

Carter, Virginia, Patricia T. Gammon, and Nancy C. Bartow
1983   *Submerged Aquatic Plants of the Tidal Potomac River.* Geological Survey Bulletin 1543. U.S. Department of the Interior. Washington, D.C.: GPO.

Chapman, Jefferson
1977   *Archaic Period Research in the Lower Tennessee River Valley.* Report of

Investigations no. 18, Department of Anthropology, University of Tennessee. Tennessee Valley Authority.

Chase, Joan W.
1990 Analysis of Skeletal Material from the Thomas Site 18CA88. Report submitted to the Maryland Historical Trust, Crownsville.

Chisolm, Michael
1968 *Rural Settlement and Land Use: An Essay in Location.* 2d ed. Chicago: Aldine.

Chretien, C. Douglas
1962 The Mathematical Models of Glottochronology. *Language* 38:11–37.

Cissna, Paul B.
1986 The Piscataway Indians of Southern Maryland: An Ethnohistory from Pre-European Contact to the Present. Ph.D. diss., Department of Anthropology, The American University, Washington, D.C.
1990 *Historical and Archeological Study of the George Washington Memorial Parkway from the Theodore Roosevelt Bridge to the Lorcom Lane Turnabout on Spout Run Parkway, Arlington, Virginia.* Occasional Report no. 4. Washington, D.C.: Regional Archeology Program, National Park Service, National Capital Region.

Clark, Wayne E.
1976 The Application of Regional Research Designs to Contract Archeology: The Northwest Transportation Corridor Archeological Survey Project. M.A. thesis, Department of Anthropology, The American University, Washington, D.C.
1980 The Origins of the Piscataway and Related Indian Cultures. *Maryland Historical Magazine* 75(1):8–22.

——, and Richard Hughes
1983 Proposal for Intensive Archeological Investigations of the Cumberland Palisaded Village Site, Calvert County, Maryland. Ms on file, Maryland Historical Trust, Crownsville.

Clarke, David L.
1968 *Analytical Archaeology.* London: Methuen.

Coe, Joffre L.
1952 The Cultural Sequence of the Carolina Piedmont. In *Archeology of Eastern United States,* ed. James B. Griffin, pp. 301–11. Chicago: University of Chicago Press.
1964 *The Formative Cultures of the Carolina Piedmont.* Transactions of the American Philosophical Society, n.s., vol. 54, pt. 5. Philadelphia.

Coleman, Gary N.
    1982   The Reedy Creek Site, 44Ha22, South Boston, Virginia. Archeolog-
    ical Society of Virginia *Quarterly Bulletin* 37(4):150–209.

Cronin, L. Eugene
    1986   Fisheries and Resource Stress in the 19th Century. *Journal of the
    Washington Academy of Sciences* 76(3):188–98.

Crosby, Constance A.
    1988   From Myth to History, or Why King Philip's Ghost Walks Abroad.
    In *The Recovery of Meaning: Historical Archaeology in the Eastern United
    States,* ed. Mark P. Leone and Parker B. Potter, Jr., pp. 183–209. Wash-
    ington, D.C.: Smithsonian Institution Press.

Curry, Dennis C., and Maureen Kavanagh
    1991   The Middle to Late Woodland Transition in Maryland. *North Amer-
    ican Archaeologist* 12(1):3–28.

Custer, Jay
    1984   *Delaware Prehistoric Archaeology: An Ecological Approach.* Newark: Uni-
    versity of Delaware Press.
    1986   Late Woodland Cultural Diversity in the Middle Atlantic: An Evo-
    lutionary Perspective. In *Late Woodland Cultures of the Middle Atlantic Re-
    gion,* ed. Jay Custer, pp. 143–68. Newark: University of Delaware Press.
    1987   Problems and Prospects in Northeastern Prehistoric Ceramic Stud-
    ies. *North American Archaeologist* 8(2):97–123.
    1989   *Prehistoric Cultures of the Delmarva Peninsula.* Newark: University of
    Delaware Press.

——, and Stephen R. Potter
    1988   Native American Sociopolitical Complexity and Trade during the
    Contact Period. Paper presented at the Middle Atlantic Archaeological
    Conference, Rehoboth Beach, Del.

Dabney, Virginius
    1971   *Virginia, the New Dominion: A History from 1607 to the Present.* New
    York: Doubleday.

Dalton, Joseph F.
    1974   The Owings Site, Northumberland County, Virginia. Archeological
    Society of Virginia *Quarterly Bulletin* 28(3):162–68.

Davidson, Thomas E., Richard Hughes, and Joseph M. McNamara
    1985   Where Are the Indian Towns? Archeology, Ethnohistory, and Mani-
    festations of Contact on Maryland's Eastern Shore. *Journal of Middle Atlantic
    Archaeology* 1:43–50.

DeBoer, Warren R.
1988 Subterranean Storage and the Organization of Surplus: The View from Eastern North America. *Southeastern Archaeology* 7(1):1–20.

Deetz, James
1988 American Historical Archeology: Methods and Results. *Science* 239:362–67.

Dent, Richard J., and Christine Jirikowic
1990 Preliminary Report of Archaeological Investigations at the Hughes Site (18MO1). Potomac River Archaeological Survey, Department of Anthropology, The American University, Washington, D.C.

Earle, Timothy K.
1987 Chiefdoms in Archaeological and Ethnohistorical Perspective. In *Annual Reviews of Anthropology* 16:279–308.

Edwards, Andrew, William Pittman, Gregory Brown, Mary Ellen N. Hodges, Marley Brown III, and Eric Voigt
1989 Hampton University Archaeological Project, vol. 1: A Report on the Findings. The Department of Archaeological Research, Colonial Williamsburg Foundation. Report submitted to Hampton University, Virginia.

Egloff, Keith
1985 Spheres of Cultural Interaction across the Coastal Plain of Virginia in the Woodland Period. In *Structure and Process in Southeastern Archaeology*, ed. R. Dickens, Jr., and H. Trawick Ward, pp. 229–42. Tuscaloosa: University of Alabama Press.

——, and Stephen R. Potter
1982 Indian Ceramics from Coastal Plain Virginia. *Archaeology of Eastern North America* 10:95–117.

Elder, John H., Jr., E. L. Henry, and R. F. Pendleton
1963 *Soil Survey of Northumberland and Lancaster Counties, Virginia.* U.S. Department of Agriculture, Soil Conservation Service. Washington, D.C.: GPO.

Emerson, Matthew C.
1988 Decorated Clay Tobacco Pipes from the Chesapeake. Ph.D. diss., Department of Anthropology, University of California, Berkeley.

Evans, Clifford
1955 *A Ceramic Study of Virginia Archeology.* Bureau of American Ethnology Bulletin 160. Washington, D.C.

Falk, Carole P.
1981   Cordage Impressed on Potomac Creek Pottery: Decoding the Corded Style, Motifs, and the Methods of Pattern Manufacture. M.A. thesis, Master of Fine Art of Ceramics Program, Visual Art Center, Columbia Cultural Institute, Columbia, Md.

Fausz, J. Frederick
1977   The Powhatan Uprising of 1622: A Historical Study of Ethnocentrism and Cultural Conflict. Ph.D. diss., The College of William and Mary. University Microfilms, Ann Arbor.
1979   Fighting "Fire" with Firearms: The Anglo-Powhatan Arms Race in Early Virginia. *American Indian Culture and Research Journal* 3(4):33–50.
1984   "Sonnes of Wrath": The Impact of the Beaver Trade and Anglo-Indian Interest Groups on the Development of the Early Chesapeake, 1620–1660. Paper presented at the Annual Meeting of the American Society for Ethnohistory.

1985   Patterns of Anglo-Indian Aggression and Accommodation along the Mid-Atlantic Coast. In *Cultures in Contact*, ed. William Fitzhugh, pp. 225–68. Washington, D.C.: Smithsonian Institution Press.
1987   Middlemen in Peace and War: Virginia's Earliest Indian Interpreters, 1608–1632. *Virginia Magazine of History and Biography* 95(1):41–64.
1988   Merging and Emerging Worlds: Anglo-Indian Interest Groups and the Development of the Seventeenth-Century Chesapeake. In *Colonial Chesapeake Society*, ed. Lois Carr, Philip Morgan, and Jean Russo, pp. 47–98. Chapel Hill: University of North Carolina Press.
1990   An "Abundance of Blood Shed on Both Sides": England's First Indian War, 1609–1614. *Virginia Magazine of History and Biography* 98(1): 3–56.

Feest, Christian F.
1966   Powhatan: A Study in Political Organization. *Wiener Völkerkundliche Mitteilungen* 13:69–83.
1973   Seventeenth Century Virginia Algonquian Population Estimates. Archeological Society of Virginia *Quarterly Bulletin* 28(2):66–79.
1978a   Virginia Algonquians. In *Northeast*, ed. Bruce G. Trigger, pp. 253–70. *Handbook of North American Indians*, vol. 15, William G. Sturtevant, general editor. Washington, D.C.: Smithsonian Institution.
1978b   Nanticoke and Neighboring Tribes. In *Northeast*, ed. Bruce G. Trigger, pp. 240–52. *Handbook of North American Indians*, vol. 15. William G. Sturtevant, general editor. Washington, D.C.: Smithsonian Institution.

Feinman, Gary, and Jill Neitzel
1984   Too Many Types: An Overview of Sedentary Prestate Societies in the

Americas. In *Advances in Archaeological Method and Theory*, vol. 7, ed. Michael B. Schiffer, pp. 39–102. New York: Academic press.

Ferguson, Alice L. L., and T. Dale Stewart
1940 An Ossuary near Piscataway Creek. *American Antiquity* 6(1):4–18.

Ferguson, Leland
1992 *Uncommon Ground: Archaeology and Early African America, 1650–1800*. Washington, D.C.: Smithsonian Institution Press.

Fiedel, Stuart J.
1987 Algonquian Origins: A Problem in Archaeological-Linguistic Correlation. *Archaeology of Eastern North America* 15:1–11.
1990 Middle Woodland Algonquian Expansion: A Refined Model. *North American Archaeologist* 11(3):209–30.
1991 Correlating Archaeology and Linguistics. *Man in the Northeast* no. 41, pp. 9–32.

Fitzhugh, William W.
1972 *Environmental Archeology and Cultural Systems in Hamilton Inlet, Labrador*. Smithsonian Contributions to Anthropology no. 16. Washington, D.C.: Smithsonian Institution.

——, (editor)
1985 *Cultures in Contact: The European Impact on Native Cultural Institutions in Eastern North America, A.D. 1000–1800*. Washington, D.C.: Smithsonian Institution Press.

Flannery, Kent V. (editor)
1976 *The Early Mesoamerican Village*. New York: Academic Press.

Flannery, Regina
1939 *An Analysis of Coastal Algonkian Culture*. The Catholic University of America Anthropological Series no. 7. Washington, D.C.

Fleet, Henry
1956 [1633] A Brief Journal of a Voyage in the Barque "Warwick" to Virginia and Other Parts of the Continent of America. *Northern Neck of Virginia Historical Magazine* 6(1):479–89.

Ford, Richard I.
1974 Northeastern Archeology: Past and Future Directions. *Annual Review of Anthropology* 3:385–413.

Gardner, William M.
1976 Excavations at Three Sites near Piscataway Creek, Maryland: 18PR141, 18PR142 and 18PR143. Ms on file, Department of Anthropology, The Catholic University of America, Washington, D.C.

1982   Early and Middle Woodland in the Middle Atlantic: An Overview. In *Practicing Environmental Archaeology: Methods and Interpretations*, ed. Roger Moeller, pp. 53–85. Occasional Paper no. 3, Washington, Conn.: American Indian Archaeological Institute.

1986   *Lost Arrowheads and Broken Pottery: Traces of Indians in the Shenandoah Valley.* Front Royal, Va.: Thunderbird Museum.

———, and Victor A. Carbone
n.d.   Man and Environment in the Middle Atlantic: A Fool's Journey down the Garden Path. Ms in possession of senior author.

———, and Charles W. McNett, Jr.
1971   Early Pottery in the Potomac. *Proceedings of the Middle Atlantic Archeology Conference.* Washington, D.C.: The Catholic University of America.

———, Carole Nash, Joan Walker, and William Barse
1989   Excavations at 18CV272. Report submitted to CRJ Associates, Camp Springs, Md.

Geier, Clarence R.
1983   *The Skiffes Creek Site (44NN7): A Multicomponent Middle Woodland Base Camp in Newport News, Virginia.* Occasional Papers in Anthropology no. 17. Harrisonburg, Va.: James Madison University.

George, Richard L.
1983   The Gnagey Site and the Monongahela Occupation of the Somerset Plateau. *Pennsylvania Archaeologist* 53(4):1–97.

Gerard, William R.
1905   Some Virginia Indian Words. *American Anthropologist* 7(2):222–49.

Gibson, Joseph W.
1978   *Soil Survey of St. Marys County, Maryland.* U.S. Department of Agriculture, Soil Conservation Service. Washington, D.C.: GPO.

Gilsen, Leland
1978   Population Adaptation to the Chesapeake Bay: Estuarine Efficiency. *Maryland Archeology* 14(1–2):11–16.

1979   The Environmental Ecology of Calvert County, Maryland, pts. 1 and 2. *Maryland Archeology* 15(1–2):1–30.

Gleach, Frederic W.
1987a   A Working Projectile Point Classification for Central Virginia. Archeological Society of Virginia *Quarterly Bulletin* 42(2):80–120.

1987b   The Reynolds-Alvis Site (44He470): A Summary Report. Archeological Society of Virginia *Quarterly Bulletin* 42(4):205–32.

1988   A Rose by Any Other Name: Questions on Mockley Chronology. *Journal of Middle Atlantic Archaeology* 4:85–98.

Goddard, Ives
1978   Eastern Algonquian Languages. In *Northeast,* ed. Bruce G. Trigger, pp. 70–77. *Handbook of North American Indians,* vol. 15, William G. Sturtevant, general editor. Washington, D.C.: Smithsonian Institution.

Graham, William J.
1935   *The Indians of the Port Tobacco River, Maryland, and Their Burial Places.* Privately printed.

Green, Paul R.
1986   *The Archaeology of "Chowanoke."* America's Four Hundredth Anniversary Committee. Raleigh: North Carolina Division of Archives and History.
1987   Forager-Farmer Transitions in Coastal Prehistory. Ph.D. diss., Department of Anthropology, University of North Carolina, Chapel Hill.

Griffith, Daniel
1977   Townsend Ceramics and the Late Woodland of Southern Delaware. M.A. thesis, Department of Anthropology, The American University, Washington, D.C.
1980   Townsend Ceramics and the Late Woodland and Southern Delaware. *Maryland Historical Magazine* 75(1):23–41.

———, and Richard Artusy
1977   Middle Woodland Ceramics from Wolfe Neck, Sussex County, Delaware. *Archeolog* 28(1):1–28.

———, and Jay Custer
1985   Late Woodland Ceramics of Delaware: Implications for the Late Prehistoric Archaeology of Northeastern North America. *Pennsylvania Archaeologist* 55(3):6–20.

Grumet, Robert S.
1980   Sunksquaws, Shamans, and Tribeswomen: Middle Atlantic Coastal Algonkian Women during the 17th and 18th Centuries. In *Women and Colonization: Anthropological Perspectives,* ed. Mona Etienne and Eleanor Burke Leacock, pp. 43–62. New York: Praeger Scientific.

Hall, Clayton Colman (editor)
1925   *Narratives of Early Maryland.* New York: Charles Scribner's Sons.

Hall, Richard L., and Earle D. Matthews
1974   *Soil Survey of Charles County, Maryland.* U.S. Department of Agriculture, Soil Conservation Service. Washington, D.C.: GPO.

Hamor, Ralph
1957 [1615]   *A True Discourse of the Present Estate of Virginia and the Success of the Affairs There till the 18th of June, 1614.* Rept. Richmond: Virginia State Library.

Handsman, Russell, and Charles W. McNett
1974 The Middle Woodland in the Middle Atlantic: Chronology, Adaptation, and Contact. Paper presented at the 5th Middle Atlantic Archaeological Conference, Baltimore.

Hantman, Jeffrey L.
1990 Between Powhatan and Quirank: Reconstructing Monacan Culture and History in the Context of Jamestown. *American Anthropologist* 92(3):676–90.

Harris, Marvin
1975 *Culture, People, Nature.* New York: McGraw-Hill.

Harrison, Fairfax
1987 *Landmarks of Old Prince William: A Study of Origins in Northern Virginia.* Richmond: privately printed, 1924. Rept. Baltimore: Gateway Press.

Haynes, John H., Jr.
1984 The Seasons of Tsenacommacoh and the Rise of Wahunsenacawh: Structure and Ecology in Social Evolution. M.A. thesis, Department of Anthropology, University of Virginia, Charlottesville.

Heidenreich, Conrad
1971 *Huronia: A History and Geography of the Huron Indians, 1600–1650.* McClelland and Stewart.

Hening, William W. (editor)
1823 *The Statutes at Large; Being a Collection of All the Laws of Virginia, from the First Session of the Legislature in the Year 1619,* vol. 1. New York: R. and W. and G. Bartow.

Hiden, Martha W.
1957 *How Justice Grew—Virginia Counties: An Abstract of Their Formation.* Jamestown 350th Anniversary Historical Booklet no. 19. Williamsburg. Rept. Charlottesville: University Press of Virginia, 1973.

——, and Henry M. Dargan
1966 John Gibbon's Manuscript Notes concerning Virginia. *Virginia Magazine of History and Biography* 74(1):3–22.

Holland, C. G.
1955 *An Analysis of Projectile Points and Large Blades.* Appendix to Bureau of American Ethnology Bulletin 160. Washington, D.C.

Holmes, William H.
1897 Stone Implements of the Potomac-Chesapeake Tidewater Province. In *Fifteenth Annual Report of the Bureau of American Ethnology,* pp. 3–152. Washington, D.C.: GPO.

1903   *Aboriginal Pottery of the Eastern United States.* Twentieth Annual Report of the Bureau of American Ethnology. Washington, D.C.: GPO.

1907   Aboriginal Shellheaps of the Middle Atlantic Tidewater Region. *American Anthropologist* 9(1):113–28.

———, William Dinwiddie, and Gerard Fowke

1891   Archeological Survey of the Tidewater Maryland and Virginia Area. Ms 2125, National Anthropological Archives, Smithsonian Institution, Washington, D.C.

Horn, James P. P.

1988   "The Bare Necessities": Standards of Living in England and the Chesapeake, 1650–1700. *Historical Archaeology* 22(2):74–91.

House, John, and Ronald Wogaman

1978   *Windy Ridge: A Prehistoric Site in the Inter-riverine Piedmont in South Carolina.* Anthropological Studies no. 3. Columbia: Institute of Archeology and Anthropology, University of South Carolina.

Inashima, Paul Y.

1985   *An Archeological Investigation of Selected Construction Locales along the Mount Vernon Memorial Highway.* National Park Service, Denver Service Center.

Isgrig, Dan, and Adolph Strobel, Jr.

1974   *Soil Survey of Stafford and King George Counties, Virginia.* U.S. Department of Agriculture, Soil Conservation Service. Washington, D.C.: GPO.

Jefferson, Thomas

1972 [1787]   *Notes on the State of Virginia,* ed. William Peden. 1955. Rept. New York: W. W. Norton.

Jennings, Francis

1978   Susquehannock. In *Northeast,* ed. Bruce G. Trigger, pp. 362–67. *Handbook of North American Indians,* vol. 15, William G. Sturtevant, general editor. Washington, D.C.: Smithsonian Institution.

1982   Indians and Frontiers in Seventeenth-Century Maryland. In *Early Maryland in a Wider World,* ed. David B. Quinn, pp. 216–41. Detroit: Wayne State University Press.

Jenny, Hans

1941   *Factors of Soil Formation.* New York: McGraw-Hill.

Jirikowic, Christine

1989   Analysis of Aboriginal Artifacts from the Potomac Creek Site, 44ST2. Ms in possession of author.

1990   The Political Implications of a Cultural Practice: A New Perspective on Ossuary Burial in the Potomac Valley. *North American Archaeologist* 11(4):353–74.

Johnson, Michael F.
1986   The Karell Site: How Archaeologists Discover the Past. *Fairfax Chronicles* 10(1):3.
1991   Middle and Late Woodland Settlement Systems in the Interior Fall Zone of the Potomac Valley: Not a Live Oyster in Sight. *North American Archaeologist* 12(1):29–60.

Kavanagh, Maureen
1982   Archeological Resources of the Monocacy River Region, Frederick and Carroll Counties, Maryland. Maryland Geological Survey, Division of Archeology File Report no. 164.

Kellock, Katharine A.
1962   *Colonial Piscataway in Maryland.* Accokeek, Md.: The Alice Ferguson Foundation.

Kent, Barry C.
1984   *Susquehanna's Indians.* Anthropological Series no. 6. Harrisburg: Pennsylvania Historical and Museum Commission.

Kidd, Kenneth, and Martha Kidd
1970   *A Classification System for Glass Beads for the Use of Field Archaeologists.* Canadian Historic Sites Occasional Papers in Archaeology and History 1(1). Ottawa: Parks Canada.

Kingsbury, Susan M. (editor)
1906–35   *The Records of the Virginia Company of London.* 4 vols. Washington, D.C.: GPO.

Kinsey, Fred W.
1972   *Archaeology of the Upper Delaware Valley: A Study of the Cultural Chronology of the Tocks Island Reservoir.* Anthropological Series no. 2. Harrisburg: Pennsylvania Historical and Museum Commission.

Kirby, Robert M., Earle D. Matthews, and Moulton A. Bailey
1967   *Soil Survey of Prince Georges County, Maryland.* U.S. Department of Agriculture, Soil Conservation Service. Washington, D.C.: GPO.

Knight, Vernon J., Jr.
1990   Social Organization and the Evolution of Hierarchy in Southeastern Chiefdoms. In *Journal of Anthropological Research* 46(1):1–23.

Kraft, Herbert C.
1975   *The Archaeology of the Tocks Island Area.* South Orange, N.J.: Seton Hall University Museum.

1986 *The Lenape: Archaeology, History, and Ethnography.* Newark: New Jersey Historical Society.

1989 Sixteenth and Seventeenth Century Indian/White Trade Relations in the Middle Atlantic and Northeast Regions. *Archaeology of Eastern North America* 17:1–29.

Lewis, Clifford, and Albert J. Loomie
1953 *The Spanish Jesuit Mission in Virginia, 1570–1572.* Chapel Hill: University of North Carolina Press.

Limbrey, Susan
1975 *Soil Science and Archaeology.* London: Academic Press.

Lippson, Alice Jane (editor)
1973 *The Chesapeake Bay in Maryland: An Atlas of Natural Resources.* Baltimore: Johns Hopkins University Press.

Luckenbach, Alvin H., Wayne E. Clark, and Richard S. Levy
1987 Rethinking Cultural Stability in Eastern North American Prehistory: Linguistic Evidence from Eastern Algonquian. *Journal of Middle Atlantic Archaeology* 3:1–33.

McCartney, Martha W.
1985 Seventeenth Century Apartheid: The Suppression and Containment of Indians in Tidewater Virginia. *Journal of Middle Atlantic Archaeology* 1:51–80.

McCary, Ben C.
1950 The Rappahannock Indians. Archeological Society of Virginia *Quarterly Bulletin* 5(1):1–15.

1953 The Potts Site, Chickahominy River, New Kent County, Virginia. Archeological Society of Virginia *Quarterly Bulletin* 8(1):no pagination.

1957 *Indians in Seventeenth Century Virginia.* Jamestown 350th Anniversary Historical Booklet no. 18. Williamsburg.

——, and Norman Barka
1977 The John Smith and Zuniga Maps in Light of Recent Archaeological Investigations along the Chickahominy River. *Archaeology of Eastern North America* 5:73–86.

MacCord, Howard A., Sr.
1952 The Susquehannock Indians in West Virginia, 1630–77. *West Virginia History* 13(4):239–46.

1965 The De Shazo Site, King George County, Virginia. Archeological Society of Virginia *Quarterly Bulletin* 19(4):98–104.

1969 Camden: A Postcontact Indian Site in Caroline County. Archeological Society of Virginia *Quarterly Bulletin* 24(1):1–55.

1984   Evidence for a Late Woodland Migration from Piedmont to Tidewater in the Potomac Valley. *Maryland Archeology* 20(2):7–18.
1989   The Contact Period in Virginia. *Journal of Middle Atlantic Archaeology* 5:121–28.
1991   The Indian Point Site, Stafford County, Virginia. Archeological Society of Virginia *Quarterly Bulletin* 46(3):117–40.
—— (editor)
1985   *Falls Zone Archeology in Virginia.* Richmond: privately printed.
1986   *The Lewis Creek Mound Culture in Virginia.* Richmond: privately printed.
——, Karl Schmitt, and Richard G. Slattery
1957   *The Shepard Site Study.* Archeological Society of Maryland Bulletin no. 1. Baltimore.
——, and C. Lanier Rodgers
1966   The Miley Site, Shenandoah County, Virginia. Archeological Society of Virginia *Quarterly Bulletin* 21(1):9–20.

McDaniel, Roland E.
1987   The Language of the Motif: An Analysis of the Walker Village Late Woodland Ceramics. Ph.D. diss., Department of Anthropology, The American University, Washington, D.C.

McKern, W. C.
1939   The Midwestern Taxonomic Method as an Aid to Archaeological Culture Study. *American Antiquity* 4(4):301–13.

McLearen, Douglas C., and L. Daniel Mouer
1989   Middle Woodland II Typology and Chronology in the Lower James River Valley of Virginia. Paper presented at the Middle Atlantic Archaeological Conference, Rehoboth Beach, Del.

MacLeod, W. C.
1926   Piscataway Royalty: A Study in Stone Age Government and Inheritance Rulings. *Journal of the Washington Academy of Sciences* 16(11):301–9.

McNett, Charles W., Jr.
1975   Potomac Valley Archeology. Ms on file, Department of Anthropology, The American University, Washington, D.C.
——, and Ellis E. McDowell
1974   *An Archeological Survey of Swan Point Neck, Maryland.* Archeological Society of Maryland, Miscellaneous Paper no. 9. Baltimore.

Manson, Carl, and Howard A. MacCord, Sr.
1985   The Stratigraphic Sequence at Patawomeke, Stafford County, Vir-

ginia. In *Falls Zone Archeology in Virginia*, ed. Howard A. MacCord, Sr., pp. 13–40. Richmond: privately printed.

——, ——, and James B. Griffin
1944 The Culture of the Keyser Farm Site. *Papers of the Michigan Academy of Science, Arts, and Letters* 29:375–418.

Marye, William B.
1935 Piscattaway. *Maryland Historical Magazine* 30(3):183–240.

Meggers, Betty J.
1955 The Coming of Age of American Archeology. In *New Interpretations of Aboriginal American Culture History*, pp. 116–29. 75th Anniversary Volume of the Anthropological Society of Washington. Washington, D.C.

Menard, Russell R., and Lois Green Carr
1982 The Lords Baltimore and the Colonization of Maryland. In *Early Maryland in a Wider World*, ed. David B. Quinn, pp. 167–215. Detroit: Wayne State University Press.

Merrell, James H.
1979 Cultural Continuity among the Piscataway Indians of Colonial Maryland. *William and Mary Quarterly* 36:548–70.

Miller, Henry M.
1983 *A Search for the "City of Saint Maries": Report on the 1981 Excavations in St. Mary's City, Maryland*. St. Maries Citty Archaeology Series no. 1. Rev. ed. St. Mary's City: St. Mary's City Commission.

——, Dennis J. Pogue, and Michael A. Smolek
1983 Beads from the Seventeenth Century Chesapeake. In *Proceedings of the 1982 Glass Trade Bead Conference*, Research Records no. 16, ed. Charles H. Hayes III, pp. 127–44. Rochester, N.Y.: Rochester Museum and Science Center.

Mook, Maurice
1944 Aboriginal Population of Tidewater, Virginia. *American Anthropologist* 46(2):193–208.

Mooney, James
1907 The Powhatan Confederacy, Past and Present. *American Anthropologist* 9(1):129–52.
1928 The Aboriginal Population of America North of Mexico. *Smithsonian Miscellaneous Collections* 80(7):1–40. Washington, D.C.

Moore, Larry E.
1990a The Little Marsh Creek Site, Mason Neck National Wildlife Refuge, Lorton, Virginia. Report submitted to U.S. Fish and Wildlife Service.

1990b   Trade and Conflict in the Potomac Valley, ca. 1625–1650. Paper presented at the Eastern States Archeological Conference, Columbus, Ohio.

1991   A Little History of the Doeg. Archeological Society of Virginia *Quarterly Bulletin* 46(2):77–85.

Mouer, L. Daniel

1981   Powhatan and Monacan Settlement Hierarchies. Archeological Society of Virginia *Quarterly Bulletin* 36(1&2):1–21.

1983   A Review of the Ethnohistory and Archaeology of the Monacans. In *Piedmont Archaeology: Recent Research and Results*, ed. J. Mark Wittkofski and Lyle E. Browning, pp. 21–39. Special Publication no. 10. Archeological Society of Virginia.

1986   DMZ or Deer Park? Buffer Zones as Boundary Systems. Ms on file, Virginia Department of Historic Resources, Richmond.

——, Frederic Gleach, and Douglas McLearen

1986   A Ceramics Temporal Typology in Progress for Central Virginia. In *Archaeology in Henrico*, ed. L. Daniel Mouer, vol. 2, pp. 119–49. Richmond: Virginia Commonwealth University.

——, Mary Ellen N. Hodges, Stephen Potter, Susan Henry, Ivor Noël Hume, Dennis Pogue, Martha McCartney, and Thomas Davidson

In press.   "Colono" Pottery, Chesapeake Pipes, and "Uncritical Assumptions." In *"I Too Am America": Studies in African-American Archaeology*, ed. Theresa A. Singleton. Charlottesville: University Press of Virginia.

Nicholson, John C.

1981   *Soil Survey of Westmoreland County, Virginia*. U.S. Department of Agriculture, Soil Conservation Service. Washington, D.C.: GPO.

Noël Hume, Ivor

1962   An Indian Ware of the Colonial Period. Archeological Society of Virginia *Quarterly Bulletin* 17(1):1–14.

Norrisey (Hodges), Mary Ellen

1980   The Pamunkey Indians Retrieve Their Past. *Notes on Virginia* 20: 24–27.

Northumberland County

1718–26   Record Book. Northumberland County Courthouse, Heathsville, Va.

Nugent, Nell Marion

1934   *Cavaliers and Pioneers: Abstracts of Virginia Land Patents and Grants, 1623–1800*. Vol. 1. Richmond: Dietz Press.

Opperman, Antony F.
  1980   A Study of Prehistoric Ceramics from Maycocks Point, Prince George County, Virginia. Senior Honors thesis, Department of Anthropology, College of William and Mary, Williamsburg.

Outlaw, Alain
  1990   *Governor's Land: Archaeology of Early Seventeenth-Century Virginia Settlements.* University Press of Virginia, Charlottesville.

Parker, Patricia L.
  1985   *The Hinterland: An Overview of the Prehistory and History of Prince William Forest Park, Virginia.* Occasional Report no. 1. Washington, D.C.: Regional Archeology Program, National Park Service, National Capital Region.

Pendergast, James F.
  1991   *The Massawomeck: Raiders and Traders into the Chesapeake Bay in the Seventeenth Century.* Transactions of the American Philosophical Society, vol. 81, pt. 2. Philadelphia.

Percy, George
  1922 [1612]   A True Relacyon. *Tyler's Quarterly* 3:259–82.
  1967 [1608?]   *Observations Gathered out of "A Discourse of the Plantation of the Southern Colony in Virginia by the English, 1606,"* ed. David B. Quinn. Jamestown Documents. Charlottesville: University Press of Virginia.

Phelps, David S.
  1983   Archaeology of the North Carolina Coast and Coastal Plain: Problems and Hypotheses. In *The Prehistory of North Carolina: An Archaeological Symposium,* ed. Mark Mathis and Jeffrey Crow, pp. 1–51. Raleigh: North Carolina Division of Archives and History.

Plowden, Sir Edmund (alias Beauchamp Plantagenet)
  1963 [1648]   A Description of the Province of New Albion. In *Tracts and Other Papers, Relating Principally to the Origin, Settlement, and Progress of the Colonies in North America, from the Discovery of the Country to the Year 1776,* comp. Peter Force, 2(7):3–35. Washington, D.C., 1838. Rept. Gloucester, Mass.: Peter Smith.

Porter, H. C., J. F. Derting, J. H. Elder, E. F. Henry, and R. F. Pendleton
  1963   *Soil Survey of Fairfax County, Virginia.* U.S. Department of Agriculture, Soil Conservation Service. Washington, D.C.: GPO.

Potter, Stephen R.
  1976   An Ethnohistorical Examination of Indian Groups in Northumberland County, Virginia, 1608–1719. M.A. thesis, Department of Anthropology, University of North Carolina, Chapel Hill.

1980   *A Review of Archeological Resources in Piscataway Park, Maryland.* Washington, D.C.: National Park Service, National Capital Region.

1982   An Analysis of Chicacoan Settlement Patterns. Ph.D. diss., Department of Anthropology, University of North Carolina, Chapel Hill.

1989   Early English Effects on Virginia Algonquian Exchange and Tribute in the Tidewater Potomac. In *Powhatan's Mantle: Indians in the Colonial Southeast,* ed. Peter Wood, Gregory Waselkov, and M. Thomas Hatley, pp. 151–72. Lincoln: University of Nebraska Press.

n.d.   An Historical Outline of Archeology in Piscataway Park. In Archeological Survey of Piscataway Park, ed. Deborah M. Vrabel and Paul B. Cissna. Ms on file, National Park Service, National Capital Region, Washington, D.C.

———, and Gregory A. Waselkov

In press   "Whereby We Shall Enjoy Their Cultivated Places." In *The Historic Chesapeake: Archaeological Contributions,* ed. Barbara J. Little and Paul A. Shackel. Washington, D.C.: Smithsonian Institution Press.

Pousson, John F.

1983   *Archeological Excavations at the Moore Village Site.* National Park Service, Denver Service Center.

Quinn, David B.

1977   *North America from Earliest Discovery to First Settlements: The Norse Voyages to 1612.* New York: Harper and Row.

1985   *Set Fair for Roanoke: Voyages and Colonies, 1584–1606.* Chapel Hill: University of North Carolina Press.

Reynolds, Elmer R.

1881   Ossuary at Accotink, Virginia. In *Abstract of Transactions of the Anthropological Society of Washington,* pp. 92–94. Washington, D.C.

Rice, Kenneth A.

1963   Climate. In *Soil Survey of Northumberland and Lancaster Counties, Virginia,* by John H. Elder, Jr., et al., pp. 2–3. U.S. Department of Agriculture, Soil Conservation Service. Washington, D.C.: GPO.

Ritchie, William

1961   *A Typology and Nomenclature for New York Projectile Points.* New York State Museum and Science Service Bulletin 384. Albany.

1969   *The Archaeology of New York State.* Garden City, N.Y.: Natural History Press.

———, and Robert Funk

1973   *Aboriginal Settlement Patterns in the Northeast.* New York State Museum and Science Service Memoir 20. Albany.

Rolfe, John
1971 [1616]   *A True Relation of the State of Virginia Lefte by Sir Thomas Dale Knight in May Last 1616.* Jamestown Documents. Charlottesville: University Press of Virginia.

Rountree, Helen C.
1989   *The Powhatan Indians of Virginia: Their Traditional Culture.* Norman: University of Oklahoma Press.
1990   *Pocahontas's People: The Powhatan Indians of Virginia through Four Centuries.* Norman: University of Oklahoma Press.
n.d.   A Guide to the Late Woodland Indians' Use of Ecological Zones in the Chesapeake Region. Ms in possession of the author.

Rouse, Irving
1986   *Migrations in Prehistory: Inferring Population Movement from Cultural Remains.* New Haven: Yale University Press.

Rust, William F., III
1986   Chronology of Prehistoric Sites at Countryside Planned Community, in Loudoun County, Virginia. Ms on file, Virginia Department of Historic Resources, Richmond.

Ryland, Elizabeth L. (editor)
1976   *Richmond County, Virginia: A Review Commemorating the Bicentennial.* Warsaw, Va.: Westmoreland County Commission for History and Archaeology.

Sahlins, Marshall D.
1958   *Social Stratification in Polynesia.* Seattle: University of Washington Press.
1968   *Tribesmen.* Englewood Cliffs, N.J.: Prentice-Hall.

Schmitt, Karl
1952   Archeological Chronology of the Middle Atlantic States. In *Archeology of Eastern United States,* ed. James B. Griffin, pp. 59–70. Chicago: University of Chicago Press.
1965   Patawomeke: An Historic Algonkian Site. Archeological Society of Virginia *Quarterly Bulletin* 20(1):1–36.

Schortman, Edward D.
1989   Interregional Interaction in Prehistory: The Need for a New Perspective. *American Antiquity* 54(1):52–65.

Service, Elman R.
1975   *Origins of the State and Civilization: The Process of Cultural Evolution.* New York: W. W. Norton.

Silberhorn, Gene M.
1975   *Northumberland County Tidal Marsh Inventory.* Special Report no. 58 in Applied Marine Science and Ocean Engineering. Gloucester Point, Va.: Virginia Institute of Marine Science.

Slattery, Richard G., and Douglas R. Woodward
n.d.   The Montgomery Focus. Ms on file, Maryland Historical Trust, Crownsville.

——, William A. Tidwell, and Douglas R. Woodward
1966   The Montgomery Focus. Archeological Society of Virginia *Quarterly Bulletin* 21(2):49–51.

Smith, Bruce D.
1989   Origins of Agriculture in Eastern North America. *Science* 246: 1566–71.

Smith, Gerald P.
1971   Protohistoric Sociopolitical Organization of the Nottoway in the Chesapeake Bay–Carolina Sounds Region. Ph.D. diss., University of Missouri. University Microfilms, Ann Arbor.

Smith, John
1986a [1608]   A True Relation. In *The Complete Works of Captain John Smith,* 3 vols., ed. Philip L. Barbour, 1:3–117. Chapel Hill: University of North Carolina Press.

1986b [1612]   A Map of Virginia. In *The Complete Works of Captain John Smith,* 3 vols., ed. Philip L. Barbour, 1:119–289. Chapel Hill: University of North Carolina Press.

1986c [1624]   The Generall Historie of Virginia, New England, and the Summer Isles. In *The Complete Works of Captain John Smith,* 3 vols., ed. Philip L. Barbour, 2:25–488. Chapel Hill: University of North Carolina Press.

1986d [1631]   Advertisements for the Unexperienced Planters of New England, or Any Where. In *The Complete Works of Captain John Smith,* 3 vols., ed. Philip L. Barbour, 3:253–307. Chapel Hill: University of North Carolina Press.

Smith, Marvin T., and Julie Barnes Smith
1989   Engraved Shell Masks in North America. *Southeastern Archaeology* 8(1):9–18.

Smith, Philip E. L.
1972   Land-Use, Settlement Patterns, and Subsistence Agriculture: A Demographic Perspective. In *Man, Settlement, and Urbanism,* ed. Peter J.

Ucko, Ruth Tringham, and G. W. Dimbleby, pp. 409–25. London: Gerald Duckworth.

Smolek, Michael A.
1984   "Soyle Light, Well-Watered and On the River": Settlement Patterning of Maryland's Frontier Plantations. Paper presented at the 3d Hall of Records Conference on Maryland History, St. Marys City, Md.

Sorensen, A. D.
1974   A Method for Measuring the Spatial Association between Point Patterns. *The Professional Geographer* 26(2):172–76.

Speck, Frank G.
1928   Chapters on the Ethnology of the Powhatan Tribes of Virginia. *Indian Notes and Monographs* 1(5):227–455.

Spelman, Henry
1910 [1613]   Relation of Virginia. In *Travel and Works of Captain John Smith*, 2 vols., ed. Edward Arber, 1:ci–cxiv. Edinburgh: John Grant.

Stearns, Richard E.
1940   *The Hughes Site: An Aboriginal Village Site on the Potomac River in Montgomery County, Maryland.* Proceeding no. 6. Baltimore: Natural History Society of Maryland.

Stephenson, Robert L., A. L. L. Ferguson, and H. G. Ferguson
1963   *The Accokeek Creek Site: A Middle Atlantic Seaboard Culture Sequence.* Anthropological Papers no. 20. Ann Arbor: Museum of Anthropology, University of Michigan.

Steponaitis, Laurie Cameron
1986   Prehistoric Settlement Patterns in the Lower Patuxent Drainage, Maryland. Ph.D. diss., Department of Anthropology, State University of New York, Binghamton.

Stewart, R. Michael
1980   Prehistoric Settlement and Subsistence Patterns and the Testing of Predictive Site Location Models in the Great Valley of Maryland. Ph.D. diss., Department of Anthropology, The Catholic University of America, Washington, D.C.
1989   Trade and Exchange in Middle Atlantic Region Prehistory. *Archaeology of Eastern North America* 17:47–78.
1990   Clemson's Island Studies in Pennsylvania: A Perspective. *Pennsylvania Archaeologist* 60(1):79–107.
In press   Observations on the Middle Woodland Period of Virginia: A Middle Atlantic Region Perspective. In *Middle and Late Woodland Re-*

search in Virginia: A Synthesis, ed. T. R. Reinhart and M. E. N. Hodges. Council of Virginia Archeologists and the Archeological Society of Virginia.

Stewart, T. Dale
1988   Archeological Exploration of Patawomeke. Ms on file, Department of Anthropology, Smithsonian Institution, Washington, D.C.

Stith, William
1747   *History of the First Discovery and Settlement of Virginia.* Spartanburg: Reprint Company.

Stocum, Faye L.
1977   An Important Ceramic Discovery at the Robbins Farm Site. *Bulletin of the Archaeological Society of Delaware,* pp. 40–48.

Strachey, William
1953 [1612]   *The Historie of Travel into Virginia Britania.* Works issued by the Hakluyt Society, 2d ser., vol. 103, ed. Louis B. Wright and Virginia Freund. London.

Swanton, John R.
1952   *The Indian Tribes of North America.* Bureau of American Ethnology Bulletin 145. Washington, D.C.

Tainter, Joseph A.
1988   *The Collapse of Complex Societies.* Cambridge: Cambridge University Press.

Thomas, Ronald, D. R. Griffith, C. L. Wise, and R. E. Artusy
1974   A Discussion of the Lithics, Ceramics, and Cultural Ecology of the Fox Creek–Cony–Selby Bay Paradigm As It Relates to the Delmarva Peninsula. Paper presented at the 5th Middle Atlantic Archaeological Conference, Baltimore.

Thurman, Melburn D.
1972   Re-excavation of the Accokeek Creek Site: A Preliminary Report. Paper presented at the Annual Meeting of the Society for American Archaeology, Bal Harbour, Fla.

Tooker, William Wallace
1894   On the Meaning of the Name Anacostia. *American Anthropologist* 7(4):389–93.
1901   *The Algonquian Terms Patawomeke (Potomac) and Massawomeke.* The Algonquian Series. New York: Francis P. Harper.
1905   Some More about Virginia Names. *American Anthropologist,* n.s., 7(3):524–28.

Trigger, Bruce G.
  1969   Criteria for Identifying the Locations of Historic Indian Sites: A
  Case Study from Montreal. *Ethnohistory* 16(4):303–16.
  1976   *The Children of Aataentsic: A History of the Huron People to 1660*, vol. 1.
  Montreal: McGill-Queen's University Press.
  1978   *Time and Traditions: Essays in Archaeological Interpretations.* New York:
  Columbia University Press.

Tuck, James A.
  1978   Northern Iroquoian Prehistory. In *Northeast,* ed. Bruce G. Trigger,
  pp. 322–33. *Handbook of North American Indians,* vol. 15, William G. Sturtevant, general editor. Washington, D.C.: Smithsonian Institution.

Turner, E. Randolph, III
  1972   An Ethnohistorical Study of the Powhatan of Tidewater, Virginia.
  M.A. thesis, Department of Anthropology, Pennsylvania State University,
  University Park.
  1973   A New Population Estimate for the Powhatan Chiefdom of the
  Coastal Plain of Virginia. Archeological Society of Virginia *Quarterly Bulletin* 28(2):57–65.
  1976   An Archaeological and Ethnohistorical Study on the Evolution of
  Rank Societies in the Virginia Coastal Plain. Ph.D. diss., Department of
  Anthropology, Pennsylvania State University, University Park.
  1978   An Intertribal Deer Exploitation Buffer Zone for the Virginia
  Coastal Plain—Piedmont Regions. Archeological Society of Virginia
  Quarterly Bulletin 32(3):42–28.
  1982   A Re-examination of Powhatan Territorial Boundaries and Population, ca. A.D. 1607. Archeological Society of Virginia *Quarterly Bulletin*
  37(2):45–64.
  1985   Socio-political Organization within the Powhatan Chiefdom and the
  Effects of European Contact, A.D. 1607–1646. In *Cultures in Contact: The
  Impact of European Contacts on Native American Cultural Institutions,* ed. William W. Fitzhugh, pp. 193–224. Washington, D.C.: Smithsonian Institution Press.
  1988   Protohistoric Native American Interactions in the Virginia Coastal
  Plain. Paper presented at the Annual Meeting of the American Society
  for Ethnohistory, Williamsburg.
  In press   The Virginia Coastal Plain during the Late Woodland Period. In
  Middle and Late Woodland Research in Virginia: A Synthesis, ed. T. R. Reinhart and M. E. N. Hodges. Council of Virginia Archeologists and the
  Archeological Society of Virginia.

Tyler, Lyon G. (editor)
1907 *Narratives of Early Virginia, 1606–1625.* New York: Barnes and Noble.

Ubelaker, Douglas H.
1974 *Reconstruction of Demographic Profiles from Ossuary Skeletal Samples.* Smithsonian Contributions to Anthropology no. 18. Washington, D.C.: Smithsonian Institution Press.
1976 The Sources and Methodology for Mooney's Estimates of North American Indian Populations. In *The Native Population of the Americas in 1492,* ed. W. M. Denevan, pp. 243–88. Madison: University of Wisconsin Press.

U.S. Department of Agriculture
1938 *Yearbook of Agriculture 1938: Soils and Men.* Washington, D.C.: GPO.

Veatch, Betty L.
1974 The Farmington Landing Site: A Cultural Sequence of the Maryland Coastal Plain. M.A. thesis, Department of Anthropology, The American University, Washington,D.C.

Vokes, Harold E., and Jonathan Edwards, Jr.
1974 *Geography and Geology of Maryland.* Maryland Geological Survey Bulletin 19. Baltimore: 1957. Rev. and rept.

Vrabel, Deborah M., and Paul B. Cissna (editors)
n.d. Archeological Survey of Piscataway Park. Ms on file, National Park Service, National Capital Region, Washington, D.C.

Wanser, Jeffrey C.
1982 A Survey of Artifact Collections from Central Southern Maryland. Maryland Historical Trust Manuscript Series no. 23, Annapolis.

Ward, H. Trawick
1965 Correlation of Mississippian Sites and Soil Types. *Proceedings of the 21st Southeastern Archaeological Conference,* Bulletin 3:42–48.
1985 Social Implications of Storage and Disposal Patterns. In *Structure and Process in Southeastern Archaeology,* ed. Roy S. Dickens, Jr., and H. Trawick Ward, pp. 82–101. Tuscaloosa: University of Alabama Press.

——, and R. P. Stephen Davis, Jr.
1989 The Impact of Old World Diseases on the Native Inhabitants of the North Carolina Piedmont. Paper presented at the 46th Annual Meeting of the Southeastern Archaeological Conference, Tampa, Fla.

Waselkov, Gregory A.
1978a Evolution of Deer Hunting in the Eastern Woodlands. *Mid-Continental Journal of Archaeology* 3(1):15–34.

1978b   Shellfish Gathering and Shell Midden Archaeology. Ms on file, Department of Anthropology, University of North Carolina, Chapel Hill.
1980   *Coosa River Valley Archaeology.* Vol. 1 of 2. Auburn University Archaeological Monograph 2. Auburn, Ala.
1982a   Shellfish Gathering and Shell Midden Archaeology. Ph.D. diss., Department of Anthropology, University of North Carolina, Chapel Hill.
1982b   Appendix 4: Analysis of Faunal Remains. In An Analysis of Chicacoan Settlement Patterns, by Stephen R. Potter. Ph.D. diss., Department of Anthropology, University of North Carolina, Chapel Hill.
1983   Indians of Westmoreland County. In *Westmoreland County, Virginia, 1653–1983,* ed. Walter Norris, Jr., pp. 15–33. Montross, Va.: Westmoreland County Commission for History and Archaeology.

——, and R. Eli Paul
1981   Frontiers and Archaeology. *North American Archaeologist* 2(4): 309–29.

Washburn, Wilcomb E.
1972   *The Governor and the Rebel: A History of Bacon's Rebellion in Virginia.* New York: W. W. Norton.

Wells, Peter S.
1980   *Culture Contact and Culture Change.* Cambridge: Cambridge University Press.

Wilke, Steve, and Gail Thompson
1977   Archeological Survey of Western Kent County, Maryland. Report submitted to the Maryland Historical Trust, Crownsville.

Willey, Gordon R., and Philip Phillips
1958   *Method and Theory in American Archeology.* Chicago: University of Chicago Press.

Wilson, Harold L.
1955   *Grain Crops.* New York: McGraw-Hill.

Wilson, Thomas
1897   Arrowpoints, Spearheads, and Knives of Prehistoric Times. In *Report of the National Museum, 1897,* pp. 811–988. Washington, D.C.: Smithsonian Institution.

Wimsatt, W. K., Jr.
1958   A Cache of Blades near the Great Falls of the Potomac. *Archaeology* 11(2):87–92.

Winfree, R. Westwood
1967   The T. Gray Haddon Site, King William County, Virginia. Archeological Society of Virginia *Quarterly Bulletin* 22(1):2–26.

Witthoft, John
    1952   Comments on the Cultural Position of the Herriot Farm Site. *West Virginia History* 13(4):249–53.

Wood, W. Raymond
    1990   Ethnohistory and Historical Method. In *Archaeological Method and Theory*, vol. 2, ed. Michael B. Schiffer, pp. 81–110. Tucson: University of Arizona Press.

Woodward, Douglas R., and George E. Phebus, Jr.
    1973   The Piscataway Site: A Stratified Woodland Site in Tidewater Maryland. Ms on file, Maryland Historical Trust, Crownsville.

Wright, Henry T.
    1973   *An Archeological Sequence in the Middle Chesapeake Region, Maryland.* Maryland Geological Survey Archeological Studies no. 1. Baltimore.

Index

Accokeek Creek site, 87, 117, 120; cultural interaction, 154, 158; defining traits, 122–23; origins, 126, 128–30, 132, 136–37; politics, 171–72, 174–75, 178; summary, 207–8

Accomacs, 19, 40

Acquintanacsucks, 20

Agriculture: crops, 102, 113–14; seasons, 40–43, 47; slash and burn, 32–33, 39; soil associations, 35–36, 39, 46, 75; soils, 95–96, 115, 175

Albemarle ceramics, 157

Algonquian culture, 1–2

Algonquian language, 1–3, 5, 11, 13–14, 19–21, 120, 132, 142, 146, 155

Algonquians, 1–2, 4, 8, 20, 22–24, 26, 28, 32–34, 40–41, 45–46, 50, 52, 94, 120, 130, 142, 146–47, 149, 152, 164–65, 167, 170, 172–80, 185, 189, 191, 195–96, 198, 209–10, 213, 220–21, 223; *see also* names of specific groups of Algonquian-speaking Indians

Amorlock, Siouan-speaking Manahoac, 176

Anacostanks. *See* Nacotchtanks

Anglo-Powhatan War. *See* First, Second, Third Anglo-Powhatan Wars

Annapolis, Md., 108

Antouhonorons (Entouhonorons). *See* Massawomecks

Appalachian Mountains, 7, 109, 154, 160

Appamatucks, 18, 183

Aquia Creek, 153, 160, 175

Archaeological components: definition, 5; description of sites, 68, 71, 79, 81, 89, 91–93; distribution, 85, 87, 89, 91–93, 109; increase, 102, 118; specialization, 104, 108–9

Archaeological contact period sites, 199–200

Archaeological phase, 103

Archaeological settlement patterns, 68–77, 79–81, 85–87, 89–102, 109–11, 115–18, 126–27, 138–48 passim, 220–21

Archaeological survey, 48, 50; definition of area, 53–55, 68; designation, 58–59; methods, 56; objectives, 52–53

Argall, Capt. Samuel, 13, 182–83

Arrohatecks, 18, 183

Assateagues, 20

Atlantic Ocean coast, 7–8, 50, 114, 161

Baltimore, Md., 119, 125

Betz Landing site, 72, 74–75

Biggs Ford site, 125

Blue Fish Beach site, 48, 75, 88, 97, 200, 203

Blue Ridge Mountains, 107–8, 181

Boathouse Pond site, 59, 68, 111, 115, 118; description and interpretation, 81, 85, 87, 89; excavation of, 48, 71; settlement pattern, 92–97, 100, 102, 140–41; site in the contact period, 202, 208

Bowmans Brook ceramics, 133, 146

Burials: of commoners, 210–11, 218–20; of the Montgomery complex, 126–27, 129–30; of the Potomac Creek